The Strange Genius of
WILLIAM BURGES
'Art-Architect',
1827-1881

Interior of door from the Yatman Cabinet (B.1)

Amgueddfa Genedlaethol Cymru
National Museum of Wales
Cardiff 1981

The Strange Genius of
WILLIAM BURGES

'Art-Architect', 1827-1881

A catalogue to a Centenary Exhibition organised jointly by the National Museum of Wales, Cardiff, and the Victoria and Albert Museum, London

EDITED BY J. MORDAUNT CROOK

CATALOGUE ENTRIES BY
MARY AXON AND VIRGINIA GLENN

© National Museum of Wales, 1981
Design: PENKNIFE
Typesetting: CHARACTERS
Print: SOUTH WESTERN PRINTERS
ISBN 0 7200 0234 6

Front cover:
stained glass cartoon for Cork Cathedral (C.20)

Back cover:
west elevation of the Crimea Memorial Church, Constantinople (C.5)

Contents

- 8   Abbreviations
- 9   Foreword
- 10   The Strange Genius of William Burges by J. Mordaunt Crook
- 13   Major Architectural Works
- 13   Major Unexecuted Designs
- 14   Catalogue A: Castles, Houses and Public Buildings
- 67   Pre-Raphaelite Furniture by Clive Wainwright
- 72   Catalogue B: Furniture
- 88   Catalogue C: Ecclesiastical Architecture, Stained Glass, Metalwork and Decoration
- 123   Burges as a Medievalist by Virginia Glenn
- 128   Catalogue D: Scholarship Sources and Collections
- 155   Select Bibliography
- 156   Acknowledgements

Abbreviations

A.: *The Architect* 'Abstract': W. Burges, 'Abstract of Diaries'
AJ.: *Art Journal.*
Arch.Rev.: *Architectural Review*
B.: *The Builder*
BN.: *Building News*
Burl.Mag.: *Burlington Magazine*
CEAJ: *Civil Engineer and Architect's Journal*
C.L.: *Country Life*
E.: *Ecclesiologist*
E. W. Godwin *AJ* (1886): 'The Home of an English Architect', 170-3, 301-5.
C. Handley-Read, *Burl.Mag.* cv (1963): 'Notes on William Burges's Painted Furniture', 498-509.
C. Handley-Read, *CL* CXXXIX (1966): 'Aladdin's Palace in Kensington', 600-604.
R.I.B.A.: Royal Institute of British Architects
R.I.B.A. Jnl: Journal of the R.I.B.A.
R.I.B.A. Trans: Transactions of the R.I.B.A.
R.I.B.A., S.N.B.: W. Burges, 'Small Note Books' in R.I.B.A. Drawings Collection.
R.A.: Royal Academy.
Tower House Sale 1933: *Catalogue of the Sale of Tower House* 1933, Chesterton & Son.
V&A: Victoria and Albert Museum.
V&A, P&D: Victoria and Albert Museum, Prints and Drawings Department.

The compilers' initials are given at the end of each entry in the catalogue section.

Foreword

Plans for a major exhibition of William Burges's work to commemorate the centenary of his death were first mooted in 1976. At first it was hoped that such an exhibition would be staged in Cardiff Castle, the architect's 'masterpiece', but when this did not prove feasible the National Museum took on the task, both of organising the exhibition and providing its first venue. During the last two years or so the exhibition has developed into a joint venture with the Victoria and Albert Museum, with financial co-operation from the Friends of the National Museum of Wales.

It would have been impossible to do justice to Burges without the generous support given by Dr. J. Mordaunt Crook, who has acted as editor of this catalogue, and the contributions made by the specialists in ninetenth century studies who have collaborated in the research. The bulk of the organisation has been undertaken at Cardiff by Virginia Glenn of the Department of Art, and in London by Michael Darby of the Museums Services Department. Mary Axon, as Exhibition Co-Ordinator, has brought together all aspects of the research and administration. Acknowledgements and sincere thanks are also due to the many people who have generously lent material and to the Keepers and their staffs in both museums for giving their time, their advice and their support.

In times of financial restrictions, the organisation of large scale exhibitions of this kind places great pressure on curatorial staff and it is only by the pooling of resources of the two national museums that this exhibition has been possible.

Dr. Douglas A. Bassett
Dr. Roy L. Strong

The Strange Genius of William Burges
by J. Mordaunt Crook

When he died one hundred years ago in 1881, William Burges was widely regarded as the most brilliant architect-designer of his generation. Brilliant but eccentric, unstable and extravagant. Burges was a Pre-Raphaelite architect in all but name, and like his Pre-Raphaelite friends he sought an artistic Holy Grail in a Victorian vision of the Middle Ages. His creative range was extraordinary. In architecture he rivals Butterfield, Street and Norman Shaw. In furniture and stained glass he matches — and occasionally eclipses — the finest work of Morris & Co. In jewellery and metalwork he is really without rival, except perhaps for his hero, Pugin.

To his friends he was always 'Billy' Burges: 'a crank, but a genius, and a really good fellow'. Robert Kerr remembered his 'playful fanaticism'. In Poynter's portrait of 1858 he wears a puckish look. In a photo taken just before his death he stares out at posterity like some petulant bulldog. Picture him at tea, as Edmund Gosse remembered him, in a letter to Austin Dobson: 'He used to give the quaintest little teaparties in his bare bachelor chambers, all very dowdy, but the meal served in beaten gold, the cream poured out of a single onyx, and the tea strictured in its descent on account of real rubies in the pot. He was much blinder than any near-sighted man I ever knew, and once, when with me in the country, mistook a peacock seen *en face* for a man! His work was really more jewel like than architecture, just because he was so blind, but he had real genius I am sure.'

William Burges was born in London on 2 December 1827, the son of an engineer in the heroic age of British engineering. He was educated at King's College School where his near-contemporaries included Dante Gabriel Rossetti and William Michael Rossetti. Their drawing-master was probably John Sell Cotman. As a schoolboy Burges was already 'excessively short-sighted' with 'a chubby face like a cherub on a tombstone'. He stayed on at King's to study engineering, but left after one year, in 1844, to take up articles in the office of Edward Blore. Five years later he moved to Matthew Digby Wyatt's office as an 'improver'. And in 1851 he formed an informal partnership with a fellow enthusiast for Gothic, Henry Clutton. But the influence of A.W.N. Pugin was greater than any of these: Burges always reverenced that 'wonderful man'.

The Burges family was never short of money: Billy left £40,000; his father left £113,000. From 1849 onwards the young architect was able to travel regularly and extensively in Europe: Northern and Southern France; Italy and Sicily; Greece and Turkey; Belgium, Holland, Switzerland, Germany and Spain. He also studied vicariously the arts of Japan, India, Scandinavia and North Africa. During the 1850s and 1860s he built up an international reputation as a medieval archaeologist — though he lacked Viollet-le-Duc's systematic mind — and developed a highly personal style, an eclectic compound chiefly based on French, Italian, Arabic, Japanese, Pompeian and Assyrian sources. He was especially intrigued by the Islamic permeation of Gothic, and by Pagan survivals in Christian art. The thirteenth century, in particular, was Burges's chosen field, and he modelled his style of draughtmanship on the famous sketch-book of Wilars de Honecort in the Bibliothèque Nationale, Paris. For visionary drawings, however (notably 'St Simeon Stylites', 1860), his model was Albrecht Dürer.

Burges's career was astonishingly diverse but unhappily brief. His early competition triumphs (Lille Cathedral, 1855; Crimea Memorial Church, 1856) proved abortive. He won his first major commission (Cork Cathedral) in 1863 at the age of thirty-five, and he died in 1881 aged fifty-three. His style, therefore, did not 'develop' from commission to commission. Once established, after twenty years' preparation, his 'design language' had merely to be applied, and he applied and re-applied the same vocabulary with increasing subtlety and gusto. Like Tennyson, he re-used and re-fashioned his favourite 'dodges' again and again. He worked for pleasure, not for profit, and he was uninterested in fashion. As Dudley Harbron wrote, 'Burges put his whole being into everything he undertook'. Several of his most extraordinary designs remained unexecuted: cathedrals from Lille to Brisbane, from Edinburgh to Truro; a multi-quadrangled university in Connecticut; a multi-domed art school for Bombay, in 'a kind of . . . quasi-Orientalising Gothic' (1865-66); a controversial scheme to make St. Paul's Cathedral out-dazzle St. Peter's, Rome, by decorating its interior with polychrome marble and Byzantine mosaics (1870-77); and a competition project for the Law Courts (1866-67) — designed, apparently, to turn London into Camelot, and which, in planning and silhouette, combined lucidity and drama to an exceptional degree. Such missed opportunities had their saving grace: Burges was rescued from Scott's prolixity, from Street's overproduction.

As an architectural theorist, Burges was neither original nor consistent. But his very confusion is valuable: in numerous lectures and public statements he speaks on behalf of the mid-Victorian generation, a generation bewildered by novelty and confused by change, a generation of architects whistling in the dark. Despite his engineering background, Burges's aesthetic was essentially atectonic. He would have applauded Lutyens's aphorism: 'architecture begins where function ends'. 'The Civil Engineer', he admitted, 'is the real nineteenth century architect'. But engineering alone, he believed, was not architecture. In his early years he followed A.J. Beresford-Hope's doctrine of 'progressive eclecticism'. And Early French — rather than Italian or English Gothic — seemed to him the most suitable matrix for a Victorian style. He admired especially its 'boldness, breadth, strength, sternness and virility'. But in the 1860s the excesses of popular Gothic led him to despair: the New Style, he admitted in 1865, 'may perhaps take place in the twentieth century, it certainly . . . will not occur in the nineteenth'. During the 1870s, however, Burges refused to follow his contemporaries in rejecting Gothic for Queen Anne. In 1875 he described the new fashion as an illiterate 'negro-language', 'the very dregs of the Renaissance'. 'I have been brought up', he announced, 'in the thirteenth-century belief, and in that belief I intend to die'. Towards the end of his life he retained only one last vestige of evolutionary optimism: the future of architecture must lie in a renaissance of the minor arts. Hence Burge's position as proto-high-priest of the Arts and Crafts movement. Generally speaking, however, he shared in the aesthetic flaccidity of the 1870s. He gave up wrestling with eclectic theory, and concentrated on private rather than public, decorative rather than structural design. He escaped into a world of architectural fantasy: at Cardiff Castle and Castell Coch — Wagnerian creations for the richest man in the world — and in his own Tennysonian retreat, Tower House, Kensington. In effect, he had abandoned doubts for dreams.

Burges was friendly with most of the leaders of the Pre-Raphaelite movement, and employed a number of Pre-Raphaelites and peripheral Pre-Raphaelites in the production of mural decoration, stained glass and painted furniture. D.G. Rossetti, E. Burne-Jones, J.E. Millais, Simeon Solomon, Henry Holiday, N.H.J. Westlake, Albert Moore, Thomas Morten, Charles Rossiter, Frederick Smallfield, J.A. Fitzgerald, W.F. Yeames, E. J. Poynter, H.W. Lonsdale, W. Gualbert Saunders, Fred Weekes, Stacy Marks, Charles Campbell, Axel Herman Haig — all these worked at different times under Burges's direction. And several (notably Burne-Jones, Poynter, Holiday, Westlake, Stacy Marks and Campbell) acknowledged a considerable debt to Burges at the start of their careers. With their assistance, Burges produced the earliest and most striking examples of painted Gothic furniture; and with the help of Saunders, Lonsdale and Weekes in particular, he produced stained glass which surpassed in originality and brilliance even the finest work of Morris & Co. He also excelled in a field Morris never entered: jewellery and metalwork. Working with several different silversmiths (Keith & Co.; Hart, Son & Peard; Hardman & Co.; Barkentin and Krall), Burges inspired work which excels in scholarship even that of his master Pugin, and anticipates in range and virtuosity the triumphs of the Arts and Crafts phase.

Burges was a key member of several fringe Pre-Raphaelite coteries: the Hogarth Club, the Medieval Society, the Arts Club, and the Foreign Architectural Book Society. He also played a leading role in a number of more obviously professional groups: the Institute of British Architects, the Archaeological Institute, the Architectural Museum and Architectural Exhibition Society, the Architectural Association and the Ecclesiological Society. His bohemian manners seem to have kept him out of the Royal Academy until just before his death — he was elected A.R.A. in January 1881 — and he never joined the Society of Antiquaries. Besides numerous lectures and essays, he published *Art Applied to Industry* (1865) and *Architectural Drawings* (1870). He was an omnivorous — almost manic — collector, and bequeathed many items — armour, ivories, illuminated manuscripts — to the British Museum.

Burges never ran a large office. His style had many imitators (especially popular were his Law Courts and Skilbeck's Warehouse designs), but he founded no school: his pupils were devotés rather than disciples. Two of them, however — Josiah Conder and Sir William Emerson — carried Burgesian eclecticism across the world. Emerson trained on Burges's unexecuted Bombay Art School project (1865-66), and was made responsible for transporting the working drawings to India. There he studied native vernacular building, and laid the foundations of a major Anglo-Indian architectural practice. In much the same way, Conder translated Burgesian Gothic into Japanese. After two years with Burges, he emigrated to Japan in 1876, married a Japanese girl, and settled down to become the leading architect in his adopted country. Apart from India and Japan, Burge's influence can be traced to the United States. His design for Trinity College, Hartford, Conn. (1873-82), remained incomplete: less than one-sixth of the quadruple-quadrangled masterplan was constructed, and even that was diluted in execution by its two local architects, F.H. Kimball and G.W. Keller. Still, through Kimball, through Keller and — most of all — through H.H. Richardson, not a little of Burges's genius lives on across the Atlantic. His influence on Richardson is a matter for debate. But Richardson's only English work — Lululaund, Bushey, Hertfordshire (1886-94), for Sir Hubert Herkomer R.A. — seems almost a tribute to Burges.

Burges's leading patrons were Roman Catholic (the 3rd Marquess of Bute; the 1st Marquess of Ripon) or High Anglican (A.J. Beresford-Hope, M.P.). But his own approach to religion was aesthetic rather than theological. As Robert Kerr put it 'Butterfield was High Church, Scott Low Church, and Burges no church'. In his art and in his writings he emphasised the visual rather than the metaphysical side of religion. His ideal was the church candescent, an aesthete's version of the church militant: Faith made manifest in Art. He loved ceremony almost for its own sake. Hence perhaps the fact that he was an enthusiastic Freemason, and may well have been a Rosicrucian.

A lifelong bachelor, enthusiastic, jokey, talkative, gregarious, Billy Burges was a popular figure in the mid-Victorian art world. Short-sighted, stocky and unkempt — he was known as 'Ugly Burges' to distinguish him from J.B. ('Pretty') Burgess, the painter — he died suddenly, at the height of his powers, in the same year as his contemporary and rival G.E. Street. Like a number of the Pre-Raphaelite generation, he seems to have enjoyed opium and alcohol. And the intensity of his vision was perhaps diluted by a luxurious lifestyle. But no Gothic Revivalist was more gifted, or better loved. Lord Bute christened him 'the soul-inspiring one'. Lady Bute wrote his epitaph: 'ugly Burges who designs lovely things. Isn't he a duck'.

Major Architectural Works

1858-65, Gayhurst, Bucks., alterations for Lord Carrington.
1859-77, Waltham Abbey, Essex, restoration.
1860-2, All Saints, Fleet, Hants.
1863-1904, St. Finbar's Cathedral, Cork.
1864-79, Worcester College, Oxford, chapel and hall.
1865-6, Skilbeck's Warehouse, 46 Upper Thames St., London.
1866-1928, Cardiff Castle, reconstruction for Lord Bute.
1866-8, Holy Trinity, Templebrady, Crosshaven, Co. Cork.
1867-8, St. Michael, Lowfield Heath, Surrey.
1867-74, Knightshayes, Devon, for Sir J. Heathcoat-Amory.
1868 and 1892-9, St. Michael, Brighton, Sussex, extensions.
1868, 1871-3 and 1881, St. Faith, Stoke Newington, London.
1870-6, Christ the Consoler, Skelton, Yorks.
1870-8, St. Mary, Studley Royal, Yorks.
1871-7, Harrow School, Middlesex, speech room.
1873-82, Trinity College, Hartford, Conn.
1875-81, Tower House, Melbury Rd., Kensington, London, for himself.

Major Unexecuted Designs

1856, Lille Cathedral (with Henry Clutton).
1856-61, Crimea Memorial Church, Constantinople.
1859, Brisbane Cathedral.
1862, Florence Cathedral, West front.
1863-4, Bradford Exchange, Yorkshire.
1865-6, Bombay Art School.
1866-7, New Law Courts, Strand, London.
1870-7, St. Paul's Cathedral, London: interior decoration.
1873, St. Mary's Cathedral, Edinburgh.
1878, Truro Cathedral.

Catalogue A:
Castles, Houses and Public Buildings

For Burges the Georgian years were 'the Dark Ages of Art'. He hated architectural 'prettiness' and 'chaste' effects. His designs — at Cardiff Castle, at Castell Coch, at Cork Cathedral, at the churches of Studley Royal and Skelton — bludgeon the spectator into applause. He loved powerful geometrical shapes, symbolic decoration, bright heraldic colours and menacing sculpture. He combined an unerring sense of mass with an insatiable relish for ornament. Above all, he understood scale. He could make small things look large, and large things look enormous. Even among his own generation of 'muscular' Goths, he stands out as a master of architectural shock-tactics. But Burges could never be described as a 'Rogue': he had too sharp a sense of humour, too keen an eye for detail. Somehow he manages to balance the precision and delicacy of the Puginian era with a severity and exaggeration which is characteristically High Victorian. Despite torments of doubt, he succeeded in creating an eclectic, personal style based on the architectural language of the Middle Ages, the Renaissance and Islam. Contemporaries christened it Burgesian Gothic.

J.M.C.

A.1 Sketch for a Fountain for the City of Gloucester

Pen and ink and watercolour over preliminary pencil, on four sheets of paper joined together, with alterations pasted on
21″ (53.5)×17¼″ (44.5)

Drawing showing the proposed fountain in situ, with an imaginary reconstruction of the medieval city of Gloucester in the background. The fountain illustrates the story of Sabrina and Estrildis, as told by Geoffrey of Monmouth; Sabrina was condemned to be thrown into the River Severn (which flows through the centre of Gloucester), from whence comes the river's name. In Burges's diary for 1856 is the entry, 'Design for Gloucester Fount'; unfortunately the fountain was not built. R.P. Pullan reproduces another version of the fountain as the frontispiece to *The Architectural Designs of William Burges*. He states that the original, in Burges's own hand, is a partly coloured perspective on vellum.

B. xvi (1858), 375 illus.   M.A.

Victoria and Albert Museum

Drawing Room chimneypiece at Gayhurst

Gayhurst, Buckinghamshire

From 1859 Burges was engaged in making alterations to a number of houses belonging to Lord Carrington, his first major patron, but it was at Gayhurst that his efforts were concentrated. Here he was responsible for a stone-built back staircase — the Caliban Staircase (1859-61) — a guard room (1859), two chimneypieces (1860 and 1865), a kitchen, chef's apartments with a spyhole to supervise cooking activities, a stew house, a bakehouse, a dog kennel and a drawing room entirely panelled and painted with fruit, flowers and birds in the manner of Catherine de Medici's 'cabinet' at the Chateau de Blois. Perhaps the most fanciful addition was the menservants' multiple privy adjacent to the service quarters. Lord Carrington was reported to be unusually concerned with sanitation and supplied closets in all the bedrooms, as well as in the female servants' attic. However, for the menservants' lavatory he built 'a quaint stone circus, lighted and ventilated by roof dormers, and surmounted at the apex of the roof by a boldly sculptured Cerberus with red glass eyes in each of his three heads'.* Burges worked on a complete scheme for redecoration, including a grand staircase, but this was never carried out. Nevertheless, the cost of the work completed was rumoured to be about £20,000.

                                                          M.A.

A.2

A.2 **Cerberus Privy**
designed 1859-60
'Abstract' 1860-61, 'Gayhurst W.C.'; R.I.B.A. S.N.B. xxvii (1859) 60 and xxviii (1860) 31, 40, 51-2, 63-4
*R. Reynolds Rowe, *R.I.B.A. Trans.* xxxii (1881-2), 195

Worcester College Chapel, Oxford

In 1863, Burges received the commission to redecorate the chapel of Worcester College designed by James Wyatt in 1776-90, and to transform the interior with a programme of Christian decoration. The cost imposed by the Fellows was to be no more than £1,200-£1,500. Burges secured the commission through influence, and his friends further assured his employment by donating generously for the more expensive items such as candelabra, testament bindings and windows.

The decorative scheme is an extraordinarily ecclectic display: Raphaelesque mural patterns; a mosaic pavement reminiscent of Pompeii or Herculaneum; beautifully carved woodwork and statuary by Thomas Nicholls; glowing stained glass designed by Henry Holiday (1839-1927) and made by Lavers and Baraud. The whole is an intricate agglomeration of High Victorian iconography which can be read horizontally as well as vertically. The roof illustrates the Temptation and Fall, the walls, the Te Deum and Benedicite, while numerous scenes and characters exemplify the unity of Man and Nature in the worship of God.

Fisher of London was the contracting decorator, though Holiday and Frederick Smallfield (1829-1915) were largely responsible for the mural decorations and Nicholls for the carving. The excessive ritualism of the iconography was the cause of much controversy; as was the continual introduction of additional expensive items. But in the end Burges achieved most of his requests. The final cost must have been in the region of £6,000. At the opening ceremony the scheme was described as 'one of the first great works where the windows formed part of the original design and are kept in strict harmony with the details of the walls and ceiling'.

M.A.

C. Handley-Read in P. Ferriday, ed., *Victorian Architecture* (1963), 202-5

Interior of Worcester College Chapel

A.3 **Elevation of East End**

Pen and watercolour on paper
18½″ (407)×24″ (610)
Inscribed 'Elevation of East End./Wor: Coll: Chapel. Oxon/
½ Inch Scale'

Some alterations in the design are pasted on.

Lent by the Fellows of Worcester College, Oxford

A.4 **Designs for Candelabrum and Lectern**

Plans and elevations of the lectern and candelabrum in ink on flimsy paper, with an old photograph and a page illustrating the candelabrum and lectern taken from the photo, from the *Building News* of March 6th, 1868
Drawing 14¼″ (360)×19″ (485)
Photo 10⅝″ (270)×8″ (205)
Lithograph 11¼″ (285) ×7⅛″ (180)
The drawing is inscribed with some instructions for the production of the pieces

Burges secured the authority for the lectern and two candelabra in December 1864; the cost of the candelabra alone was estimated to be £60 for they were to be made of finest white alabaster. The latter were eventually donated by Rev. J.D. Collis (1816-79), Freemason, Headmaster of Bromsgrove School, Vicar of Stratford-on-Avon, member of the Worcester College Senior Common Room and later Bishop of Nova Scotia.

Thomas Nicholls supplied the models in Quattrocento style, working from designs by Burges. Both lectern and candelabra were carved by Jacquet of Stanford Street, Vauxhall Bridge Road, London. The photo was evidently taken whilst the lectern and candelabra were in the sculptor's studio.   M.A.

Lent by the Fellows of Worcester College, Oxford

A.5 **Old Testament Binding**

Silver with a copper back panel
h 9½″ (24.1) w 6¼″ (15.8)
Inscribed 'DD.HENRICUS.DANIEL.SOC.'

The front panel in silver illustrates the theme 'Jacob and Rachel at the Well'. The spine and chain fastenings are of silver, the back panel is a copper inset of 'the Adoration of the Magi'. The Chapel Committee minutes for 25 November, 1869 give the passing of authorisation for silver bindings for both Old and New Testaments to be made by Barkentin to Burges's designs, each incorporating 17th century Flemish panels, at £25 each. The binding was donated by the Rev. H.C.O. Daniel (1836-1919), a Fellow, member of the Worcester College S.C.R. and future Provost of the College.
                    M.A.

Lent by the Fellows of Worcester College, Oxford

A.6 **Organ Stool**

Walnut, inlaid with ivory bosses
1865
h 3′1″ (94) w 4′5″ (134.6) d 1′ (30.4)

Burges's diary for 1865 contains the entry 'Organ seat Worc.Coll.'. The seat has ornate sides formed by female griffons, as the supports, with leopard heads forming the hand rests. A sketch may be found in the Worcester College archives (TD.4.MS290). The animal ends are a feature which is repeated in the pew ends for the chapel; there are over 30 small wooden animals such as the swan, boar and tortoise. These were modelled by Thomas Nicholls, and it seems reasonable that the organ stool may also be his work. The organ itself is by Nicholson of Worcester.   M.A.

Lent by the Fellows of Worcester College, Oxford

Regrettably this item was not available for exhibition.

A.7

A WAREHOUSE IN UPPER THAMES STREET, LONDON.—Mr. W. Burges, Architect.

Perspective view of the smithy, Bombay School of Art

Bombay School of Art

Burges accepted the invitation in 1865 to submit designs for a capacious new building for the Bombay School of Art. He made 129 drawings for the building, which were sent to India accompanied by a formal report. The Indian officials refused to offer more than 2½% commission, which Burges felt unable to accept. The project was abandoned, though not without his design causing considerable interest in the architectural press.

The basic plan is E shaped, combining a central hall, lecture rooms, studios, museum, library, staff and servants quarters. The most original feature being the smithy, 'a circular domed building somewhat in the shape of a medieval kitchen', (it resembles the Benedictine kitchen at Marmoutier, published in A. Lenoir, *Architecture Monastique* ii, 1865, Pl. 495, which Burges possessed.) It also resembles the tulip vases Burges designed for himself and for Lord Bute, and the lily vases designed for St. Andrew's, Wells Street.

The building incorporates small windows and several staircases with deep eaves and double walls, allowing free passage of air and protection from the sun. The basic style is that of 'the architecture of Europe at the end of the twelfth century', which he felt retained a European character while associating more closely 'with Eastern pointed architecture than any other style'.
                                                          M.A.

Report, May 1866 (Weller MSS)
RIBA *Special Papers* ix (1867), 43
Pullan, *Architectural Designs of Williams Burges* i (1883), 28-9, and ii (1887), 23-8

A.7 **Skilbeck's Warehouse**

An extract from Burges's diary for 1865-6 reads, 'Skilbeck Warehouse'. It was a most unusual commission; Burges was employed to remodel Skilbeck's drysalters' warehouse at 46 Upper Thames Street, in the City. The addition of a fifth storey and refacing of the street frontage was hardly a large commission, but Burges's application of medieval forms to commercial purposes was innovative, successful and much adopted by other architects of his generation. Burges divided the frontage vertically, giving the attic storey twin arches linked by a gable, and topped the parapets with finials. The surface became a curious mixture of nineteenth century materials and medieval decoration. An exposed iron girder, stencilled and painted, surmounts a ground floor of glass and iron; two pulleys are supported by lions, the crane by a corbel in the form of an Oriental maid. The decoration is further enhanced by symbolic sculpture by Thomas Nicholls. The contractors were J. & C. I'Anson and the cost £1,413. 11s. The effect was much admired; Burges's associates found it 'plucky', 'strikingly clever', 'a great success'; the *Ecclesiologist* thought it displayed 'great solidity and firmness, plenty of light, every accomodation, and very considerable artistic effect'.*
                                                          M.A.

R.I.B.A. S.N.B. xxxii (1865), 64
B. xxiv (1866), 850-1
**E.* xxvii, NS xxv (1866), 310-11
BN. xiii (1866), 780

A.10

A.8 **Section Through Bombay School of Art**
Photograph
9″ (23)×11⅜″ (34)
Inscribed 'Bombay School of Art. No. 14'
    'Section on line AB'

Lent by the British Architectural Library/R.I.B.A.

A.9 **Front Elevation of Bombay School of Art**
Photograph
9″ (23)×11¾″ (35)
Inscribed 'Bombay School of Art. No. 9'

Lent by the British Architectural Library/R.I.B.A.

A.10 **Perspective of the Bombay School of Art**
Photograph
6½″ (16.5)×10¼″ (26)

Lent by the British Architectural Library/R.I.B.A.

Plate 1. The proposed Law Courts from the Strand

The Law Courts

The Law Courts' competition of 1866 had eleven invited entrants, all of whom produced designs in the Gothic style. Burges went to Blackheath with Godwin to work on his design, he also employed Phéné Spiers as a draughtsman. Burges's published *Report* gave diagrams of several possible basic plans, and the reasons why each was unsuitable; in 54 points he answered all the paragraphs of the instructions, and gave details of the methods and materials of his design and the reasons for their use. It was a very thorough report and an exciting and grandiose plan. His estimated cost was £1,584,589.0.0. His reasons for choice of style were equally grandiose: 'It is by no means favourable to architecture of the nineteenth century that an Architect should have to say anything about the choice of Style. In every other age but our own, but one style was in fashion at the time, and every artist designed in that style. Now, however, it is very different. When we consider the traditions with which our English laws and constitution are surrounded, we naturally seek for some style of architecture which will recall those traditions, and at the same time be the best of its kind. These conditions are fulfilled by the architecture of the thirteenth century .... In selecting the exact variety of the thirteenth century architecture to be adopted, we naturally give the preference to that of our own country'.

Burges excused the rather broad decorative details being French in manner, on the basis that the small mouldings of English thirteenth century architecture would be destroyed by the acids and smoke of the city. The *Ecclesiologist* found his designs ... 'the work of a master mind ... the very best architectural work we have seen since the commencement of the Gothic Revival ... [In] architectural power, artistic talent, and ability to plan ... none ... can compete with Mr. Burges'. To another there was 'no doubt that, whatever may have been the defects of his Law Court design, the facades, the clock tower, and the bridge with which he proposed to span the site of Temple Bar, were among the best efforts of his constructive and artistic ability, and worthy to rank with the best compositions of our age'.* There was criticism among the architectural profession that Burges had rather 'overdone it' in some areas, but on the whole his drawings were acknowledged superior. The judges were less united: some placed Barry first and Scott second; the architectural judges placed Scott first and Waterhouse second. In 1868 a decision was reached with Street the winner, and even then his design was subjected to many cuts and alterations.

M.A.

W. Burges, *Report to the Courts of Justice Commission* (1867)
B. xxv (1867), 89-91, 144, 309-11, 593, 885
BN. xiv (1867), 202-3, 270
C.E.A. Jnl. xxx (1867), 97-8
E. xxxviii NS xxv (1867) 113-20, 292
**R.I.B.A. Trans* (1881-2), 17-30

A.11 **'Report to the Courts of Justice Commission', by William Burges**
1867
Inscribed on the title page: 'Department of Science & Art/Library/From/W. Burges'

This is the official report, as specified by the Commission, containing explanations, plans, and perspectives. Burges lists 54 points answering all the points of the Commission's instructions, and explaining how his plan is suitable, providing for, among other things, ventilation, refreshments, window cleaning and particularly, fire precautions. Also included is the estimate, by Burges's reckoning, a space of 24,583,923 cubic feet at an average cost of 12.685 pence or 1s 0¾d per cubic foot, equalling £1,299,409, which with the added expense of heating, water, approaches and bridges equalled £1,584,589. The explanation is accompanied by five photographs of watercolour perspectives of parts of the interior and exterior of the proposed Law Courts, and twelve printed plans, elevations and sections.

Here open at the second of the photographs, showing an aerial perspective of Burges's proposal for the Law Courts.
M.A.

Victoria and Albert Museum

A.12 **Interior View of the Law Courts**
Pencil and wash on Whatman paper
20" (50.5) ×14¾" (37.5)
Signed W. Burges and A.H. Haig

This perspective shows the interior of a law court, with court in session. One of two watercolours of the interior by Haig, both of which appeared in Burges's *Report to the Courts of Justice Commission*, showing the prospective interior decoration.

W. Burges, *Report to the Courts of Justice Commission* (1867), Pl.3

Victoria and Albert Museum

A.13 **Interior View of the Law Courts**
Pencil and wash on Whatman paper
21½" (54.6)×14¾" (37.5)
Signed W. Burges and A.H. Haig

Perspective showing the interior of the hall of the Law Courts, with small figures representing members of the profession. One of two watercolours by Haig, showing prospective interior decoration.

W. Burges, *Report to the Courts of Justice Commission* (1867), Pl.4

Victoria and Albert Museum

Chimneypiece in the Hall, Worcester College

Worcester College Hall
Burges produced a rough estimate and design for the redecoration of the Hall in June 1873, and a detailed report in November. The walls were to be red, the ceiling filled in compartments with arabesques as in the chapel, the windows were to be of grisaille glass, the columns covered with marble, a new dado was to be installed and a massive inlaid walnut sideboard was to stand at one end. An ornate chimneypiece was to rise to ceiling level, and all the portraits were to be removed or copied and made of uniform size. All this was to be accomplished for £3,035. The Fellows were unhappy with the expense, the 'florid' decoration and particularly the banishment of the college portraits. Burges stood firm over his dislike of dark and ugly portraits, and he refused to diminish either the abundance of Italian decorative work, which he considered 'proper', or the size of the St. Laurence fireplace. The Fellows then asked J.D. Crace to submit designs; Burges capitulated, made reductions and work began in 1876. The finished result was a very subdued version of the original design: plain walls, small dado, ungilded and unstatued chimneypiece, the walls largely red and buff yellow with stencilling. The walnut sideboard survived the cuts, as did the glass, but successive redecorations have since removed all trace of the Burgesian scheme.
M.A.

Worcester College Archive; (J. Campbell) 'The Hall' *Worcester College* (1964-66), 10-20
C.H. Daniel and W.R. Barker, *Worcester College* (1900), 200

A.14 **Perspective of the Hall**

Pencil and watercolour on Whatman paper
10½″ (265)×11¾″ (300)
Unsigned, in the style of A.H. Haig

A finished watercolour showing the Hall completely redecorated as Burges first intended, including several small figures of scholars.

Lent by the Fellows of Worcester College, Oxford

A.15 **Elevation of the South Side of the Hall**

Pencil and watercolour on Whatman paper.
21½″ (545)×30½″ (775)

Inscribed 'WORCESTER.COLLEGE.HALL./N⁰ 2'
top
'W.BVRGES ARCHT/15
BVCKINGHAM ST STRAND W.C.'
bottom
'SOUTH SIDE'

This detailed elevation shows the fireplace wall of the Hall, with the enormous canopied St. Laurence chimneypiece. St. Laurence stands in the middle of the tiled canopy holding his attributes, the martyr's palm and the gridiron, while below him putti hold a laurel wreath within which are the College arms. When asked to design a fireplace both cheaper and less ostentatious Burges replied: 'I should be most unwilling to alter a work which I think is pure art for the mere debased vitruvian of the last century'.

Lent by the Fellows of Worcester College, Oxford

A.16 **Elevation of the West End of the Hall**

Pencil and watercolour on Whatman paper
21½″ (545)×30½″ (775)

This elevation of the West end clearly shows the enormous sideboard of walnut inlaid with tarsia which Burges designed for the Hall, here covered in the College silver, ewers, plates and dishes. In the walled panel can be seen the date MDCCCLXXIII — 1873. The sideboard is currently at Knightshayes, Devon.

Lent by the Fellows of Worcester College, Oxford

A.17 **Design for the Inlay Panel for the East End**

Pencil and wash on three sheets of cartridge paper, joined. The central shield pasted on and outlined in ink
26″ (66)×61″ (154.9)
Inscribed 'This drawing to be/ returned to/ W. Burges Archt/ 15 Buckingham Str Strand/ 6 Aug 1877' Bottom l.h.s.
'Worcester College. Oxford/centre panel in East end.'

This full size drawing for the panel depicts a merman and mermaid flanking an heraldic shield carrying the College arms.

Lent by the Fellows of Worcester College, Oxford

A.18 **Stained Glass Cartoon for part of the East Window**

Pen and ink and wash over pencil on Whatman paper
12¼″ (31)×12¼″ (31)
Inscribed 'ADAM.AND.EVE'

A hexagonal section of the window for the East end of the Hall, showing Adam and Eve with the Angel.

Lent by the Fellows of Worcester College, Oxford

A.19 **Stained Glass Cartoon for Part of the East Window**

Pen and ink and wash over pencil on Whatman paper
12″ (30.5)×12¼″ (31)
Inscribed 'SLENDER.AND.ANNE.PAGE'

A hexagonal section of the window for the East end of the Hall, showing Slender and Anne Page in a bower, from *The Merry Wives of Windsor*.

Lent by the Fellows of Worcester College, Oxford

A.20 **Elevation of the East End of the Hall**

Pencil and watercolour on Whatman paper
21½″ (545)×30½″ (775)
Inscribed 'WORCESTER.COLLEGE.HALL./N⁰3.' top
'W.BVRGES ARCHT 15 BVCKINGHAM ST STRAND. W.C.' bottom
'EAST END/Half inch Scale'

This elevation shows the East window with the hexagonal stained glass panels (A17, 18) and the inlaid panel (A16) as well as a side elevation in pencil of the chimneypiece.

Lent by the Fellows of Worcester College, Oxford

A.18

A.19

The Garden Front at Knightshayes

Knightshayes, Tiverton, Devon

Sir John Heathcoat-Amory (1829-1914), local MP and lace-making magnate, employed Burges to build him a house near Tiverton in Devon. For Burges it was a significant commission, the first house he had been asked to design from scratch; he began work in 1868 and the foundation stone was laid on 16th April 1869 ('Abstract' 1869 — 'First stone at Knightshayes... Knightshayes going on'.) The house is unquestionably High Victorian; solid, gabled and crenellated with a multitude of windows, chimneys and roof lines and an asymetry which C.L. Eastlake found to be 'no doubt adopted for convenience of internal arrangement, and an instance of the ease with which a Gothic elevation may accommodate itself to exigencies of pain without sacrifice of artistic effect'. The builder was Fletcher of Salisbury and the contract for the building of the house, without facing stonework or details, was fixed at £14,080.

In 1873 Burges presented Heathcoat-Amory with an ornate album of designs for his proposed decorative scheme. Decoration was certainly begun, but it seems unlikely that it got beyond the interior corbelling and some of the woodwork. On grounds of economy Burges was replaced by J.D. Crace (1838-1919) in 1874. Changing taste meant that the Crace-Burges interiors were almost entirely eclipsed over the years, but they are now being replaced, where possible, by the National Trust.
M.A.

A. iv (1870), 7
J. Mordaunt Crook, 'Knightshayes, Devon: Burges versus Crace', *National Trust Yearbook* i (1975-76), 44-55.

A.21 **Album of Designs for the Decorative Scheme at Knightshayes**

The 'Abstract of Diaries' for 1873 reads: 'Amory's book finished', and evidently refers to the magnificent album of finished designs for a complete and intricate scheme of decoration for the interior of Knightshayes. Heathcoat-Amory evidently approved the scheme and instructed Burges to continue, but a year later he had lost patience with the time and the expense necessary to bring about Burges's scheme and turned instead to Crace.

Burges was in the habit of collecting his drawings into albums both for himself and as presentation albums of finished drawings of a high quality for his patrons; similar albums were prepared for the alterations at Gayhurst, Cardiff Castle and Castell Coch.

The album contains detailed coloured drawings for the decorative schemes for the hall, passage to garden entrance, library, drawing room, billiard room, staircase, minstrel's gallery, gentleman's room, boudoir and two bedrooms. There are schemes for walls, chimneypieces, ceilings, panelling and bookcases. The album is signed, 'This book was finished Nov 21.1873/William Burges'.

The album is open at the page inscribed 'Knightshayes No 24/Drawing Room/Looking West', and shows the pillared window embrasure with deep buttoned seating and a section of the ceiling. The latter has recently been revealed following the removal of a false ceiling erected in the late 19th century.
M.A.

Lent by The National Trust (Knightshayes, Devon)

'Knightshayes No 24 Drawing Room' (detail)

A.22 **Section from the north, 'Knightshayes No. 7'**

Pencil, pen and wash on Whatman paper
18½″(47.0)×25¾″(65.4)

A proposal for the main block, featuring the hall, main staircase, bedrooms and service wing.

Inscribed 'William Burges Archt, 15 Buckingham Street, Strand W.C.'
Signed '

Like the following six items, taken from a dismembered volume of working drawings, details and proposals recently discovered among the estate papers. V.G.

Lent by the National Trust (Knightshayes, Devon).

A.23 **Elevation from the north, 'Knightshayes No. 10'**

Pencil, pen and wash on Whatman paper
18½″(47.0)×25¾″(65.4)

A proposal for the exterior of the main block, showing minor variations from 'Knightshayes No. 7', particularly in the chimney arrangements.

Inscribed 'William Burges Archt, 15 Buckingham Street, Strand W.C.' V.G.

Lent by the National Trust (Knightshayes, Devon).

Drawing Room ceiling at Knightshayes

A.24

A.24 **Section through the main staircase at Knightshayes**
Pencil, pen and wash on Whatman paper
23½″(59.7)×16⅞″(42.8)

A design for the staircase looking north, showing the turned and carved bannisters in detail.

Inscribed (in pencil) 'W. Burges Archt, 15 Buckingham St W.C.'   V.G.

Lent by the National Trust (Knightshayes, Devon)

A.25 **Elevation from the south, 'Knightshayes No. 11'**
Pencil, pen and wash on Whatman paper
18½″(47)×25¾″(65.5)

Inscribed 'William Burges. Archt./15 Buckingham Street/Strand. W.C.'

Signed 'Robert

A proposal for the south face of the main block, showing some details of the decorative stonework.   M.A.

Lent by the National Trust (Knightshayes, Devon)

A.26 **Three sections, 'Knightshayes No.6'**
Pencil, pen and wash on Whatman paper
17⅞″(45.5)×25½″(65)
Inscribed 'William Burges Archt/15 Buckingham Street/Strand W.C.'
Signed 'Robert Walden'

Three sections through the Library, the Drawing Room and the Gentleman's Room, showing the doors, windows and fireplaces. Each room is annotated to show its purpose.   M.A.

Lent by The National Trust (Knightshayes, Devon)

A.27 **Design for the Construction of the Drawing Room Ceiling, Knightshayes**
Pencil and wash on Whatman paper
21″(53.5)×26″(66)

A section and details for the construction of the Drawing Room ceiling showing the proposed timbering and some of the decoration. The ceiling has recently been revealed at Knightshayes, following the removal of a lower ceiling which had previously obscured Burges's ornate blue and gold timbered original.

Inscribed 'Knightshayes No.33. Drawing Room Ceiling'. 'W. Burges. Arch., 15, Buckingham Street, Strand, W.C.' and signed 'Robert Walden'   M.A.

Lent by The National Trust (Knightshayes, Devon)

A.28 **Sketch for the Hall Chimneypiece at Knightshayes**
Pencil and pen on cartridge paper
8″(20.3)×7½″(19.1)

A very free perspective sketch of the hooded chimneypiece, with a fire blazing in the grate and a roughly indicated standing figure. Possibly by Burges himself. From a sheet labelled 'Knightshayes No. 21'.   V.G.

Lent by The National Trust (Knightshayes, Devon)

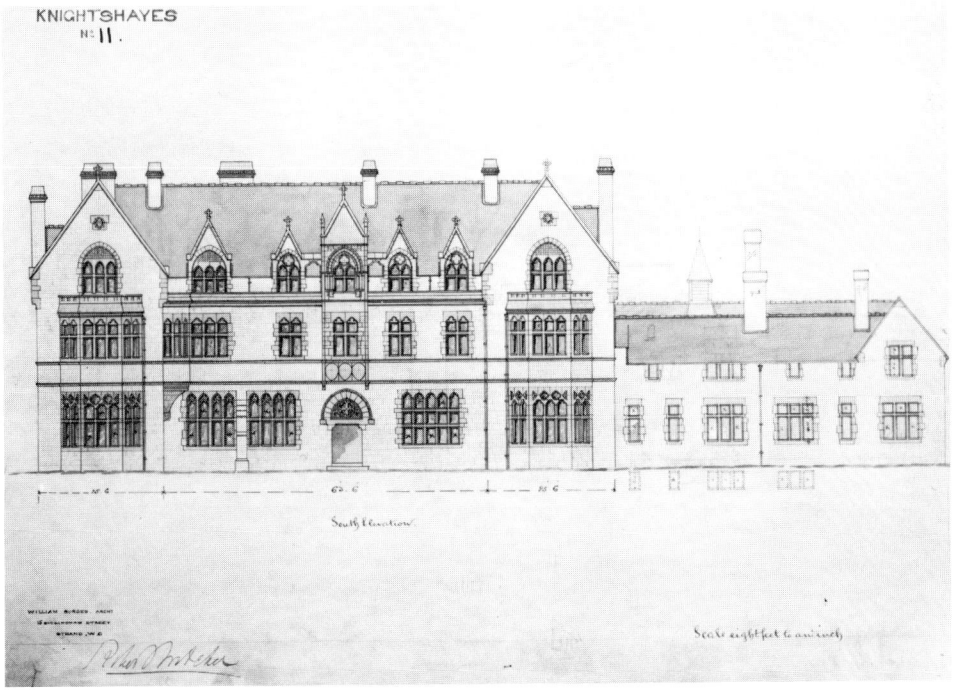

A.25

Harrow Speech Room

For the Speech Room at Harrow, Burges devised a semi-circular plan, employing the sloping site to give a raked section. His aim was a Gothic Revival theatre. The building was of brick, flat roofed and designed to seat a thousand people. In addition, the original intention was also for a museum, laboratory, two science lecture rooms, an art gallery, four classrooms and a gymnasium. These were largely accomplished by refurbishment of the old Speech Room, and with the assistance of Burges's friend, C.F. Hayward (1830-1905). Burges commenced drawing in 1871; the foundation stone was laid in 1874. The nature of the site involved much time and money in engineering and pile sinking, thereby reducing the funds available. The Speech Room was opened in 1877 following some redesigning; the roof became pitched, and the open arcades became towers. Of the latter, one was finished in 1919 and the other by another architect in 1925. Restricted economy also left the interior largely unadorned, and like Trinity College, Hartford, a humble reflection of the original conception. M.A.

Report, 23 Dec 1871 (Weller MSS)
A. viii (1871), 8

A.29 Reproduction from 'The Architect' of July 6, 1872, showing the Interior of the 'Proposed New Speech-Room' at Harrow

One of the early proposals for the interior decoration of the Speech Room, which was never completed. 'The wooden roof over the main body of the auditorium is elaborately decorated, in the centre with a cluster of small inset domes. Concentrically grouped and bordered by delicate tracery, the domes and curves were intended to echo the plan of the seating below. The roof is supported by cast-iron pillars, very tall and thin, at present with gilded capitals. In the auditorium these pillars are arranged in pairs along one of the higher rows of seats, a few yards away from the rear wall; and they follow the same curve. Springing from the capitals a system of arches and vaults, constructed of wood, links the pillars with the roof.' (C. Handley-Read in P. Ferriday, *Victorian Architecture*.) Burges had used iron in the warehouse for Messrs. Skilbeck in 1866, but here he has used it on a much grander scale. M.A.

Lent by J. Mordaunt Crook

A.30

A.30 Reproduction from 'The Architect' of July 6, 1872, showing the Proposed New Speech Room at Harrow

The design is in the form of a bold two storey facade of polychromatic brickwork with pointed arches and a flat roof on a D-shaped plan. This early design is not entirely as executed. M.A.

Lent by J. Mordaunt Crook

Cardiff Castle

The commission to rebuild Cardiff Castle for the 3rd Marquess of Bute was undoubtedly the artistic opportunity of a lifetime for William Burges. For him, Bute was the ideal patron. Held to be the richest man in Britain — his gross annual income was £300,000 when he attained his majority in 1868 — he had the resources to realise the most fantastic schemes which he and his architect could concoct. Intellectually there was also much common ground between the two men. Both were inveterate and curious travellers, both published assiduously on antiquarian and historical subjects; both shared a romantic passion for the Middle Ages. Burges became a frequent guest, treated with affection by both Lord and Lady Bute.

Burges and Bute first met in 1865 when the Marquess was only 18 years old but by the following year a report on how the castle could be developed had already been prepared. Work began immediately after Lord Bute's coming of age in 1868 and the foundation stone of the Clock Tower was laid on 12th March, 1869. The building campaign continued for the rest of Burges's life, and after his death was carried on under William Frame who adhered more or less strictly to his predecessor's designs. Well into the present century the Roman Gateway and the outer walls were still under construction.

The architect had by no means taken over a clear site. Remains of Roman, Norman and Plantagenet masonry punctuated the flat square area. In 1774 Capability Brown was brought in to remove the debris and landscape the central court and Henry Holland to convert the West Wing into habitable living quarters. Further works were carried out about 1817, leaving Burges with a sizeable structure to incorporate into his plans. He first conceived a great tower which would change the landscape of Cardiff, and a sunken medieval garden around the moat to which the citizens could be admitted from time to time. Both conceptions were realised and to them he added the richly varied silhouette and the majestically juxtaposed masses of the present building. For his sources, Burges drew on his extensive travels and the studies he had made of the campanili of San Gimignano, Florence and Siena. He included recollections of Nuremburg and Palermo, of the Château de Chillon on Lake Geneva, the Castello at Milan and the Palais des Papes at Avignon. Nearer home, he took elements from Conway, Caernarvon and Durham Castle.

Exh. *Marble Halls*, V. & A., 1973; *Plans and Prospects*, Welsh Arts Council, Cardiff, 1975; *The Act of Design*, Cardiff Castle, 1977; *Stained Glass Cartoons from the Cardiff Castle Collection*, Cardiff Castle, 1977

Cardiff Castle Drawings Collection; Mt. St. MSS; R.I.B.A. Drawings Collection; N.M.W. John Ward Papers; Clark, G.T., 'Cardiff Castle' *Archaeologia Cambrensis*, 3rd series viii (1862) 249-71; 5th series vii (1890), 283-92; Burges, W., *Architectural Drawings*, pl.22, 1870; Sesom-Hiley, H., 'Cardiff Castle', *Cardiff Times* and *South Wales Daily News* (1912, 1921); Girouard, M., 'Cardiff Castle'. *Country Life*, cxxix (1961) 760-63, 822 *et seq*.; Rees W., *Cardiff — A History of the City*, 1962; Davies, J., *Cardiff and the Marquises of Bute*, Cardiff, 1981; Hilling, J., *Cardiff and the Valleys*, 1973; Glenn, C., *The Lords of Cardiff Castle*, 1976; Girouard, M. *The Victorian Country House*, revised edition, 1979

Cardiff Castle Before Burges

A.31 **Cardiff Castle from the West with the River Taff in the Foreground**
Pencil on paper
4″ (10.2)×12½″ (31.7)

A general view of the landscape with the castle in the centre. Inscribed on the reverse 'By Swayne of Bristol/c 1850'.

National Museum of Wales

A.32 **The South Gate of Cardiff Castle in Glamorgan Shire**
Aquatint, after Paul Sandby
1775
8½″ (21.6)×10½″ (26.7)

This view shows part of the West front of the castle with the octagon tower in the centre. The river has been diverted some distance away in modern times and a canalised moat, part of Burges's schemes, now takes its place.

National Museum of Wales

A.33 **Cardiff Castle from the West**
Aquatint; after Paul Sandby
1777
8″ (20.3)×11½″ (29.2)

A view taken from the north walls showing the rear of the Keep and the west wall running down to the west wing in the centre of the composition; the 13th century Black Tower which forms the present entrance is also just visable.

National Museum of Wales

A.34 **Cardiff Castle from the Outer Ward**
Lithograph after a daguerrotype by Jacquier
11¾″ (29.8)×19½″ (49.5)

A mid-19th century view of the Castle from the grounds, taken from the east, with the medieval Keep on the right hand side, the West Wing in the centre and the Black Tower on the left.

National Museum of Wales

A.35

A.35 **Survey Drawing of Cardiff Castle from the South West**
Pencil, pen and wash on Whatman paper
9⅞"(25.1)×14"(35.6)

A carefully ruled perspective drawing of the west range of the castle, tinted in sepia, with rough pencil sketches above. Probably dating from the second quarter of the 19th century and possibly associated with shemes for redevelopment under the Second Marquess.

Signed, 'J.D.' V.G.

National Museum of Wales

A.36 **Survey Drawing of Cardiff Castle from the North West**
Pencil, pen and wash on Whatman paper
9⅞"(25.1)×14"(35.6)

A companion piece to the previous drawing, showing the same part of the building from a different angle.
V.G.

National Museum of Wales

A.37 **A Photograph of the West Wing with Alterations Sketched in**
Photograph, with ink alterations
9"(229)×11⅜"(288)

A photograph by Mr. Collings of Cardiff pre-dating the works of the 1870s, with the rough shapes of the Bute, Herbert and Beauchamp Towers brushed in, probably by Burges himself.

Lent by Cardiff City Council

The Patron

A.38 **John Patrick Stuart, Marquis of Bute and Earl of Dumfries Baron Cardiff of Cardiff Castle**
Lithograph, after a daguerrotype by Jacquier
11¾"(29.8)×8½"(21.6)

A portrait of the 3rd Marquess as a child in front of the residential west wing of Cardiff Castle in the form in which he inherited it.

National Museum of Wales

A.39 **The Marquess and the Marchioness of Bute in 1872**
Steel engravings
1872
8½"(21.6)×6"(15.2) each

Head and shoulders portraits of the bride (Lady Gwendolen Howard) and groom taken to celebrate their marriage on 16th April 1872.

National Museum of Wales

A.40 **Caricature Sketches of the Marquess of Bute**
Pen on cartridge paper
10½"(26.7)×8½"(21.6)

Humorous sketches of Lord Bute as Lord Mayor of Cardiff, an authority on ghosts, an antiquarian and a handsome figure 'stands over 6ft.' along with one of Disraeli incorporating him as hero of his novel *Lothair*.

National Museum of Wales

A.41 **The 3rd Marquess of Bute**
Photograph
11½"(29.2)×9¼"(23.5)

A portrait of Lord Bute as an older man.

National Museum of Wales

A.37

Cardiff Castle — After Burges

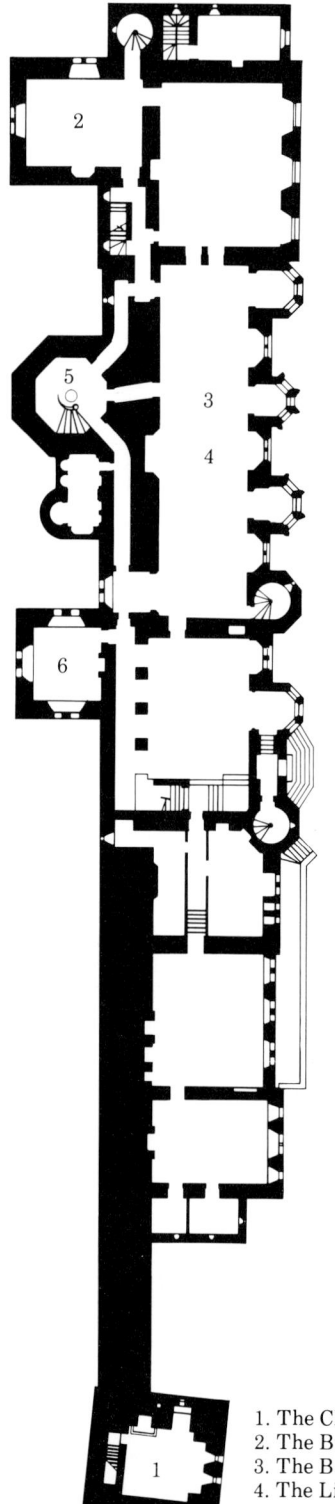

1. The Clock Tower
2. The Bute Tower
3. The Banqueting Hall
4. The Library
5. The Beauchamp Tower
6. The Herbert Tower

A.42 **Two Sections of the Main Block Looking West**
Pencil and wash on flimsy, pasted to Whatman paper; further details in pen and wash on Whatman paper
19⅞″ (50.5)×26⅛″ (66.5)

Showing the Herbert Tower, the Guest Tower, the Staircase and the Entrance Hall in fine detail with 'medieval' figures; annotated with written instructions at many points. There are two sections of the building at different stages moving west. The section on flimsy is more impressionistic and less functional than the other; a very small sketchy version of the Grand Staircase has been pasted over the main drawing.

Lent by Cardiff City Council

A.43 **The Grand Staircase, a Perspective View of the Proposed Design**
Watercolour on paper
24½″ (62.3)×19¾″ (50.2)
By A.H. Haig
1874

This would have been the gothic high point of the whole Cardiff Castle transformation. The combination of tracery, polychromy and intricate spatial relationships at different levels all flowing around the central monumental figure of the equestrian knight was to have been intensely theatrical. Its position in the house can be seen in the previous drawing. In the event only part of the scheme was executed, and that was cleared away early in the 20th century, leaving the Castle with only minor turret stairs and the brilliantly decorated but small staircase in the Octagon Tower.

R.P. Pullan, *The Architectural Designs of William Burges, ARA*, 1883, Pl.33
Exh *Marble Halls*, V.&A., 1973, 29 ill.
Exh *RA* 1874, no. 1146

Lent anonymously

The partially completed Grand Staircase in 1891

The Clock Tower

This contains three important interiors—the Winter Smoking Room entered from the level of the covered walkway, the Bachelor's Bedroom immediately above and the Summer Smoking Room occupying the top floor with a gallery and a domed ceiling rising into the interior of the lantern. The exterior ornamentation and the decorative schemes of these three rooms all have linked iconographic themes. On the outside, the faces of the clock are surrounded by statues (painted by Weekes and Smallfield) of the seven planets on plinths carved with their respective signs of the zodiac. The Winter Smoking Room has illustrated cycles of the seasons, the months and the days of the week taken from sources as diverse as Norse legends and Greek mythology. Alchemy is the basis of the decoration of the Bachelor Bedroom with precious stones representing the zodiac once again, labelled 'Gems' on the walls, actual polished stones from the Bute estate set into the chimneypiece and historical goldsmiths portrayed on the vaulting. Allegories of six precious jewels fill the windows. Further zodiac symbols appear on the tiles of the Summer Smoking Room, complemented by emblems of the five Continents on the floor, where they are depicted along with the Holy City and the life patterns of birds and beasts. Astronomy is the inspiration of this room. Great swooping sculptures of the eight winds of Greek fable form the supporting corbels for the gallery. Together they represent the divisions of Time and the organisation of the Cosmos. These thematic complexities combined with the extreme theatricality of the individual rooms amazed and bewildered Burges's contemporaries. *The Building News*, perhaps, spoke for many of them when it wrote, 'the portentous corbellings (in the Summer Smoking Room) are of a character of design which we honestly allow we fail to comprehend.' V.G.

A.44 Section of New Tower—No.9

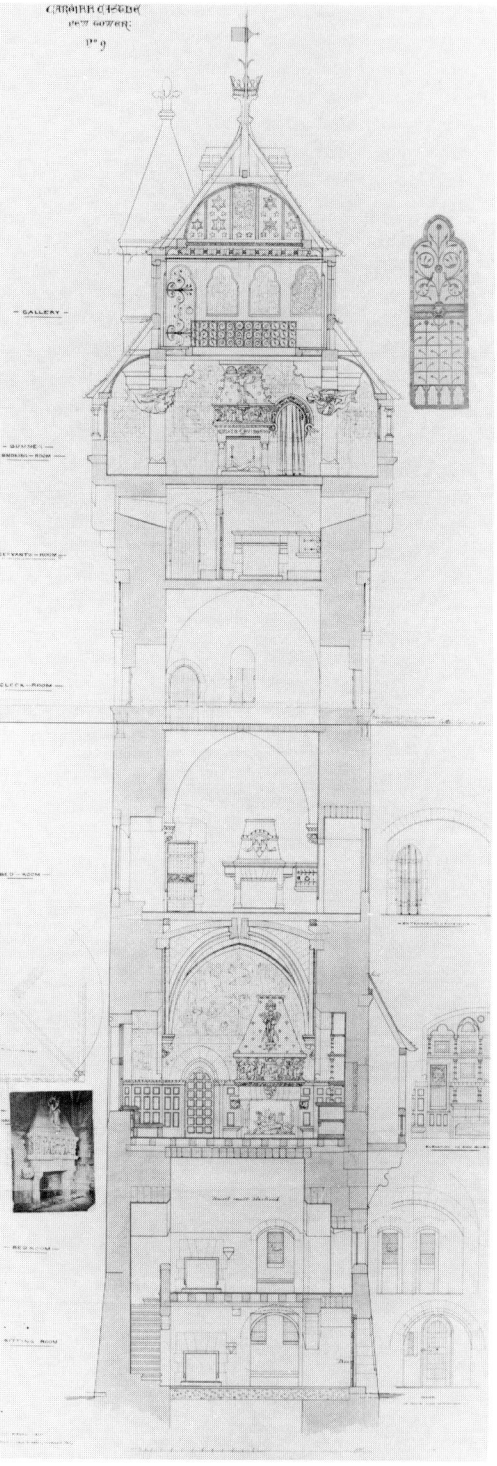

A.44

Pencil, pen and wash on cartridge paper
In two parts respectively 34⅜″(82.7)×24½″(62); 34¾″(88.3)×24⅝″(67)

One of a series of at least ten proposals for the Clock Tower, none of the surviving examples exactly as built. These sheets show a section with plan and elevations of details. Two early photographs have been attached.
Inscribed 'William Burges, Arch't 15 Buckingham Street, Strand, WC. Cardiff Castle'

Lent by Cardiff City Council

A.45 **Winter Smoking Room—Perspective of Corner**
Pencil and watercolour on cartridge paper
17″(44.9)×13½″(34.5)

An unfinished sketch showing chimneypiece, door, window embrasure and vault.

Lent by Cardiff City Council

A.46

A.46 **View of the Winter Smoking Room with Medieval Figures**
Watercolour on paper
By A.H. Haig
1870
14″(35.5)×16″(40.6)

A fanciful view of the room with two gentlemen before a blazing fire with smoking pipes, ivory caskets and exotic vessels on the table and a lady seated in the window embrasure.

Exh., R.A. 1870, No. 744/752
Lent by The National Trust (Knightshayes, Devon)

A.47 **Winter Smoking Room—Design for Mural Decoration**
Pen and watercolour on cartridge paper, with pasted on additions and alterations
Original measurements obscured

A design for chimneypiece, ceiling and vault
The walls and spandrels were painted by Weekes with the twelve signs of the zodiac. Lonsdale contributed murals of the origins of music and dancing, and four seasons appear in pictorial form. The apple gathering shown here represents autumn, while the indoor amusements of winter are carved on the chimneypiece

Lent by Cardiff City Council

A.48 **Winter Smoking Room—Design for Mural Decoration**
Pen and watercolour on cartridge paper, with pasted on additions and alterations
1874
Cut down from original measurements

Fragments from a scheme of painted decoration for the upper walls and lunettes, showing Aries, Taurus and Leo in roundels flanked by pastoral scenes.
Signed and dated 'Mr Hobart March 14/74.'
Very similar in technique to the previous item, but rather more precise in execution.

Lent by Cardiff City Council

A.49

A.49 **Winter Smoking Room—Designs for Marquetry Panels**
Pen and wash on paper
1872
Original measurements obscured

18 small designs to be carried out in coloured woods, shell and mother of pearl; the motifs being foliage and comic grotesque monsters.
This sheet was formerly inscribed in pencil 'Thomas John 1872'

Lent by Cardiff City Council

A.50 **Designs for the Doors to the Winter Smoking Room and the Bachelor Bedroom**

(a) Pen and wash on paper
1872
12¾"(32.4)×13½"(34.2)

A detailed design with an early photograph mounted alongside; a lancet top opening, the inner face with a leafy tree inhabited by an 'orchestra' of birds and animals.
Signed 'W. Burges/Architect/June 17 1872'
Inscribed in the same hand 'Cardiff Castle/New Tower/Entrance door to winter/smoking room/Material—Walnut/executed at Lord Bute's own workshops—/the inlays of box wood/also executed at the same/place. The exterior covered with red leather/Mr Shrivell of/London. The iron work is gilt/and the birds coloured green/with red heads—one of the birds acts/as the handle/and lock. Mother o'pearl/is used for the/little dots/at A and the other/details of Marquetry'.

(b) pen and wash on paper
1872
12¾"(32.4)×13½"(34.2)

Detailed designs for the interior and exterior of the door, with enlarged detail of the inlay and a section below.
Signed and dated as (a).
Inscribed 'DOOR IN BEDROOM./New Tower/Cardiff Castle/door to bedroom/material teak/Marquetry border ivory/and ebony'
'The carving deeply/cut like the arab/and Norwegian doors/the ground of carving/gilt and glazed with red./Iron work tinned (r.d.)/executed by Mr Shrivell/of London'
'The carving executed by Lord Bute's workmen/from models by Mr./Nicholls the sculptor/ The hinges are pierced and red and black velvet placed beneath them'.
In pencil is the note 'The shields are blazoned in their proper colors'.

Lent by Cardiff City Council

A.51 **The Summer Smoking Room in use in the late 19th century**

A plate from *Historic Houses of the United Kingdom* (1892).

A.52 **'Corbels in Summer Smoking Room—New Tower, Cardiff Castle'**
Reproduction from 'The Architect', Sept. 14 1872

The four great corbels with the figures identified as AQUILO, SEPTENTRIO, SUBSOLANDS, EURUS, AFRICUS, AUSTER, ZEPHYRUS and CORUS.
Inscribed 'T. Nicholls, Sculptor'
'W. Burges, Architect'

National Museum of Wales

The Summer Smoking Room

(detail)

A.53

A.55

A.53 Tulip Vase
Porcellaneous stoneware
1874
Height 14½″/37.0)

A central vase with four tulip holders arranged around the neck, the lower parts decorated with scale pattern, the upper parts with parakeets amid blue foliage. Round the body, between two coats of arms of the third Marquess of Bute, is the legend 'IOHNS PACTS.MARQ.DeBUTE', and around the top of the central tulip-holder 'ANNO:DOMINI:1874' One of four vases designed by Burges for the Summer Smoking Room at Cardiff Castle. Similar shapes in monochrome glazes appear among the furnishings at Buckingham Street and Tower House. The form is drawn in the 'Vellum Sketchbook' where it is called 'Pot from Java', but it also owes much to the silhouette of a favourite Burges medieval structure —the kitchen at Marmoutier   V.G.

Victoria and Albert Museum

A.54 Sketch for Entrance to Summer Smoking Room
Pencil, pen and wash on Whatman paper
15″(43)×11¾″(27)
Watermarked WHATMAN 1871

A rough sketch probably in Burges's own hand, showing a plan, section and elevation.
Signed 'W. Burges Archt.
    15 Buckingham St
      Strand W.C.'
Inscribed 'CARDIFF CASTLE/Parapet to landing for Summer Smoking Room'.

Lent by Cardiff City Council

A.55 Tile Designs for the Summer Smoking Room
Pen, pencil and wash
Original measurements lost

Fragments of designs for painted tiles for the walls in a style close to that signed 'Mr Hobart', they show romanticised medieval figures representing the signs of the zodiac. The cartoons were undertaken by Frederick Smallfield.

Lent by Cardiff City Council

The Bute Tower

The foundation stone of the Bute Tower was laid on 24th April 1873. Here the embellishments are a splendid mixture of religious imagery and exotic ornament. The Small Dining Room which is on the same level as the Library, that is an elevated ground floor, illustrates the life of Abraham in the windows and the *Annunciation to Sarah* on the chimneypiece. Two storeys above, Lord Bute's Sitting Room has a frieze of the *Life of St. Blane* and the Seven Deadly Sins on the door. Lord Bute's Bedroom immediately above takes as its inspiration St. John, his patron saint. The Evangelist and his symbol, the eagle, appear cast in bronze over the mantel and the Seven Churches whom he addressed in his Revelation are portrayed in the stained glass. Even the Roof Garden which crowns the tower is presided over by a freestanding Madonna and Child and the painted tiles of the walls carry suitable Hebrew inscriptions and stories from the Book of Kings. However, the overall impression is far from being that of ascetic piety, due in the main to a strong admixture of Moorish and Arab elements culled by Burges from his travels and studies in Sicily and the Near East. The gilded ceiling of the Small Dining Room, with its fat round beams and domed coffering, the elaborate latticed partitions screening Lord Bute's Bathroom and the very conception of a courtyard garden with a fountain, produce an atmosphere of Oriental luxury overriding the iconographic solemnities.   V.G.

The Small Dining Room

A.56 **Small Dining Room—Designs for The Abraham Chimneypiece**
Pencil, pen and wash on paper
18⅞"(48)×24¼"(61.4)

A design and a series of details, with two early photographs pasted on. The chimneypiece shows Sarah to the left hand side and Abraham to the right, on corbels. On the face of the overmantel are the three angels, under a crocketed gothic arcade below a square-towered spire. On the frieze below are battling figures in medieval dress and a coat of arms in a shield. The Greek inscription above the fireplace itself translates as 'Entertaining Angels Unawares'
Signed 'W. Burges Archt'
Inscribed 'Liveries/Howard red and white/Stuart blue and gold/Hastings black and white/Crichton blue and white'
This chimneypiece was originally designed as part of the Hartford commission and recurs frequently in Burges' notebooks. It was carried out here in Painswick sandstone for the lower part, the frieze at least being carved by Nicholls; the upper sections are either Caen stone or Corsham Bath stone. The room was first planned in 1872, and it was for its decoration the following year that Campbell, Smith and Co. were introduced into the Cardiff Castle works. Burges had taught Charles Campbell to draw and also trained him in composition and the use of colour.   V.G.

Lent by Cardiff City Council

A.57 **Designs for the Small Dining Room Ceiling**
Pencil and wash on paper
17⅜"(44)×15¼"(38.8)
A plan, section and small perspective sketch
Inscribed 'W. Burges/15 Buckingham Street/Strand W.C.'

Burges possessed a number of books on Moorish design in Spain, Sicily and the Arab world. It appeared to be these artistically and geographically peripheral examples of Islamic art which appealed to him most, with their additions of local and antique motifs. His own personal favourite among such buildings appears to have been the Cathedral at Messina, which he rather improbably compared with San Paolo fuori le Mura in Rome.

Lent by Cardiff City Council

A.58 **Designs for the Small Dining Room Windows**
Pen and wash on paper
7"(17.8)×11⅞(30)

A set of small designs showing marrative scenes from the life of Abraham. The windows were carried out by Lonsdale and Saunders about 1873.

Lent by Cardiff City Council

A.56

A.58

Lord Bute's Bedroom and Bathroom beyond in the 19th century

A.59 **Designs for the Chimneypiece for Lord Bute's Bedroom**
Pencil and wash on paper, the inscription on a sheet of attached flimsy
19″(48.3)×26¾″(68)

A plan, section and elevation, with sketches of architectural detail. A very worn version of Burges's signature.
Inscribed 'Cardiff Castle/Lord Bute's own Room/Chimney piece/inch scale'.

Lent by Cardiff City Council

A.60 **Design for Statue of St. John the Evangelist for Lord Bute's Bedroom**
Pencil, pen and wash on paper
18½″(47)×26⅛″(66.3)
A design with numerous details of engraving, enamelling, filigree and other decoration for the figure of St. John
Inscribed 'Bronze figure to Chimneypiece/Details of Gilding, Engraving &c'.
With instructions probably in Burges's own hand 'Bird to have the tips of/feathers gilt and the head/Mercury gilding. Beak and claws silver/Breastplate copper enamel/and gilt jewels real/also chains/Engraved cross hatched or cut down all the lines to be deep./Eagles 20/Stole—cut right side of stole off/'

Lent by Cardiff City Council

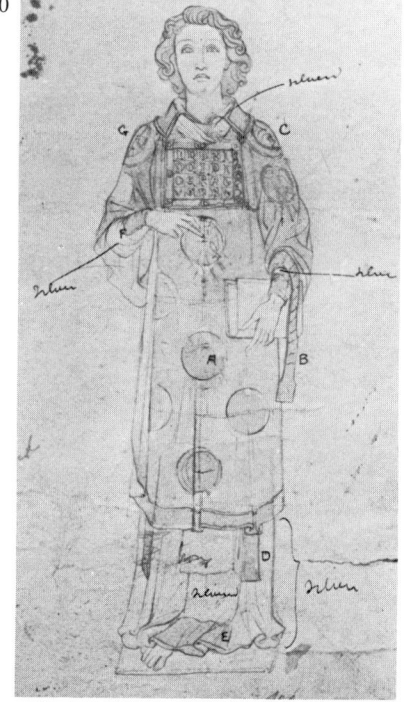

(detail)

A.61

A.62 **Lord Bute's Bedroom—Perspective Drawing of Window Embrasure**
Pencil and wash on Whatman paper
Original measurements obscured.

An unfinished sketch of a corner of the room indicating the great richness of the decoration and the combination of Moorish and religious elements, Probably in Burges's own hand.

Lent by Cardiff City Council

A.63

A.61 **Statue of St. John the Evangelist**
Bronze, hollow cast, partly gilt, partly oxidised and partly silvered; the frontal *basse taille* enamel, the eyes set with onyx, the robe with copper inlays
H. 34″ (86.5)

A standing figure of the young St. John, his robe scattered with splayed eagles and engraved inscriptions, the rays around them inlaid in copper. The enamel inscription reads 'IN PRI/NCIPI/O ERAT/VERBM'

The figure was modelled by Fucigna and cast by Barkentin between 1874 and 1876. Ceccardo E. Fucigna exhibited ten works of sculpture at the Royal Academy between 1863 and 1879. The subjects were varied; genre pieces like 'the first bouquet' and 'the fortune teller', allegorical subjects such as 'Meekness' and 'Spring' and religious scenes including the 'Last Supper', executed for Lightcliffe Church, Halifax. He had been chief assistant to John Birnie Phillip and on the latter's death took over many of his workshop's commissions, a move which was supported by Birnie Phillip's widow, W. Calder Marshall and Sir G. Gilbert Scott. His other outstanding work in Cardiff Castle is the altar in the Oratory. This has the dead Christ entombed, carved in marble behind a grille under the altar table, and the sleeping soldiers outside cast in bronze. V.G.

Lent by Cardiff City Council

A.63 **Basin from Lord Bute's Bedroom**
Earthenware, tin glazed in the fashion of maiolica
Diameter 18⅛″ (47) Depth 8¼″ (21)

A deep round bowl designed to be set into a shelf and to swivel. In blue, green, ochre, brown and grey; the arms of Bute and Howard quartered are at one side. A mermaid combs her hair in the bottom of the bowl and monsters swim above her under an arcade of stone arches. An inscription taken from Tennyson runs round the bowl 'WHO:WOULD:BE:A:MERMAID:FAIR: SINGING:ALONE:COMBING:HER:HAIR: UNDER: THE:SEA:IN:GOLDEN:CURL:WITH: A:COMB: OF:PEARL'.
Burges was much taken with the motif of the Mermaid which recurs frequently in his notebooks and sketches. He had a very similar bowl with the same inscription made for his own house in gilt brass with silver and niello decoration.
Lord Bute's bathroom was very luxurious. It is separated from the bedroom itself by screens with Turkish style wooden grilles; the latticed windows were originally filled with translucent alabaster and the walls are inset with thirty-six types of marble. V.G.

Lent by Cardiff City Council

The Roof Garden

A.64 Design for the Roof Garden
Ink and wash on tissue
In two parts, original measurements obscured

One of a series of designs prepared by Burges for the Roof Garden, none of them as executed. The statue of the Madonna and Child form the central feature along with the fountain in this version, whereas in the final arrangement they are separated. Fucigna and Barkentin were also responsible for this statue, which is very close to some late 13th century French prototype, probably the *Vièrge Dorée* at Amiens.

Lent by Cardiff City Council

A.65 Designs for Roof Garden Wall Tiles
Pen, pencil and watercolour on paper
Original measurements lost

Twelve fragments pasted together showing the story of Elijah and the prophets of Baal. These too vary considerably from the scheme as carried out.

Lent by Cardiff City Council

A.65

(detail)

The Library and the Banqueting Hall

These two great apartments, by far the largest Burges rooms in the Castle, occupy the greater part of the original medieval structure. The three octagonal bay windows and the matching staircase turret were retained and the medieval form of the great hall was reinstated in the Banqueting Hall with the screens passage and gallery over it. The first drawings for the Library appear in 1873, for the Banqueting Hall directly above a little later. Work on both continued well into the decade after Burges's death. The Library is peopled by scholars, prophets and kings. They fill the windows, they appear in marquetry on the bookcase ends and their names—from Sophocles to Schiller—are written on the walls. Over another spectacular chimneypiece are sculpted personifications of the Greek, Assyrian, Hebrew and Egyptian alphabets alongside a portrait of Lord Bute himself in the guise of Celtic learning. In all this the hand of the patron is surely evident. To a writer, commentator and translator who published on subjects ranging from Celtic history to contemporary Russian novels, from the *Alleged Haunting of B(allechin) House* to Wagner, and produced his *magnum opus* on the *Roman Breviary*, the design of his library would have been of particular personal interest. Lord Bute must also have enjoyed the story of Robert the Consul which rampages round the upper walls of the Banqueting Hall and takes three-dimensional form in the miniature castle over the fireplace. This very piece of Glamorgan's history had formed the greater part of his own address to the Archaeological Institute at the opening of their annual meeting in Cardiff in 1871 when he took office as President of the Meeting. The architectural details of the room are a cross between the Continental Flamboyant and the English Perpendicular styles, to which Burges has added a hammer-beam roof complete with angels taken from some East Anglian ecclesiastical source.

V.G.

The Library chimneypiece

A.66 **Elevation of the Fireplace Wall of the Library**

Pen, pencil and wash
12¼"(31.2)×39¼"(100)

The elaborately crocketed doorcase to the Beauchamp Tower and the chimneypiece. The latter is not in the most characteristic Burges hooded shape, but takes the form of a Perpendicular arch over an arcade of five vaulted Flamboyant niches under ogee arches heavy with cusping, crockets and leafy finials; the whole being recessed into the plane of the wall in contrast to the marked sculptural projection of most of the other major chimneypieces in the Castle.

Lent by Cardiff City Council

A.66

A.69

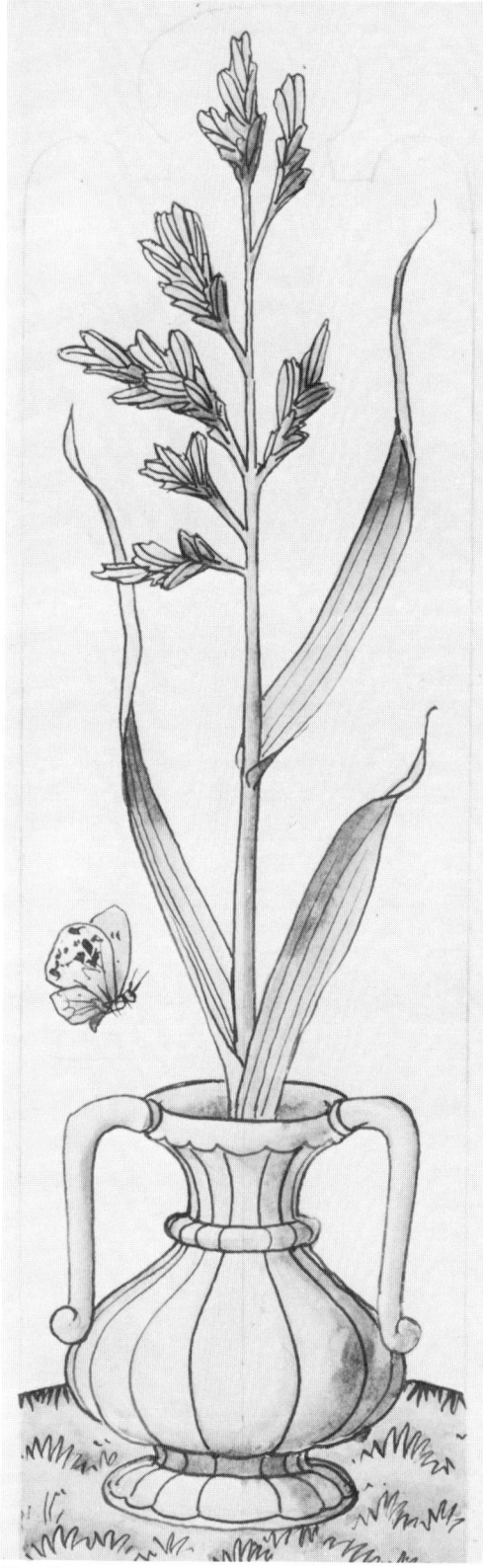

(detail)

A.67 **Design for the Library bookcases**
Pencil and wash on thick cartridge paper.
20″(51)×27″(68.5)

These show the principal ranges of bookcases with an alternative idea for cupboards below the shelves. Three flaps with further options are stuck on.
Inscribed 'These figures to be the same size as windows in the Library'
Lonsdale and Worrall did the stained glass in question, while the fittings which are of mahogany, inlaid with Californian marble and tulip wood marquetry were made by Gillow.

Lent by Cardiff City Council

A.68 **Marquetry Design—Figure for the End of a Library Bookcase**
Pen, wash and pencil on Whatman paper
32⅝″(830)×19⅝″(497)
A seated figure of Euripedes for the end of the Herbert bookcase, on a trilobate lancet.
These cartoons were drawn out by Lonsdale about 1876. All the major ranges of bookcases were called after branches of Bute's family (Herbert, Crichton, Stuart etc.). But they have usually been more familiarly known by the names of the animals carved on their ends by Nicholls. These include charming beasts like the armadillo, the wombat and the beaver.

Lent by Cardiff City Council

A.69 **Marquetry design—Panels for a Library Door**
Pencil, pen and wash
29″(73.6)×21″(53.4)

Eight lancet shaped reserves with trilobate tops containing formalised plants, with insects and small animals in the spaces between the tracery above.
Inscribed 'Cardiff Castle Library/Door to back stairs/No. 1 Juniper/No. 2 Hop/No. 3 Potato/No. 4 Barley'.
Also 'Cardiff Library/Door to Octagon stairs/No. 1 papyrus/No. 2 flax/ No. 3 gall nuts/No. 4 reed'.

Lent by Cardiff City Council

A.70 **Design for Marquetry for a Seat in the Library**
Pencil, pen and wash on paper
1880
15⅜″(39)×15½″(39.2)

Two lancet panels with lobed tops, one bearing the Stuart arms the other a formalised plant.
Inscribed 'Cardiff Castle. Library seat/inlay in panels of back. Full size. W.Burges, Archt/15 Buckingham St Strand/April 1880'.

Lent by Cardiff City Council

A.72

A.71 Fireplace Wall and Portion of West Wall of the Banqueting Hall
Pencil, ink and watercolour on Whatman paper
1877
26½"(67.3)×26½"(67.3)

The chimneypiece is a miniature battlemented castle with waving ladies and trumpeting heralds on top of the towers. A bellicose Robert the Consul rides out from under the portcullis, while his unfortunate uncle, Robert the Norman, watches from his dungeon window.
Inscribed 'Banqueting Hall Chimneypiece', there are numerous notes and instructions for painting and the order 'To be returned to/W.Burges, 15 Buckingham St/Feb 23. 1877.'
Burges had previously used a similar medieval castle motif in a chimneypiece design for Knightshayes. Its origins probably lay in one of the 15th. century French domestic buildings of which he was so fond, and of which he made so many sketches.

Lent by Cardiff City Council

A.72 North Wall of the Banqueting Hall
Pencil, pen and wash on paper
20⅛"(51.1)×26⅞"(68.2)

This elevation shows the sideboard wall flanked by doorways, their ogee tops elaborately crocketed, under large foliate finials. In the tympanum of each is a shield, the left labelled 'Dumfries' and the right 'Windsor'.
Inscribed in pencil 'This sideboard approved'.
The sideboard was part of the Banqueting Hall woodwork to be executed in Burges's lifetime. It was designed in 1874 and carried out between 1878 and 1879.

Lent by Cardiff City Council

A.73

A.73 **Design for Mural Decoration for the North Wall of the Banqueting Hall**
Pencil, pen and wash on paper
1875
18″(47)×24⅝″(66)

The scene is the marriage of Robert the Consul with Mabel Fitzhamon. In the background is the facade of a church somewhat resembling Poitiers. Signed 'H.W. Lonsdale May/75'.

Lent by Cardiff City Council

A.74 **Design for Mural Decoration for the East Wall of the Banqueting Hall**
Pen, pencil and watercolour
18″(47)×24⅝″(66)

The narrative continues with Henry I on his death bed seeking Robert's support for Matilda; and Robert and Stephen swearing allegiance to her cause. All the murals are carefully set in the midst of early Romanesque architecture appropriate to the historical dates (*Circa* 1116-1147) of the events portrayed.

Lent by Cardiff City Council

The Banqueting Hall looking north

The Beauchamp Tower

It is the Beauchamp Tower which lends most excitement and variety to the masses of the Castle as seen from the West. Between its bulky square neighbours, its slender shape, dictated by its octagonal 15th century foundations, and its elaborate wooden filigree spire (surely drawn by Burges from the *flèche* of Amiens Cathedral which he had studied so laboriously) bring to mind a detail from the *Très Riches Heures* of the Duc de Berry. It contains one magnificent Burges apartment, the Chaucer Room. This has a gallery and a clerestory extending up into the timber structure. The murals, the glass and the carving illustrate the *Canterbury Tales* and a statue of Chaucer himself presides over the chimneypiece. The *flèche* was first thought of as early as 1872, but the decoration of the room inside was still in progress in the year of Burges's death.   V.G.

The Chaucer Room

A.75

A.75 Proposals for the Construction of the Chaucer Room

Pencil and wash on Whatman paper
In two sections respectively 23″(58.5)×11¼″(28.5) and 12″(30.5)×11″(27.5)

The smaller sheet is an alternative design for the upper parts of the room. A perspective sketch, possibly in Burges's own hand showing arrangements of the gallery, balustrading and vault.

Lent by Cardiff City Council

A.76 **Window Designs for the Chaucer Room**
Pencil, pen and watercolour on Whatman paper
Sixteen panels 12″(30.5)×4⅜″(11.2)

From the set of thirty-two windows designed for the clerestory by Lonsdale and carried out by Worrall, each showing a different character from the *Canterbury Tales*.

Lent by Cardiff City Council

A.77 **Design for the Floor of the Chaucer Room**
Pen and wash on flimsy, pasted on Whatman paper
28⅜″(72)×18⅝″(47)

A design for the tiled 'maze' on the floor and some of the passage, with the type of tile to be used denoted by letters.
Inscribed 'Cardiff Castle/floor of Chaucer Room'. Burges was certainly familiar with the famous 'labyrinth' on the floor at Reims Cathedral and may well have taken his inspiration from there.

Lent by Cardiff City Council

A.78 **Tile Patterns for the Chaucer Room**
Pen and watercolour, small printed section pasted on
12⅛″(31)×8″(20.5)

A selection of tiles for the fireplace; lotus motifs for the sides and an alphabet for the hearth.
Inscribed 'Chaucer Room—Octagon Tower Cardiff Castle'.
The tiles were supplied by Simpson.

Lent by Cardiff City Council

The Herbert Tower
Basically a sixteenth-century structure, this tower houses two of Burges's finest miniature interiors. These are the Study and the Arab Room, both belonging to the last months of his work in 1880-81. The Arab Room, near the top of the Herbert Tower is the culmination of the architect's experiments as already seen in Lord Bute's Bedroom and the Small Dining Room. Under a breathtaking coffered and domed ceiling, richly painted and gilded, marble, tiles, fretwork shutters at the windows and arcades of tiny arches along the upper walls combine to produce an effect of hazy, romantic, Oriental opulence. V.G.

The Arab Room chimneypiece   *Detail of the Arab Room ceiling*

A.79 **An Elevation and Section for the Fireplace Wall of the Arab Room**
Pen and wash on flimsy
17⅜″(44.2)×26⅛″(66.3)

The fireplace is treated as an Islamic lobed ogee arch in panels of scrolling foliage. Round the border is the inscription 'Ioannes Marchio Bute—erected MDCCCLXXXI—William Burges Arc'. The overmantel is composed of a series of Moorish niches with vases flanking the low four-centered arch; the whole topped with a cornice of fleurons and two parakeets.
Neither this drawing nor the next in the catalogue show the room as actually carried out.

Lent by Cardiff City Council

A.80 **A Proposed Scheme of Decoration for the Window Wall and Ceiling of the Arab Room**
Ink, wash and pencil on flimsy
22½″(57.2)×18″(45.7)

Here the scheme in the fireplace wall drawing is carried round two lobed lancet windows, with elaborate pierced and bobbin-turned screens and decorated shutters. Alongside is a section of the proposed vault with angels and winged beasts.

Lent by Cardiff City Council

A.80

Cardiff Castle Chapel, a memorial to the 2nd Marquess

A.81

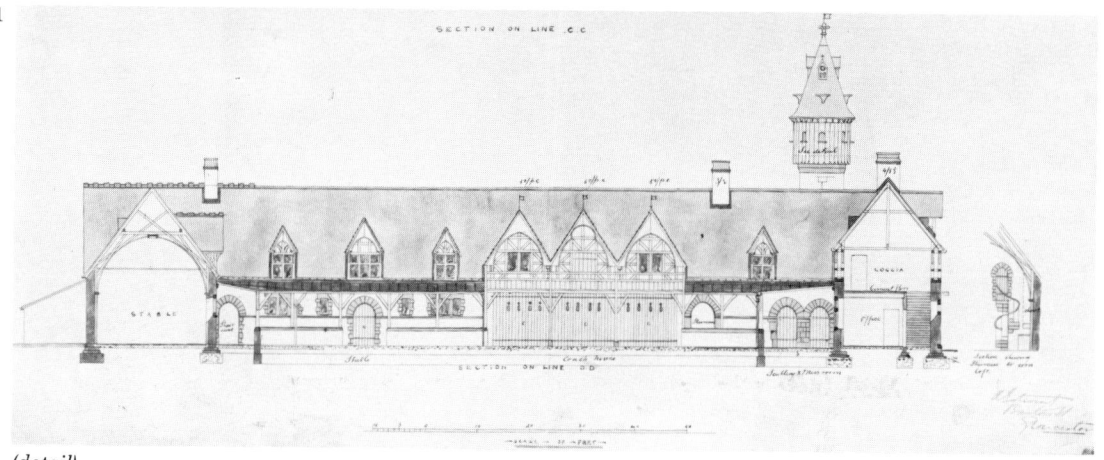
(detail)

A.81 Design for the Stables at Cardiff Castle

Pen and wash on linen backed paper
26¼"(66.6)×18¼"(46.7)

A section and a side elevation inscribed 'New Stables at Cardiff for the Marquess of Bute—No.4' Signed 'A. Estcourt/Baitory Street/Gloucester'. In 1868-69 Burges designed a new set of stables to the north of the castle compound. 'It forms an entire quadrangle' noted the *Building News*, 'entered by gateways on opposite sides; a lean-to roof, on wooden supports, gives shelter cloister-wise all round the interior. A fountain, which, if it would not frighten the horses, would certainly form an effective feature, occupies the centre of the quadrangle, and the inevitable turret, dedicated to pigeons, sticks up at one corner, but hardly so as to gather the grouping together as well as it should. (Still) the design is one which we should be glad to see carried out.' Carried out it was, in 1872-75. But the skyline was shorn of its staircase turret and pigeon tower, to say nothing of the fountain. The result is plain and unexciting. Lord Bute was not interested in horses. J.M.C.

B.N. XVIII(1870), 387.
A. XI (1874), 150-51.

Lent by The British Architectural Library/R.I.B.A.

A.82 **The Rustic Bridge**
Photograph

The bridge—modelled on a Swiss prototype—connected the Herbert Tower with the park and the recently excavated Blackfriars monastery. It was intended in Burges's earliest plans that part of the moat become a sunken medieval garden. The gardener, who would occupy the lower levels of the Clock Tower, would be able to supervise as the citizens of Cardiff, admitted at certain hours, came to enjoy the orderly gravelled paths and raised beds, comprising flowers, grass, potted plants, fountains and statues. The rustic bridge cum summerhouse was composed of sturdy piers with steeply tiled roofs, with broad eaves and ornate finials adorned by weather vanes sporting the letter 'B'. The estimate for the bridge without finials and minor details, was £1108 in 1875. The bridge was dismantled in the 1930s, though the supporting timbers are still visible in the moat.

M.A.

Lent by J. Mordaunt Crook

A.83 **Plaster Casts for the Animal Wall**
c. 8″(21) high

Nine models for the animals which surmount the wall surrounding part of the Castle. The models are probably by Thomas Nicholls, who was responsible for most of the carving for the Castle. They consist of two shield bearing lions, two lionesses, a bear, a wolf, a beaver, a hyena and a pair of baboons. The wall itself has been considerably altered, and once extended at least as far as the main entrance; additional animals were added in the 1920's, and restoration of some of the badly weathered sculpture has recently taken place.

M.A.

National Museum of Wales

Castell Coch

On 27th December 1872 Burges presented Lord Bute with an album of drawings, plans, explanations and sources for his proposed reconstruction of Castell Coch. Burges offered two courses for dealing with the ruins of the medieval fortified 'Red Castle' in the Taff valley: 'One is to leave them as they are and the other to restore them so as to make a Country residence for your occasional occupation in the summer'. Lord Bute, attracted by the plans for an elaborately roofed and silhouetted medieval castle, combined with his own interest in archeology and restoration, opted for a rebuilding programme.

In 1875 the Gloucester builder, Estcourt, accepted the contract for the first part of the scheme. Burges worked from the surviving thirteenth century foundations, but the upper parts of the castle are entirely his own creation; three tall towers are joined by a curtain wall, all steeply roofed and tiled, with high chimneys that sink into the conical roofs, themselves topped by tall weather vanes. The commanding height and impressive silhouette of the structure combine to produce an effect of power and strength and of dramatic fantasy. The result is a convincing example of Burges's mastery of three dimensional form.

Burges supported his plans for the reconstruction with examples from similar fortified structures both in Britain and abroad; for towers and parapets he linked Castell Coch with L'Aigle and Chillon in Switzerland, for the pointed towers he quoted the dubious example of the castles depicted in several of the well known manuscripts of the period in the British Museum. He skirted the fact that no such roofs existed by saying '... nearly every Castle in the Country has been ruined for more than two centuries and ... the few that remain have been converted to modern uses (like Cardiff)', though he also admitted that he had 'selected the high roof as being more picturesque'. Burges also had great delight in fitting the castle as for war, with portcullis and drawbridge, bretaches, arrow slits and holes in the wall from which boiling oil could be poured. For these he quoted examples from Carlisle, Caerphilly, Winchester and the Tower of London.

Having crossed the drawbridge, passing beneath Fucigna's statue of the Virgin and Child carved in 1878, one enters the courtyard. From here steps lead to the four major apartments, Banqueting Hall, Drawing Room and the two principal bedrooms. Building was completed in 1879, thus the design of the structure and rooms is entirely Burges's own, but at his untimely death in 1881, much of the decoration remained incomplete. William Frame took over as architect, and by employing J S Chapple and other craftsmen who had worked under Burges, attempted to finish the decorations in the same spirit. This was completed in 1891.

The Hall is simple in shape and austere in detail. Under a pine and cedar-panelled tie-beam roof, a

Ruins of Castell Coch before restoration

stone figure of St Lucius, legendary king of Britain, sculpted by Nicholls takes central position on the chimney breast. Frame's 'Letter Book' records that this was 'now being decorated' in October 1886. The Gable end walls are covered in pale murals, the furniture designed by Chapple and made in the Bute workshops in Cardiff is simple and unadorned.

The Drawing Room was intended as two rooms, one above the other. A dated drawing in the Cardiff Castle collection suggests that the alteration was not made until February 1879. The result is an octagonal vaulted room with interior gallery and deep window embrasures. Nicholls' 'Three Fates', erected in 1886 fill the wall above the fireplace, but the most attractive feature of the Drawing Room is the glittering decoration; gilded beams covered in butterflies of every hue divide the brilliant blue sky of the vault. Here birds and stars fill the heavens, while on the walls themselves, Earth is depicted in the form of scenes from Aesop's Fables, filled with flora and fauna and the Bute family portraits, hanging from the boughs.

Lord Bute's bedroom is contrastingly austere; stencilled walls and chunky furniture, but Lady Bute's bedroom is once again alive with colour and imagination. At the top of the tower, the room is circular and surmounted by a curved dome covered in painted and gilded panels of animals and plant life. The walls are lined by pillars from which spring arches to frame windows, fireplace and furnishings. The centre of the room is dominated by an enormous red and gilt bed with railed head and carved sides, the knops topped by glittering crystal. The dressing table and washstand, designed by J S Chapple date from 1891. The latter, an ornate two towered architectural creation, has towers designed to hold hot and cold water. The execution of this room dates largely from after Burges's death, but the combined talent of Frame, Chapple, Nicholls and Hart (who designed the grate) produce an undoubtably Burgesian result. The overall effect is a magnificent fairytale, an ideal setting for the 'Sleeping Beauty' suggested in the decoration or for the Lady of Shalott to espy her Lancelot.

A Well Tower chapel was originally intended to project over the courtyard, the windows were ordered and executed, but the project was abandoned, as was the hoard, a defensive structure which was intended to surround the base of the roof. Burges further proposed that 'the outworks could contain the Stables and the rest of the Domestics', but this also remained only an idea. The completed castle is the flowering of the vision of two men, Burges and Bute, both fervently interested in the middle ages and in archeology. Thanks to these efforts, a medieval fortress rises again from the slopes of the Taff valley. Its architecture and decoration, is the product of profound scholarship diluted by sheer exuberance and wit. The resulting structure is certainly one of the foremost creations of the High Victorian Dream.

M.A.

A.84

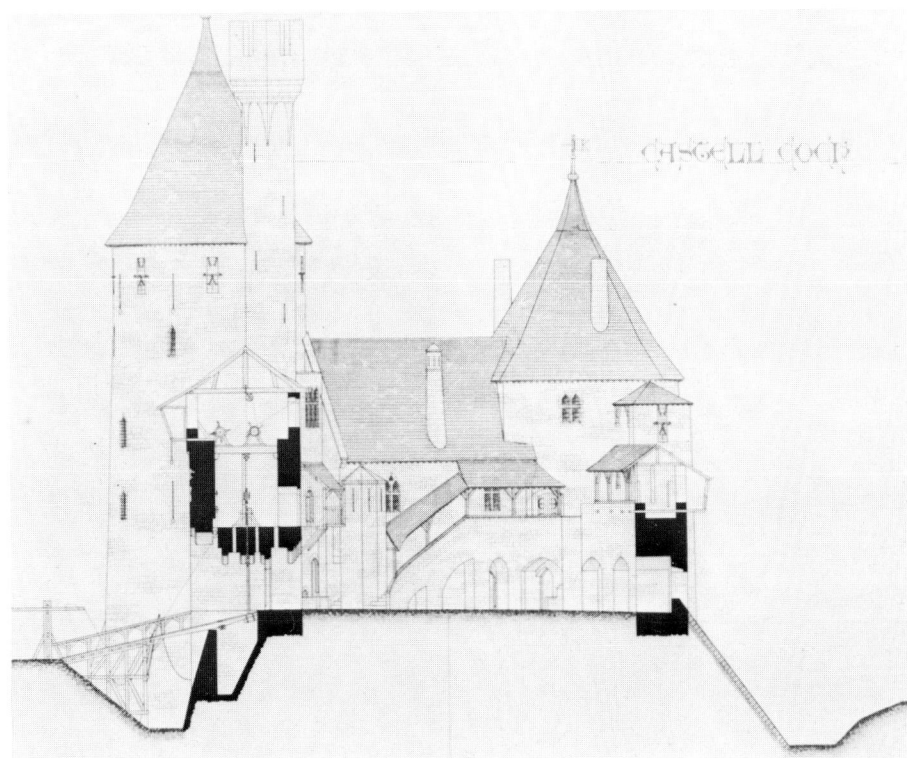

(detail)

Castell Coch

A.84 **Album of Designs for the Restoration of Castell Coch**

The album is comprised of Burges's report on the condition of the ruins of the medieval castle in the Taff valley, known as the 'Red Castle', or Castell Coch. It also contains Burges's suggestions for the future of the castle, offering Lord Bute two alternatives, preservation or restoration. Burges's own intention was clear—the album contains plans, sections and elevations of his proposed reconstruction, combined with archaeological facts and comparisons with similar contemporary fortifications and manuscript illustrations to give authenticity to his conjectural restoration.

The seventeen page hand written report has tracings from illuminated manuscripts and drawings of machinery which he proposed to include pasted at the side of the text. It also includes an extract taken from G.T. Clark's paper in *Archaeologia Cambrensis* of 1850, which deals with the history and excavation of the site at that time. The album is dated December 27th 1872 and signed 'Your Lordship's faithful Servant, William Burges'.

The report is here open at page 24 showing a section through the ruins as they then stood, and above, a section through the proposed reconstruction of the castle along the same line. This reveals elevations of the Keep and Kitchen towers as well as the courtyard, with a section through the entrance showing the workings of the portcullis and drawbridge. To the left are detailed drawings of this machinery. M.A.

Lent by The Welsh Office

Figure of St. Lucius in the Hall at Castell Coch

A.85 **Designs for the Mural Decorations of the Banqueting Hall, Castell Coch**

Pen and watercolour on Whatman paper
In three strips, height 10″(25)×45″(145)
×37″(94)
×26¾″(68)

The subject of the mural is evidently that of the life and work of a female saint, and though Burges's fondness for somewhat obscure symbolism, and the lack of any written hint makes identification uncertain, the story bears relation to the life of St Margaret of Scotland. The murals were probably by H.W. Lonsdale, and were executed by the firm of Campbell and Smith in 1878. M.A.

Lent by Cardiff City Council

Drawing Room at Castell Coch

A.86 **Designs for the Mural Decorations of the Banqueting Hall, Castell Coch**

Pen and wash on Whatman paper. Three pieces pasted together
10″(25.5)×15″(39)
Inscribed 'No 1' '½ Inch scale'.

As in the previous entry, the designs follow the life and martyrdom by burning at the stake, of a British female saint, the designs have been squared up for enlargement, in preparation for their being drawn full size on the canvas for the gable end wall. Burges's 'Estimate Book' for March 12 1878 records 'Painting tracery in brown and yellow; canvas etc., 22 figs, 24 figures'. Campbell and Smith were the contractors at 4s 4d per figure. M.A.

Lent by Cardiff City Council

A.87

A.87 Stained Glass Panel for the Proposed Chapel at Castell Coch. 'Christ in Majesty'
39½"(100)×15½"(39)

The window is in the form of a lancet. Against a ground scattered with stars is a seated figure of Christ with crown and orb in a mandorla filled with winged cherub heads; the sun and moon in roundels below. The glass is principally in shades of green, with pinkish red for the flesh and other small areas, though in the cartoon, Christ's robes and the main ground area are shown as plain white.
V.G.

Lent by Cardiff City Council

A.88 Stained Glass Panel for the Proposed Chapel at Castell Coch. 'S. Lucius'
28½"(72.5)×14½"(37)

The figure of the saint stands, facing sinister, within a rectangular panel. At his feet are grass and plants while he holds a martyr's palm; he wears a red mantle over a green robe with embroidered borders. On his head is a crown, surrounded by an amber halo. St. Lucius was a legendary king of Britain; a large statue of him by Thomas Nicholls was installed in the Banqueting Hall in 1866. This figure was also richly attired and crowned, carrying both martyr's palm and a simple church.
M.A.

Lent by Cardiff City Council

A.89 Stained Glass Panel for the Proposed Chapel at Castell Coch. 'S. Magnus'
28½"(72.5)×14½"(37)

Within a rectangular panel, the figure of the saint is standing facing dexter, on grass and plants. He is wearing a circlet and carrying a martyr's palm, with a plain green halo. The ground is in shades of pale green, the saint in a yellow mantle lined with vail, over a blue robe.
V.G.

Lent by Cardiff City Council

A.90

A.90 Cartoon for a Stained Glass Panel for the Proposed Chapel at Castell Coch 'S. Gwendolen'
Pencil, pen and watercolour on paper

A standing figure of St Gwendolen attired in an ochre robe and blue mantle, she carries a martyr's palm and a model of a church. The figure is reputed to be a portrait of Lady Bute, the spelling of the saint's name is the same as that of the Marchioness.
M.A.

Lent by Cardiff City Council

A.91 Cartoon for a Stained Glass Panel for the Proposed Chapel at Castell Coch
Pencil, pen and watercolour
33¼"(84.5)×19¾"(50)

The cartoon represents the standing figures of three saints, St Michael in a white robe and armour, with a blue halo, with two attendant saints, St Uriel in a red robe with yellow halo and another saint in a mauve robe with orange halo. St Michael carries the sword and scales, the other saints have staves. Burges's 'Estimate Book' for July 16 1878 has the entry 'Castell Coch Chapel Glass — 20 lights @ £3.10.0' for which Saunders and Co. were responsible at a cost of £62.0.0.
M.A.

Lent by Cardiff City Council

Mr. McConnochie's House, Cardiff

James McConnochie, chief engineer for the Bute docks, friend of Lord Bute and later Mayor of Cardiff, commissioned Burges to design him a house in 1871. It was virtually complete by 1874 though its interior decorations remained unfinished until 1880. Simplified Early French in style and built in Caerphilly stone by workmen from the Bute docks, Park House is solid, 'satisfactory looking' and irrefutably neo-Gothic. Asymmetrically planned with arched loggias to the front and North side, the house bears a strong resemblance to the garden front of Tower House, though in the latter Burges corrected the only flaw in the design of McConnochie's house: its interior planning is hindered by the introduction of an over grand timber staircase with mahogany balustrade. The exterior detailings in stone are more elaborate than those Burges was to design for his own house, but of course much less elaborate than his renovations to Cardiff Castle only a short distance away. McConnochie's House is now used as offices by the Vale of Glamorgon Borough Council.   M.A.

H.-R. Hitchcock, *Architecture, Nineteenth and Twentieth Centuries* (1958), C. Handley-Read, *CL* CXXXIX (1966), 600-604

A.92 **Perspective View of McConnochie's House**

Watercolour on heavy Whatman paper
17¾"(45)×21"(53.4)
Unsigned and undated, perspective view by A.H. Haig

Exh *RA* 1872, No. 1210
Exh *Plans and Prospects*, Welsh Arts Council, 1975
C. Handley-Read, *CL* CXXXIX (1966), 600-604 ill.

Lent by The British Architectural Library/R.I.B.A.

A.92

Trinity College, Hartford, Connecticut, USA

In 1872 Burges was commissioned to design a new university college for Hartford, Connecticut. £80,000 was the fund raising target, and Burges's first plan reflected this ambitious aim, with a multi-quadrangled structure, complete with chapel, library, museum, theatre, art gallery and observatory. The scale was enormous and the many lofty towers and spires would have made a fabulous sight. Early French Gothic in style and bold in conception, Trinity was a marvellous ideal. Unfortunately as the true nature of the available funds emerged, Trinity shrank in size. Foundations were laid in 1875, but by 1878 only two blocks had been completed; a third linking Gateway block was added in 1882. The lack of close supervision and the shortage of money forbade the inclusion of Burgesian detail; the resulting structure is a fragment of the original dream.   M.A.

A.93 **Trinity College, Hartford**
Early photograph
1909

Panoramic view of the front of Trinity College. The style is evidently Burgesian, but lacking in the exterior adornment and sculpture that he would have preferred, had the funds been available. The massive scale of the handling of the architecture had it been expanded to his original four quadrangles, would have produced a building of cathedral like power and proportions.   M.A.

Lent by J. Mordaunt Crook

A.94 **The Architectural Designs of William Burges, A.R.A.', ed. R.P. Pullan**
1883

R.P.Pullan, Burges's brother-in-law, published several books relating to Burges's designs, including many photographs of his work and house. In the introduction Pullan says he hopes the book will 'afford evidence of Mr. Burges's marvellous powers of adapting Gothic architecture to the requirements of every day life without altering or degrading its characteristic features. It will tend also to exhibit his profound knowledge of style, his thorough acquaintance with iconography, the great versatility of his genius, and his great imaginative power . . .' *Architectural Designs* contains seventy five plates, some previously published in periodicals, others from his work shop. There are plans, sections and perspectives as well as details of Burges's architectural designs, many of them never built.
Here open at page 68. An aerial perspective of Burges's proposal for Trinity College, Hartford, Connecticut.   M.A.

Victoria and Albert Museum

Tower House, Melbury Road, Kensington

When William Burges began to design his own home in July 1875, it was with the experience of twenty years learning, travelling and building. It was to be a synthesis of his career and a glittering tribute to his achievement. Outwardly simple, the house is similar to that designed for Mr. McConnochie, the major alteration being the removal of the staircase to a stair turret, giving greater space within the interior and an interesting exterior silhouette composed of cylinder, cone, triangle and cube. Surface ornament is scarce, the imposing bulk of the London guage red brick being relieved only by a sunken porch with carved capitals, stone mullions over the library windows, a pair of gargoyles and two weather vanes proudly flying his symbols from the roof tops: the mermaid and the heart threatened by spears.
The garden 'may be described as an open lesche approached by a low flight of steps. Jura marble seats sweep round its semicircular ends, and a marble statue stands above a fountain, in the centre of its mosaic floor. Here on a summer's afternoon, Burges would delight to give tea to a few friends, who lounged on the marble seats or sat on Persian rugs and embroidered cushions round the pearl-inlaid table, brilliant with tea service composed of things precious, rare, and quaint'.*
The contractors, Ashby Bros. of Kingsland Road, began work early in 1876, for an agreed sum of £6,000 for the carcass. By 1st January 1878, the house was sufficiently ready for the furniture to be moved in.
If the exterior of Tower House is an agglomeration of the influences and designs of a successful career, it is still deceptively simple: its massive handling giving little hint of the exotic interior to be found within. Burges was a rich man, and a dreamer of medieval worlds, fantasies, jokes, myths and legends, and it here within his own 'Aladdin's Palace' that his nature is freely revealed.
Everywhere there are stories and patterns, gold and silver, stars, jewels, rich woods, mirrors, massive furniture, stained glass, marvellous and singular antiques and curios, and above all, colour. Visitors were frequently overawed by the splendour and dazzled by the profusion of colour and detail, and by the fascinating mixture of history and fantasy, reality and illusion.
Burges used his considerable antiquarian knowledge and vivid imagination to devise the interior decorative scheme of his 'Palace of Art'. Each chamber has its theme, and to it conforms the decoration of the walls, ceiling, floor and furniture, and — most importantly — the enormous chimneypiece which dominates each room.   M.A.

Mrs Haweis, *Beautiful Homes* (1882)
R.P. Pullan, *The House of William Burges, ARA*, (1885)
*E.W. Godwin, *AJ* (1886)
B. lxiv, (1893), 12.
C.Handley-Read, *Burl. Mag.*, cv, (1963), 496-509
C.Handley-Read *CL*, CXXXIX (1966), 600-604
Survey of London XXXVII (1973), 144-8.

Tower House

A.95

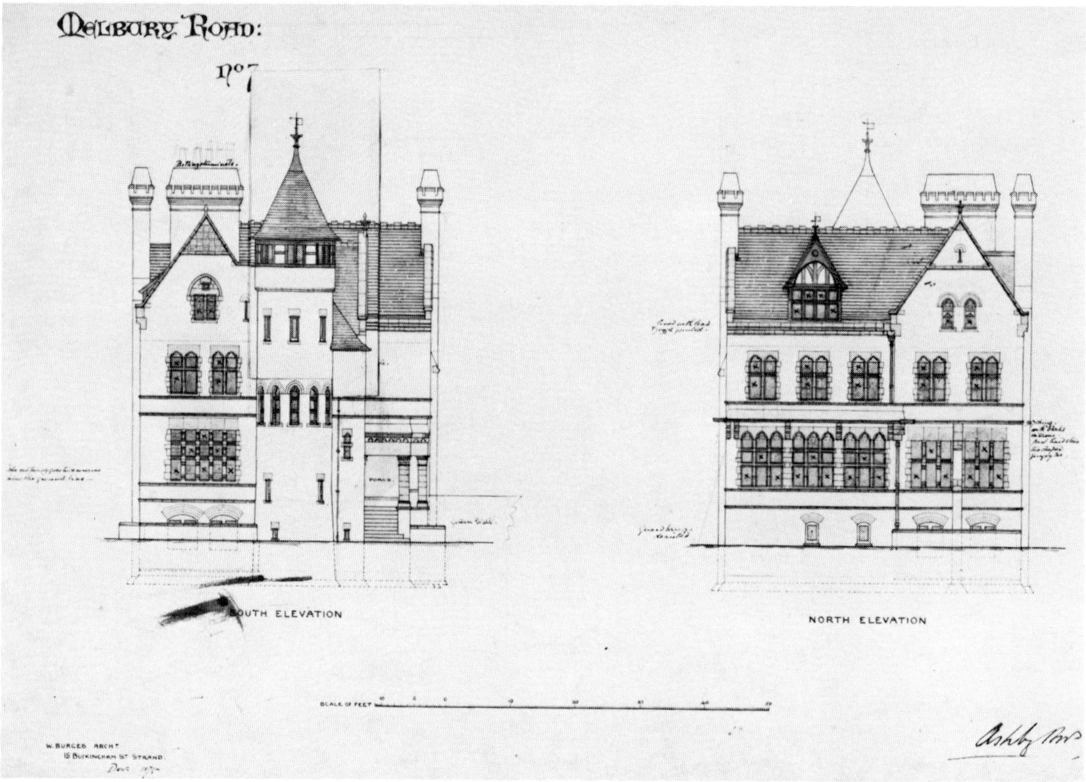

(detail)

A.95 **North and South Elevations of Tower House**
Pen and wash on two sheets of flimsy pasted on cartridge paper
19¾"(50.1)×25⅝"(65)
Inscribed 'North Elevation', 'South Elevation' 'No 7'
    'W. Burges Archt 15 Buckingham Street Strand WC.'
    '8ft=1 in'

A highly finished drawing, one of several such proposals for Tower House.

Lent by the British Architectural Library/R.I.B.A.

A.96 **Two Sections of Tower House**
Pen and wash on flimsy, pasted on cartridge paper
20"(50.8)×25⅜"(64.5)
Inscribed 'No. 5' 'W. Burges Archt 15 Buckingham Street Strand WC.'

Lent by the British Architectural Library/R.I.B.A.

The Hall, Tower House from 'The House of William Burges' by R.P. Pullan (1885)

The Hall

The porch floor is a representation of Burges's last favourite dog, Pinkie: a mosaic that might have come from a 'Cave Canem' in Pompei. Past the bronze front door, the hall is entered; here the floor is again mosaic, 'The Labyrinth of Theseus and the Minotaur', a design which formerly adorned the ceiling of his Buckingham Street bedroom. The walls are painted, a frieze of dragon monsters running round the upper section. Coloured light pours through the stained glass of the staircase windows, their theme 'The Storming of the Castle of Love'; the upper levels of the hall are filled with the sun and the moon and time, while the ceiling reflects the constellations in the positions they occupied when Burges first moved into the house. From the hall five doors lead, each marked with a symbol representing the room beyond. M.A.

A.97

A.97 'Pinkie' Porch Mosaic Design

Pencil and wash on cartridge paper
26″(66)×21″(53.1)

The drawing has been folded, stamped, addressed and postmarked.
Inscribed on the back 'Book Post' to 'Monsieur G.Burke/Rue Perignon 8/Paris'.

Lent by the British Architectural Library/R.I.B.A.

A.98 Hall Mosaic Design

Pen and wash on Whatman paper
20″(50.6)×27″(68.6)

Inscribed 'Theseus and the Minotaur' 'Inch scale'
The design for a mosaic depicting the Labyrinth of Theseus and the Minotaur was taken from Burges's Buckingham Street rooms where it was previously painted on his bedroom ceiling.

Lent by the British Architectural Library/R.I.B.A.

A.99 Design for a Stencilled Frieze

Gouache on paper
21″(53.2)×26″(66.4)

The stencilled dragon monsters formed a frieze running round the upper portion of the hall wall. In style they are similar to the miniature grotesques often found in mediaeval manuscripts. Similar creatures appear throughout Burges's work, in marquetry, metalwork and decoration.

Lent by the British Architectural Library/R.I.B.A.

A.100 Design for 'The Storming of the Castle of Love' Windows

Pencil and watercolour on paper, 15 fragments pasted onto a sheet of cartridge paper
20″(51)×26¾″(68)

Small cut out designs for fifteen windows representing the 'Storming of the Castle of Love' which adorned the main semi-circular staircase well. Sketches for a 'Chateau d'Amour' appear in the small note book of 1870-71, while the 'Abstract' for 1870 contains the words 'Drew Castle of Love'. These fifteen drawings were reduced to nine final ones which appear in 'Own Furniture' Pl. 28 and are attributed to Weekes. The Castle of Love was a theme frequently used on mediaeval mirror cases in ivory, two examples were available from 1876 in the form of plaster casts, when they were manufactured by Elkingtons and sold through the South Kensington Museum and the Arundel Society. The original of one of these, a German mirror case of 1350-60 was in the hands of a London dealer from 1866 until it was sold to the South Kensington Museum (now the V&A) in 1872. M.A.

Lent by the British Architectural Library/R.I.B.A.

The Library

From the hall, a door marked with an open book leads to the library. Burges was both a scholar and an antiquarian and had a large collection of books. To house these he designed a room lined with bookcases, each door panel portraying a different letter of the alphabet. Here also stood the magnificent giant bookcase covered with panels representing Christian and Pagan history. The theme of the room, 'Literature and the Liberal Arts' is further exemplified by its most striking feature: the gigantic and imposing 'Parts of Speech' or 'Babel' chimneypiece. Nimrod rules from the upper archway of a huge castle, below him Queen Grammar despatches the parts of speech, Pronouns, Verb, Articles, Noun, Adjective, Adverb, Conjunction and Preposition, personified by mediaeval figures of the court on their journey. Around the base of the castle run the letters of the alphabet, with one exception: the mason is presumed to have had trouble with his aspirates, and so the 'H' has been dropped below the level of the frieze.   M.A.

A.101 **Miniature Designs for the Painted Door Panels of the Library Bookcases**
Pencil, pen and wash on cartridge paper, the designs pasted onto a sheet of paper
21″(53.3)×26″(66)

Caricatures representing the letters of the alphabet. 'A' for Architect is reputed to be the figure of Burges, directing the building of Tower House; 'B' is a builder, and so on, all the figures relating to architecture. These figures are by Fred Weekes, and formed the painted panels for the front of the bookcases.

Lent by the British Architectural Library/R.I.B.A.

A.102 **Panel Design for Library Bookcase**
Pencil on Ingres paper
25½″(64.5)×18¾″(46.5)

Full size figure, 'Architecture', for the side of one of the Library bookcases.
Lent by the British Architectural Library/R.I.B.A.

A.103 **The Library, Tower House**
Watercolour
1879
By A.H. Haig

Perspective watercolour of the interior of the library in Tower House, showing the fireplace wall with the famous Tower of Babel chimneypiece. The watercolour was exhibited at the Royal Academy in 1880 where it received much acclaim. Burges's Estimate Book for 28 Oct. 1879 records 'coloured drawing of library' for Self, 'Haig £30.0.0.'.   M.A.

Exh *RA* 1880, No. 1178.

Lent anonymously

The Library, Tower House

The Drawing Room

In the Drawing Room 'Love, its fortunes and crosses' is the theme, Cupid looks down from the ceiling, legendary lovers encircle the walls in a frieze by Weekes and fabulous heroines from history and literature fill the stained glass of the windows. The chimneypiece, illustrating Chaucer's *Romaunt of the Rose*, is one of the finest examples of the combined talent of Burges's design and Nicholls's carving. On either side of the fireplace Burges installed pairs of cupboard doors from a tall painted cabinet of 1869 that had been in Buckingham Street: to the left the Winds; to the right, the Oceans; and in a side wall, the Flowers and Fairies (B22). Here also stood an ornate bobbined armchair similar to that at Castell Coch, and another famous Buckingham Street piece, the zodiac settle (B23). The room also contained much of Burges's collection of objets d'art: jades and crystals from China and Japan, rich embroideries, interesting ivories, exquisite enamels, precious inlays, marvellous metal-work in bronze and silver and gold', as well as items of his own design, including the marvellous elephant ink stand. M.A.

A.104 Design for the Drawing Room Chimneypiece

Pen, pencil and wash on cartridge paper
12½"(31.9)×9¾"(24.8)
Inscribed 'W.Burges. Archt/14 Sept 1875'

Sketch showing the details, names and positions of the figures for the *Romaunt of the Rose* chimneypiece with some instructions for painting. A medieval crowned and winged Cupid forms the centrepiece, surrounded by birds and butterflies; below, the Garden of Love. To either side Burges's own symbol of the heart threatened by spears is to be seen.

Lent by the British Architectural Library/R.I.B.A.

A.105 Sketches of Figure Subjects for Cabinet Doors

Pencil, wash and brush on paper
26"(66)×21"(53.5)

Sketches for the Oceans, one of three pairs of cabinet doors installed in the walls of the Drawing Room at Tower House. The sketches are probably by Weekes. The top four panel designs are those used, and are in the same positions as they occupy here.

Lent by the British Architectural Library/R.I.B.A.

A.105

(detail)

A.106 **Stained Glass Cartoon for the Drawing Room**
Pencil, brush and watercolour on cartridge paper
26″ (66)×21″ (53.4)

Full size cartoon for trilobate lancet window showing an owl with other small birds perched upon foliage. Burges also used these bird windows for Lord Bute's bedroom in Cardiff Castle, each cartoon featuring a different group of birds.

Lent by the British Architectural Library/R.I.B.A.

A.107 **The Drawing Room, Tower House**
Early photograph

A photograph of the Drawing Room of Tower House, looking towards the *Romaunt of the Rose* chimneypiece. Visible on either side are the Winds and the Oceans, gilded doors (A105) which were transferred from the tall cabinet at Buckingham Street. M.A.

R.P. Pullan, *The House of William Burges* (1885), Pl.15

Lent by the British Architectural Library/R.I.B.A.

A.106

A.107

The Guest Bedroom

In the Guest Bedroom Burges's love of glitter and colour reaches full expression. Mrs Haweis, a Victorian arbiter of taste, was enchanted by its opulence: 'The guest chamber is made of fire and flowers . . . the bed, toilet-table, washstand, cabinets, are all plain gold. The shutters are plain gold. The windows glow with colours of the Alhambra . . . What is not pure gold is crystal; the knobs on the bedposts, the shelves of the tables, scintillate with facets. The whole room is like an ancient shrine or reliquary'. Butterflies cover the gold ceiling, frogs and mice at war cover the beams; in the centre of the ceiling Burges placed a small convex mirror and four emu eggs hung from the centre of the panels. In this splendour glistened the great golden bed, the 'Vita Nova' washstand, a marble-topped table and a wide variety of Eastern ceramics in a gilt china case.

M.A.

A.108 **Design for the Ceiling of the Guest Bedroom**
Pencil and watercolour on cartridge paper with alterations pasted on
20″ (50.5)×26½″ (67.8)

The ceiling is divided into four sections, three containing circles and the fourth an octagonal pattern. All are infilled with scrolls and butterflies. E.W. Godwin records: 'The ceiling, with its four square compartments formed by massive cross-beams, was decorated with butterflies of all colours symmetrically arranged in circles, the beams themselves being decorated with comic illustrations of battles between those relentless enemies, the frogs and the mice'.

M.A.

Lent by the British Architectural Library/R.I.B.A.

Early photograph of the Mermaid chimneypiece

(detail)

Burges's Own Bedroom

Burges's own bedroom is painted a deep blood red, a frieze of sea creatures surrounds the walls, and the ceiling is studded with tiny mirrors set in lead stars. The Mermaid fireplace dominates the room; similar to other mermaids found in his work, both in metalwork, decorative work and ceramics, she combs her hair and looks into her glass, a fabulous example of a symbol Burges had adopted as his own. In this room stood several pieces of furniture which he brought with him from Buckingham Street; his bed, the 'Narcissus' washstand, the 'Crocker' dressing table, as well as a cupboard for 'Clean clothes' and 'Dirty clothes' decorated with allegorical figures of its contents, and a 'cabinet stand' (c.1876) of a lighter nature than his earlier furniture.

M.A.

A.109 **Design for the Mermaid Chimneypiece**
Pencil, pen and wash on cartridge paper
20″ (50.8)×13½″(34.5)

Inscribed top 'ornament on bracket on shelf/the colour is grey on white ground'.

Bottom 'The Mermaid. The fish and/the shells to be painted/in the natural colours/with etchings of gold and platinum./The carving to be delicately/outlined in black./The foam of sea to be/etched with platinum./'.

Lent by the British Architectural Library/R.I.B.A.

A.110

A.110 **Design for Wallpaper**
Stencil on card
19½" (49.6)×22¼" (56.5)

A design of black ibis-like birds on a pink ground.

Lent by the British Architectural Library/R.I.B.A.

A.111 **Design for Wallpaper**
Stencil on card
19¼" (48.8)×20¾" (52.5)

Fishes, birds and stylised floral decorations within a squared pattern, in brown, on a black ground.

Lent by the British Architectural Library/R.I.B.A.

Pre-Raphaelite Furniture by Clive Wainwright

The history of English furniture design in the 19th century has yet to be fully written. When the story is eventually told the name of William Burges will certainly occupy a prominent place. In effect, he was the creator of a type of interior decoration, so new as to be almost bizarre: we call it Pre-Raphaelite furniture.

Innovation in furniture design in the nineteenth century followed the pattern set in previous centuries and depended upon architects rather than cabinet makers. Though virtually all architects since the middle ages have interested themselves in furniture and interior design, certain of them stand out as innovators with a special interest in and talent for furniture design. In this respect Burges ranks with William Kent, Robert Adam, A.W.N. Pugin and Owen Jones. Burges in fact shared with Robert Adam in particular the ability to design, and with the help of a trained team of craftsmen and artists to see carried to completion elaborate schemes of interior decoration including painted decoration of both an abstract and a figurative character. Pugin, though brilliant as a designer of schemes of interior polychromatic decoration, was far more dependant upon abstract and floriated ornament than Burges who exploited the possibilities of figurative schemes of great iconographical complexity. Burges's furniture was specifically conceived to fit in with elaborate and richly painted interiors. Being painted it could tie in very closely with programmes of decoration painted upon walls and ceilings. With Pugin or Adam it had been different. Their furniture was unpainted, and so the only close connection between it and the painted interior lay in carved or inlaid motifs. In relating his painted pieces directly to the interiors which housed them, Burges was carefully following medieval principles. In the medieval interior painted furniture had stood within a decorated environment specifically designed for it by the architect of the building. In 1865 Burges wrote in his essay 'Furniture' in his book *Art Applied to Industry*: 'Say we were in the royal palace of Westminster, we should find the ceiling boarded, with paintings on it . . . But the great feature of our medieval chamber is the furniture; this in a rich apartment would be covered with paintings both ornaments and subjects; it not only did its duty as furniture but spoke and told a story'.

Burges certainly had a sound archaelogical basis for painting his furniture, and it is worth examining the background to the designing of his first piece. Pugin seems never to have designed a piece of domestic painted furniture though he was well aware of the surviving pieces of medieval painted furniture on the continent. He did however design painted ecclesiastical furniture in the form of altar pieces and shrines, items which are only distantly related to domestic cabinet furniture. He did design the painted organ case for Jesus College Cambridge in 1849, which still survives in the College Chapel. This organ case being a three dimensional cabinet with doors is in effect a piece of cabinet furniture, but it is the nearest Pugin ever came to designing a piece of painted domestic furniture.

Pugin died in 1852 and it is interesting to note that in 1856 Burges designed as part of his prize-winning design for the new Lille Cathedral an elaborate painted organ case. He also designed painted confessionals, but they and the organ — like the building — were never executed. Another competitor in the Lille competition travelled over to Lille with one of his pupils to look at the exhibition of the designs. The competitor was George Edmund Street; the pupil was William Morris. Perhaps it was not altogether a coincidence that when Morris left Street's office and moved to London, he and Burne Jones, with D.G. Rossetti, started to paint furniture.

In December 1856 Rossetti wrote concerning Morris and Burne Jones's rooms in Red Lion Square, Holborn: 'Morris is rather doing the magnificent there, he is having some intensely medieval furniture made . . . he and I have painted the back of a chair with figure and inscriptions in gules and vert and azure and we are all going to cover a cabinet with pictures'. None of these pieces survive, but by that time Burges's first, albeit small, piece of painted furniture had been made: the Yatman casket. This casket had an iconography far more sophisticated than Morris and his circle ever achieved. Its programme of painted decoration includes such diverse characters as Prester John and the Jackdaw of Reims.

Meanwhile, for Burges and Morris and all those interested, a number of illustrations relating to medieval painted furniture were being published. The two crucial pieces were both painted cabinets: one at Bayeux — which still exists — and one at Noyon, both in Northern France. That at Noyon had been published in *Annales Archéologiques* as early as 1846 and they were both published in 1858 in volume 1 of Viollet-Le-Duc's *Dictionnaire Raisonné du Mobilier Francais,* that from Noyon in colour. Burges however knew at least the Noyon piece at first hand. He made frequent trips to the continent and was in Noyon in 1853. There is in the Victoria and Albert Museum a watercolour by Burges of one of its painted panels probably painted on this visit. By 1862 the Bayeux cabinet was also available in colour in W. E. Nesfield's *Specimens of Mediaeval Architecture . . . .* Burges's first large scale piece of painted furniture, the Yatman cabinet of 1858 (B1) was closely modelled upon the Noyon cabinet, but with two details taken from that at Bayeux. They are the finials and the locks and bolts; the Noyon cabinet had locks but no bolts.

The earliest extant piece of painted furniture made by Morris and his circle is the Chaucer Wardrobe in the Ashmolean Museum. This was inspired by Burges's example, but its creators failed to understand either the medieval principles or Burges's use of them. The Chaucer Wardrobe is a well designed piece of Reformed Gothic furniture in the tradition of Street and Pugin, designed by Phillip Webb, which has been painted. Whereas the Yatman cabinet, like the medieval pieces which inspired it, is a piece of 'painted furniture'. The distinction between furniture which is painted and painted furniture is a very real and important one. With a piece of painted furniture the programme of decoration is designed to fit the object and the figurative painted panels are contained within an architectonic framework of abstract borders and frames. The whole front of the Chaucer Wardrobe by contrast is painted with a picture, so that when the door is opened the picture splits in the middle. On the Yatman, Noyon and Bayeux cabinets each door has a separate picture and carefully defined frame.

There is one other aspect of painted furniture which the Morris group also failed to grasp, namely the relationship of the subject matter of the paintings to the purpose of the piece of furniture. Does the presence of Chaucer and his Prioress on a wardrobe actually relate to its function as a wardrobe? Or indeed is the viewer warned what its use might be and what he might find inside? The Bayeux and Noyon cabinets are covered with pictures of saints and angels which relate closely to their function as containers for church plate. Several angels even carry pieces of plate. The whole iconography of the paintings on the Yatman cabinet — including as they do events from the life of Cadmus who introduced the alphabet to ancient Greece, also Caxton the great printer — is emblematic of writing and thus of the function of the cabinet: when its secretaire flap is down the cabinet is a writing desk. The same principle applies to most of Burges's painted pieces, for instance his own great library bookcase (B6) of 1859 which was designed to house his art books. This extraordinary piece is decorated with scenes emblematic of both Christian and Pagan art.

Burges also used in the decoration of the Yatman cabinet a medieval technique which he almost certainly took from *An Essay upon the various arts by Theophilus . . . of the eleventh century* (1847). This translation was published from several manuscript sources and was avidly read by all the Goths. One technique which particularly interested Burges was that of applying tin foil to an area of wood, then painting in colours over some of the surface. Alternatively the whole surface of the foil could be painted, thus imparting a special quality to the appearance of the colour. In either case the whole surface was varnished to prevent oxidation of the tin. Theophilus put it thus: 'A picture is likewise made upon wood, which picture is called transparent, and after some it is called aureola which you compose in this manner. Take tin leaf, not covered with varnish nor coloured with saffron, but simply as it is, and diligently polished, and with it you cover the place on which you wish to paint. Then grind the colours to be laid on most carefully with linseed oil, and when very fine lay them on with a pencil and so allow to dry'.

The roof of the Yatman cabinet and parts of Burges's bookcase are decorated in this way. The technique was copied firstly by Richard Norman Shaw in decorating the top of his celebrated cabinet now in the Victoria and Albert Museum, and later that year by Morris and Company for the interior of their St. George Cabinet also in the Victoria and Albert Museum. This technique is expensive and complicated, and only one other contemporary piece of furniture decorated in a similar way is known: a painted chest in the Victoria and Albert Museum which was probably made by Morris and Company for the 1862 Exhibition.

The International Exhibition of 1862, and more especially the Medieval Court within it, represents the high water mark of the Gothic Revival in England. The Medieval Court was laid out by Burges himself for the Ecclesiological Society. In this Court was represented the work of such a galaxy of Goths as were never to be assembled again under one roof. They included Burges, Bodley, Butterfield, Seddon, Teulon, White, Shaw, Morris, Webb, Scott, Slater, Forsyth, Street, Skidmore, Parry, Hardman, Clayton, Bell, O'Connor, Bentley, Heaton, Butler and Bayne. Whilst elsewhere in the vast building continental Goths such as Viollet-Le-Duc, Didron, Lassus, Cuypers and many more were represented. Several of the Burges pieces of painted furniture and one of the Morris pieces had been

The Medieval Court of 1862

shown at small private exhibitions, but never before had such a wide range of painted pieces been shown in public. Burges wrote in his account of the Exhibition in *The Gentleman's Magazine*: 'In the Medieval Court there are no less than five exhibitors of furniture, more or less painted . . . Messrs Morris Marshall and Company send six articles, Mr. Burges five, Prichard and Seddon five, Mr. Forsyth one, and Mr. Fisher one, making eighteen articles of furniture all more or less painted'. Burges differentiated thus between the Morris pieces and his own: 'The general characteristic of their furniture is an Eastern system of diaper combined with rather dark toned pictures . . . it is only fair to state that their furniture is more what would have been used by the middle classes in the times of our forefathers than that of other exhibitors . . . The work of Mr Burges is equally painted all over, but the tone of colouring is much brighter and the articles are more what would have been found in the houses of the nobility'. Those commentators who liked the painted furniture — and many did not — generally praised the Burges pieces and also condemned the Morris pieces for crudeness and insubstantial construction. Typical was an anonymous critic in *The Parthenon*: 'A casual comparison of this display with the customary furniture of our drawing rooms . . . enables us to see that these mere beginnings show mental power, a professional skill and indications of reading, in which the fashionable furniture is utterly destitute . . .'. After praising Burges the same critic says of Morris: 'We are almost afraid they are their own carpenters; if so, we would humbly counsel a little less roughness of work in some goods and a little more strength in others'. No doubt the hundreds of thousands of visitors from throughout the world could make up their own minds. But historically speaking it was this exhibition which established painted furniture as the offspring of Pre-Raphaelitism and the Gothic Revival.

Furniture which was painted was not an aesthetic or a commercial success. The Morris and Company pieces did not sell well and they seem to have made few pieces after the 1862 Exhibtion itself. Painted furniture however thrived, and Burges went on designing it until his death in 1881. By the later 1860s it was not the preserve of Goths alone. E.W. Godwin, who was a close friend of Burges, designed pieces in both the Anglo-Japanese and the Neo-Classical styles and by the mid 1870s painted pieces in every style then in fashion were being produced. The idea was shortly to be taken up by both Arts and Crafts and Art Nouveau designers, a very far cry from the Ecclesiological Society and the 1862 Exhibition. Burges himself was not just a narrow-minded Goth. As the present exhibition demonstrates, he was eclectic in the extreme. He was for instance a pioneer in the study of Japanese art. But however interesting the later manifestations of painted furniture are for furniture historians, any serious study of the subject must start with William Burges and the wonderful fusion of Pre-Raphaelite painting and Gothic furniture which he achieved and showed to the world in the Medieval Court of 1862.

B.13

(detail)

Catalogue B: Furniture

More than most of his generation, Burges despised Georgian and Regency furniture. Veneering he regarded with suspicion; upholstery he hated. His furniture therefore—boxy and aedicular; painted with heraldic colours and Pre-Raphaelite panels—was conceived as the ultimate answer to the 'dark ages' of Georgian joinery. Drawing upon the talents of a veritable galaxy of artistic friends, Burges in effect created the perfect medium for his talents: the art of Pre-Raphaelite furniture. By integrating joinery, architecture and painting in miniature form, he revolutionised furniture design. Bookcases and cabinets; cupboards and chairs; bedsteads and escritiores; washstands fit for Narcissus or Edward II—Burges's furniture bespeaks an artist of dazzling virtuosity. More than anyone, it was Burges, with his eye for detail and his lust for colour, who created the furniture appropriate to High Victorian Gothic.

J.M.C.

B.1 **Cabinet/Escritoire**
Carved, painted and gilt mahogany and pine
1858
Made by Harland and Fisher.
h 7′(213.3) w 4′7″(139.7) d 1′2″(35.5)

B.1

The tiling of the roof is formed by painting on a surface of silver leaf, a medieval technique, as is the use of painted vellum for the calendars in the dormer windows. The rest of the cabinet is painted and stencilled on a red ground. The figure painting is by E.J. Poynter (1836-1919), after sketches by Burges, and illustrates the legend of Cadmus, the cutting of cuneiform letters, Dante and Caxton, as examples of inscription, composition and publication. The gables contain heads of Poetry and History while Anaxagoras and Pericles are found within medallions.

On the inside of the doors, accompanying portraits of Poynter and Burges are the inscriptions 'WILLIAM BURGES ARCH: INVENIT' and 'EDWARD J POYNTER: PICTOR PINXIT'. On the righthand side of the cabinet are the words 'IN THE YEAR OF OUR LORD MDCCCLVIII', and on the left hand side 'HERBERT GEO. YATMAN CAUSED ME TO BE MADE', above, 'YATMAN CREAT'.

The elaborate roofed, tiled and gabled structure with its finials and dormers intimates that Burges was guided by his knowledge of the armoires at Bayeux and Noyon. 1858 appears to be the year that Burges first designed furniture in this medieval painted style. Criticism of the extraordinary mixture of myth, history, architecture and furniture was varied; the *Art Journal* found the six items exhibited at the 9th Architectural Exhibition to be 'a group of furniture such as Piers Gaveston might have sat in', while Christopher Dresser saw the mixture as quite unsuitable for a piece of furniture and described the Yatman cabinet as 'a mere doll's house in appearance'.

M.A.

R.I.B.A. Arc IV
V&A P&D 93.E.8 p5
Exh *Architectural Exhibition* London 1859
Exh *International Exhibition* London 1862
Exh *English Cabinets* V&A 1972, ill cover and P135
AJ (1859), 125
J.B. Waring, *Masterpieces of Industrial Art and Sculpture at the International Exhibition*, Vol 2. (1862), Pl 155.
C. Dresser, *Principles of Decorative Design*. (1873), fig 42.
T. Hughes 'English Decorated Furniture' in *Homes and Gardens*, IV, (1974), 52.

Victoria and Albert Museum.

B.2

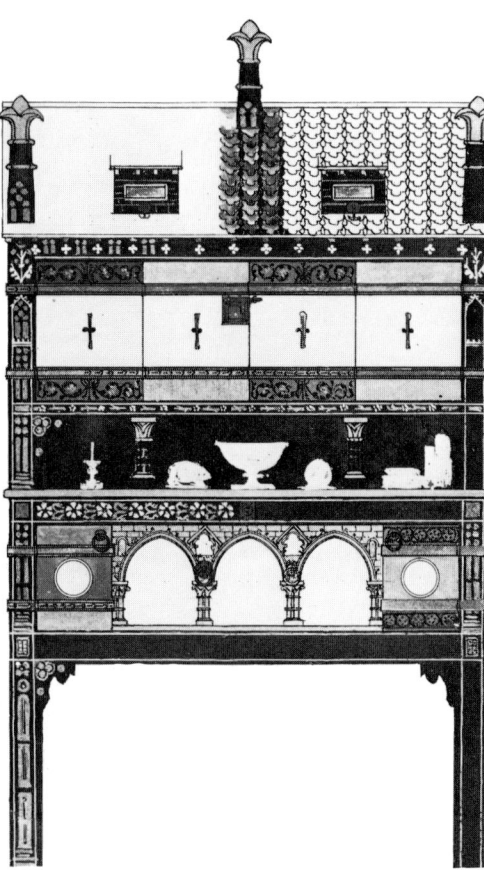

(detail)

B.2 Design for the 'Yatman' Cabinet, and two other Cabinets

Pen and watercolour over pencil with gold paint details
Eight fragments of paper and one photograph pasted onto cartridge paper. Page 1 of the 'Furniture' album
12″ (33)×19¼″ (49)

This sheet contains front and side elevations of the 'Yatman' cabinet as built, lacking only the figurative scenes. There is also an elevation of a cabinet similar to that exhibited at the 1862 International Exhibition, it has six sides and a studded backboard with shelf. The third cabinet has a pitched roof and painted decoration, there is no proof that it was manufactured. The photograph represents part of the Medieval Court at the 1862 Exhibition, which Burges was responsible for designing.

M.A.

Victoria and Albert Museum

B.3 Designs for a Table, Wardrobe and Bench

Pencil with pen and ink on flimsy paper. Page 9 of the 'Furniture' album
18⅜″ (46.5)×12″ (30.5)

Front and side elevations of each piece with their prices. At the top, the table, '£4.15.0', in the middle, the wardrobe under which is inscribed 'Wardrobe £7.0.0', 'Inch scale', and at the bottom 'Bench £2.0.0'. The sturdy construction of the furniture is typical of the less decorative pieces, they would probably be painted and stencilled. The table was of a design used frequently in Tower House, the top being of various marbles or other materials. Examples may be seen in the Birmingham City Art Gallery and Lotherton Hall, Leeds.

M.A.

Victoria and Albert Museum.

B.3

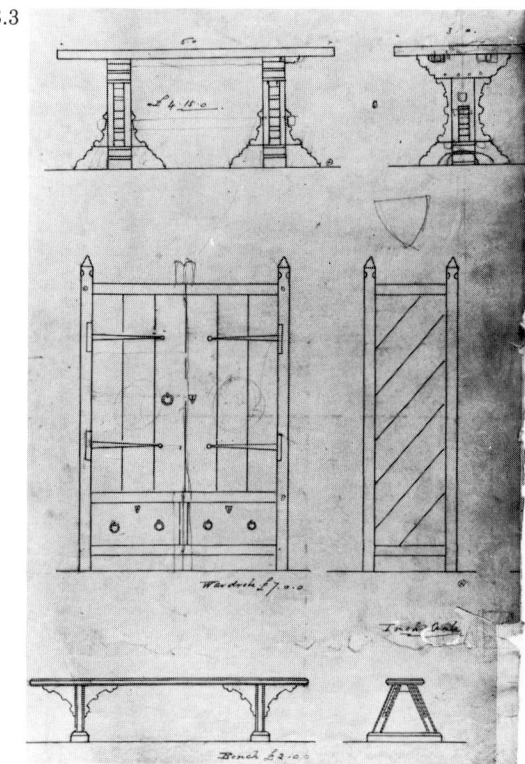

B.4 **Design for a Table**

Pencil, pen and wash on Whatman paper. Page 19 of the 'Furniture' album
19″ (48.5)×23″ (58.5)
Inscribed 'Drawing room table', '2″=1 Foot'

Plan, elevation and some details for a circular table, with some notes for the manufacturer. Burges's 'Abstract' for 1858-62 contains the entry 'Col. Cocks' table'. The table, marquetried and inlaid with a coloured allegory of the 'Wheel of Fortune' was made up by J.G. Grace for C.L.S. Cocks's house Treverbyn Vean in Devonshire.
M.A.

Victoria and Albert Museum

B.5 **Detail for a Table**

Pencil, pen and wash on Whatman paper. Page 20 of the 'Furniture' album
14″ (35.5)×12¼″ (31)

Detail for the decorative top of the table designed for C.L.S. Cocks. The lady within a wheel surrounded by shields illustrating the theme 'Wheel of Fortune'. The drawing also has notes concerning the wood to be used and minor instructions for the manufacturer. M.A.

Victoria and Albert Museum

B.6

B.6 **Bookcase**

Carved, painted and gilt wood
1859-62, 1878
h 10′5″ (317.5) w 5′8½″ (173.9) d 1′7½″ (49.5)

The simple rectangular structure is adorned by a roof with gables at the front and a gallery. Drawings in the R.I.B.A. relate to each panel and give the artist responsible and often the mythological or historical sources.

E.W. Godwin describes the bookcase as 'quite the most ambitious (of his early furniture) in size and quite the most remarkable for its historical and artistic associations'. The doors and surfaces are divided into a painted architectural arrangement, which with the use of gables and parapets again recall the Noyon armoire. Each panel contains a figure composition relating to the bookcase's purpose — to hold art books. Burges employed his young friends Westlake, Weekes, Burne-Jones, Rossetti, Poynter, Yeames, Simeon Solomon, Stacy Marks, Fitzgerald, Storey, Moore, Smallfield, Holiday, Morten and Rossiter to paint panels reflecting art subjects from Christian and Pagan history. The minor details of the decoration represent the Sea, the Earth, the Air and the Stars in rising stages. This fabulous piece originally enhanced Burges's Buckingham Street rooms, and was exhibited in the Medieval Court of the 1862 International Exhibition. It was later transferred to Tower House, and suffered some damage when it collapsed in 1878; the repairs entailed the repainting of the section immediately above the shelf — the Metals — now by Weekes. It is the largest piece of Burges's furniture and unrivalled for the richness and profusion of its decoration.
M.A.

R.I.B.A. Arc 1V
Exh *International Exhibition* London 1862
Exh *International Exhibition* Paris 1889
Exh *Victorian and Edwardian Decorative Arts* V.&A. 1952, J.1
W. Burges, 'Own Furniture', R.I.B.A., Pl.14, 15
R.P. Pullan, *The House of William Burges* (1885), Pl.14
E.W. Godwin, *AJ* 1886
H.S. Marks, *Pen and Pencil Sketches*, vol 1 (1894) 220
P. Floud, *The Concise Encyclopedia of Antiques*, (1957) 22

Lent by
Ashmolean Museum, Oxford
(Now at Knightshayes, Tiverton, Devon)

B.7

B.7 Cabinet

Early photograph
Inscribed 'Cabinet for Letters of WB.'

The 'Architecture cabinet' is one of Burges's more idiosyncratic pieces. Exhibited in 1859, it may have been designed the previous year; it is certainly among Burges's earliest painted furniture. It resembles the Yatman cabinet in its use of finials, roof and square-cut legs with folding doors. E.W. Godwin said that the armoires at Bayeux and Noyon had been at the bottom of it all. 'Designed more than twenty years before (his death) . . . it stood at his elbow all the best years of his life, and though designed to contain only a few pigeon-holes for letters, it is both contrivance and decoration full of quaint conceits.' The base of the cabinet is used to support portfolios. There are also two small upholstered and painted chairs with monsters on the back.　　　　　　　　　　　　M.A.

W. Burges, 'Own Furniture', R.I.B.A., Pl.11
BN. xix (1870), 352, 354
Furniture Gazette 6 Sept. 1873, 345

National Museum of Wales

B.8

B.8 **Sideboard or Buffet**
Painted and gilt wood with a marble top and shelf
1859
Made by Harland and Fisher
h 5′6″(167.6) l 4′7″ (139.7) d 1′5″ (43.1)

Supported by four square cut legs, the simple rectangular structure of the 'Wines and Beers' sideboard is lavishly patterned and coloured. The central panels depict 'The Battle Between the Wines and Beers' painted by E. J. Poynter (1836-1919). Bacchus, supported by personifications of Burgundy, Hock and Champagne, threatens the knightly figure of Sir John Barleycorn and his companions — Porter, Pale Ale and Scotch Ale. To either side are portrait heads within quatrefoils, and the whole is adorned with a range of gold stencilled designs on a red ground. Inside are four Neo-Classical cameos — Ginger Beer, Lemonade, Seltzer Water and Soda Water.

A reference in Burges's 'Abstract' suggests that the piece was intended for James Nicholson, but following its exhibition in the Medieval Court of the 1862 International Exhibition, it was acquired by the South Kensington Museum for £40.

With the Yatman cabinet and four other pieces, the sideboard was shown in the Architectural Exhibition at the Conduit Street Galleries in 1859 and caused one critic to remark: 'Both as articles of furniture and as ornament, while there is much to admire, it may be questioned whether there is not as much to regret; for with all the evident pains that the designer has bestowed, the unrestricted display of his exuberant fancy in gilding and colours, the results, taken as a whole, are not altogether pleasing.'* M.A.

V.&A. P.&D. 93. E.8 p27
Exh *Architectural Exhibition* London 1859 No19
Exh *International Exhibition* London 1862
CE & AJ (1859), 142
The Artist xx (1897), 396-7, ill
E. Aslin, *Nineteenth Century English Furniture* (1962), 60, 61 Pl.60

Victoria and Albert Museum

B.9 **Wash-hand-stand**
Carved, painted and gilt wood
1865-7

The wash-hand-stand is dark red in colour, adorned with gilt arabesques and inlaid with pieces of vellum and mother of pearl. The upper section is crenellated and contains the cistern; this is supported by two metal rods and has candle holders attached at either side. This section is embellished with three paintings illustrating the Narcissus legend, by Weekes, and bears the inscription 'THIS IS THE MIRROUR PERRILUS IN WHICH THE PROUDE NARCISSUS SEY AL HIS FAIR FACE BRIGHT', which is taken from Chaucer's *Romaunt of the Rose*. The splashback and top are of marble and the whole is supported on four square cut legs.

The panels appear to have been painted by J. A. Fitzgerald (1832-1906), and then repainted in 1872 by Weekes from sketches by Burges. ('Abstract' 1872 — 'Washstand pictures Weekes'.) The 'Jennings patent' tip-up basin is of marble inlaid with five gold and silver fish. The taps take the form of bronze creatures.

The washstand was moved to Tower House after many years at 15 Buckingham Street and lodged in Burges's own red bedroom. Some years ago it was presented to Evelyn Waugh by John Betjeman and featured as the fabulous wash-stand which haunted the central character in Waugh's fictional autobiography *The Ordeal of Gilbert Pinfold*. M.A.

R.I.B.A. Arc. 1V
R.P. Pullan, *The House of William Burges ARA* (1885), Pl.31
C. Handley-Read, *Burl. Mag.* cv. (1963)

Lent by Auberon Waugh, Esq.

B.10 **Bedstead**

Carved, painted and gilded mahogany
1865-1867
h (of head) 5′9″ (175.2) h (of foot) 4′1″ (124.4)
l 6′11½″ (212) w 3′½″ (92.7)

The bedstead is inset with paintings on glass, shell and coloured tinsel, the semi-circular head containing a panel in oil, 'The Sleeping Beauty', by Henry Holiday, of 1868. Beneath, in small square panels are the recumbent maids and servants; Beauty herself is asleep on a bed very similar to the one she adorns. The head posts are surmounted by winged lions, the foot posts by bulbous bobbins. Inscribed on the head in Gothic lettering are the words: 'WLELMVS:BURGES:ME:FI:FECIT:AD: MDCCCLXVII:'.

The 'Abstract of Diaries' for 1865 contains the reference 'red Bedstead and Washstand' and in 1866 'Sleeping Beauty for bed done'. The bed was originally designed for Buckingham Street. There it dominated his small bedroom beneath a ceiling painted with the maze of Thesus and the Minotaur, and surrounded by the mermaid and monster frieze. It was later transferred to Tower House, Melbury Road, where the whole room matched the blood red of the bed, the decorations illustrating the theme of 'The Sea and its Inhabitants'. It was originally covered with a Chinese Mandarin's robe, richly embroidered on a purple ground. Burges died in this bed in March 1881 following three weeks of semi-paralysed illness.   M.A.

R.I.B.A. Arc 1V
Exh *Victorian and Edwardian Decorative Art* R.A. 1972 Bl.2
Drawings R.I.B.A. and V.&A. P.&D.
W. Burges, 'Own Furniture', R.I.B.A., Pl.1, 2, 3
R.P. Pullan, *The House of William Burges ARA* (1885), Pl.26, 28
E. W. Godwin, *AJ* (1886), ill.
C. Handley-Read, *CL* (1966), 600-604

Lent by The Trustees of The Cecil Higgins Art Gallery, Bedford

B.11 **Design for the Painted Panel of a Bedhead**

Pencil, pen and wash on flimsy paper pasted onto cartridge paper. Page 37 of the 'Furniture' album
14″ (36.5)×23⅛″ (59)
Inscribed 'Bedstead'.

This sketch is for the panel in oil, by Henry Holiday, which is the centrepiece of the bedhead of Burges's own red bedstead. It illustrates the scene from the legend of the Sleeping Beauty in which the Prince awakens the Princess. In this portrayal Beauty is nude, while the Prince is attired in medieval costume.   M.A.

Victoria and Albert Museum

B.10

B.12 **The Interior of the Bedroom, 15 Buckingham Street**

Early photograph
Inscribed 'Life under the Sea' 'Wall of Bedroom. W.B.'

The photograph shows the mermaid and sea monster frieze which surrounded the upper wall of Burges's bedroom in Buckingham Street. Also just visible is the Minotaur frieze on the ceiling, and Burges's red bedstead.
                                                                M.A.

W. Burges, 'Own Furniture', R.I.B.A., Pl.1

National Museum of Wales

B.13 **Bedstead**

Early photograph
Inscribed 'Bedroom W.B.'

The photograph shows Burges's own red bedstead in situ in his bedroom at 15 Buckingham Street. It is adorned with the Chinese mandarin's robe. Also visible is a small painted chair, one of several visible in photographs of Burges's rooms and house.   M.A.

W. Burges, 'Own Furniture', R.I.B.A., Pl.3

National Museum of Wales

B.14 **Dressing Table**
Carved, painted and gilded mahogany
1867
h 5′1″ (154.9) w 3′2″ (96.5) d 2′ 3½″ (69.8)

The dressing table is painted red with some stencilling, inset with marble mosaic inlay, tinsel and shell and three portraits. The central circle enclosing bevelled mirrors, the whole revolving within hoops. It is fitted with steel mounts, tinned iron handles and finger rings of nickel plated brass. The R.I.B.A. notebooks of 1867 contain drawings for the finials and the top, there are also drawings for the table, some executed, some not, in the V. & A. The 'Abstract of Diaries' for 1867 states 'Smallfield did Crocker portraits for dressing table'.

Henry Holiday states that Burges had been 'sweet' on Emma Crocker, but that marrying 'would not agree with his favourite tastes'. Nonetheless the dressing table containing portraits of three members of the Crocker family remained in his bedroom throughout his life.

Stylistically the dressing table is a product of Burges's imagination, combining the lattice work of Constantinople with the finials he probably saw in Viollet-le-Duc's *Mobilier*, tome 1, which shows an armoire from Beauvais. The unusual circular multi-mirrored centrepiece is similar to that used by Burne-Jones in 'Fair Rosamund and Queen Eleanor', and to that in Van Eyck's 'Arnolfini Marriage' portrait.

'The cleverness and thought displayed in the dressing table show the immense amount of labour and consideration Burges expended on almost trifling subjects — the glass on double pivots — can be placed at almost any angle. The table-shelf is formed of a very fine mosaic, in which are inserted plaques of porphyry, lapis lazuli, verde-antique, gallo-antico and other semi-precious marbles.'*   M.A.

R.I.B.A. Arc 1V
V.&A., P.&D. 93.E8.38 (70)
W. Burges, 'Own Furniture', R.I.B.A., Pl.4
Exh *Victorian and Edwardian Decorative Art.*
R.A. 1972, B13
R. P. Pullan, *The House of William Burges, ARA* (1885) No. 30
E.W. Godwin, *AJ.* (1886)
Henry Holiday, *Reminiscences* (1914)
*R.A. Briggs, *R.I.B.A. Journal*, XXIII (1916), 'The Art of William Burges'
C. Handley-Read, *CL* (1966), 600-604

Lent by the Trustees of The Cecil Higgins Art Gallery, Bedford

B.14

B.15 **Design for a Secretaire**
Pen and watercolour over pencil on cartridge paper
Original measurements lost.

Signed and dated 'W. Burges Archt/15 Buckingham St Strand Oct 17/1867' 'Inch Scale'. Front and side elevations of a secretaire showing the proposed decorative scheme.
Page 5 of the 'Furniture' album.   M.A.

Victoria and Albert Museum.

B.15

B.16 **Design for a Cabinet**
Pen and watercolour over pencil on cartridge paper
Original measurements lost.

Side and front elevations of a tall cabinet with sloping roof and finials showing part of the planned decorative scheme. The front elevation has the doors open to reveal the nest of pigeonholes within. The large space beneath was intended for the storing of art books. The cabinet is similar to that in the photograph album given to Sir John Benson, which is also found in 'Own Furniture'. Page 5 of the 'Furniture' album.

M.A.

Victoria and Albert Museum

B.17 **Writing Cabinet**
Carved, painted and gilded wood with clock, bells and a gong
1867
h 8′ 5½″ (257.8) w 3′ 6½″ (108) d 1′8¾″ (52.7)

B.17

Below the tiled roof, a counterbalanced door is painted with representations of Adolescentia and Virilitas, the sides with Puerilia and Senectus. The clock has a three train movement with chimes on eight bells and one gong; the dial being engraved 'HOROLOGIUM MONET TEMPORIS FUGACIS OMNE SUBEO SCRIPTUM SIT BENEDICTUM A DEO PACIS' above three small independently operating bells. An arched panel contains figures of the Butcher, the Baker and the Candlestick Maker and coins of the realm, some dated 1867. Below are calendar dials, signed 'GUALBERT SAUNDERS MADE ME AD 1865'. The hinged door has figures of Historia and Poesia, flanking a recess with embossed 17th century leather panels. The writing flap has Miles, Rex and Mercator above five hand painted Minton tiles, one initialled GS; the footwell has 'ACCOUNTS' and 'LETTERS' boxes. The polychrome cabinet is entirely painted with animals, insects and heraldic devices, with stencilling and gilding on a red ground.

Burges worked with Saunders in 1865. It is therefore likely that the design is a collaboration, employing many familiar features of Burges's furniture design, such as the finials, pitched roof and tiling as well as the sturdy construction and red ground covered with stencilling and paintings, all of which are to be found on the Yatman escritoire and the giant bookcase. Saunders later went into brief partnership with Henry Holiday and it is possible that Holiday may be responsible for the painting. Pencil designs of small animals, attributed to Burges, which form part of the decorative scheme are to be found in the V. & A.

M.A.

V.&A., P.&D. 93.E.3
Sotheby's Belgravia Sale, 6 December 1978, lot 166
J. Mordaunt Crook, in *Morris and Company* Fine Art Society (1979), 14, 16.

Manchester City Art Gallery
Regrettably this item was not available for exhibition.

B.18 **Litany Desk**
Walnut, carved and inlaid with maple
1867
Made by Robinson of High Holborn
h 3′5″ (104) w 3′5″ (104) d 1′10″ (56)

The central arch of the litany desk frames a figure of St. Andrew, while on either side in spandrels are St. George and St. Michael each with a dragon. The sides enclose the figures of Zacharias and the Prophet Joel, all the figures being under arched openings. The coved underside of the desk is inlaid with the inscription 'Domine libera nos', 'AD mdcclxvii'. The surface of the desk is inlaid with emblems of the Passion.

St. Andrew's Church, Kingsbury was designed by S. W. Dawkes and Hamilton in 1847, and built on a site in Wells Street, W1. It was removed to its present site in 1933. St. Andrew's was in some ways the mecca of Victorian ecclesiology, thanks to the influence of Beresford-Hope, who was church warden from 1853, and Benjamin Webb, co-founder of the Cambridge Camden Society and Editor of the *Ecclesiologist*, who was vicar from 1862 to 1885. They employed several major art-architects from the Gothic Revival to design the church furnishings. As well as the litany desk, Burges designed a monument to James Murray, Webb's predecessor; a cusped niche in the south wall with a recumbent effigy of the Vicar. Street

B.18

designed the chancel screen, metal pulpit, and reredos, Pearson the font cover, and Butterfield the lectern while the windows are filled with stained glass manufactured by Clayton & Bell, with the exception of the east window which contains glass by Hardman, from a design by Pugin. M.A.

Exh *Oxford Movement Centenary Exhibition*, Imperial Institute, London 1933, ill facing p.128
Exh *Victorian and Edwardian Church Arts*, All Hallows Church, London Wall, 1967
Exh *Victorian Church Art* V.&A. 1971 D4. ill.
B.N. (1868), 163 ill.
E, xxix (1868). 63-4. ill. facing p.218
Athanaeum, 9 May 1868, 668

Lent by St. Andrew's Church, Kingsbury, Middlesex.

B.19 **Escritoire**
Early photograph
Inscribed 'Portrait of W.B.' 'Escritoire of W.B.'.

The escritoire combines a writing desk, pigeon-holes for letters, drawers and shelves. Its solid structure, strapped doors and ornate stencilling are typical of Burges's painted furniture. Figure subjects within gilded frames illustrate the uses of writing. A young man kisses a love letter before posting it in a tree trunk, a merchant fills his ledger, an urchin learns to write, while his tutor, a monk, punishes him for his tardiness by pulling his ear, and an old man makes his will. The panel below illustrates the different estates of life: Priest, King, Warrior, Merchant and Labourer. Beside the escritoire stands a heavy arm chair with turned legs and rails and large bobbin knobs. A similar chair may be seen at Castell Coch, among Lady Bute's bedroom furniture. Both the escritoire and chair are missing. M.A.

W. Burges, 'Own Furniture', R.I.B.A., Pl.7
R.P. Pullan, *House of William Burges*, Pl.10

National Museum of Wales

B.20

B.21 Design for a Bookcase

Pen and ink and watercolour over pencil with gold details, on cartridge paper. Page 26 from the 'Furniture' album
10¾" (27.3)×8¼" (21)

This design resembles those bookcases Burges installed in the Library of Tower House, which were painted with the letters of the alphabet in the form of figures from the architectural world.

M.A.

Victoria and Albert Museum

B.22

B.20 Bookcase

Early photograph
Inscribed in the margin 'Paradiso, Purgatorio, Inferno', and at the bottom 'Subject/Dante's Comedia' 'Bookcase of W.B.'.

The 'Armoury bookcase' is photographed here, as it stood in Burges's rooms at 15 Buckingham Street. The shelves are lined with books and several pieces of Burges's metalwork, including the fantastic pair of antelope-necked decanters with matching cup (C45, 46). On the lower doors there are figures of Cerberus, the centaur, Nessus, the Minotaur and Geryon; the heads of the monsters are portraits of Burges's friends. On one side are medallion heads St. Thomas of Canterbury, Etnizza and Justinian, a full-length figure of Leah, and below Dante and Virgil. On the other side are the medallion heads of St. Benedict, Costanza and Trajan, a full-length figure of Rachel, and below Charon.

M.A.

W. Burges, 'Own Furniture', R.I.B.A., Pl.24
R.P. Pullan, *House of William Burges*, (1885) Pl.35

National Museum of Wales

B.22 Pair of Cupboard Doors

Carved, painted and gilded wood with inset oil paintings
1869
h 2' (60.9) w 1'2½" (36.8)

The gilded wood of the doors frames sixteen paintings of flowers containing shadowy fairies, probably by N. H. J. Westlake (1833-1921). The doors were originally one of three pairs which formed the front of a tall cabinet in Buckingham Street. This was later broken up and the ornamental doors were inserted in the walls of the drawing room in Tower House. The other pairs, 'the Winds' and 'the Oceans', both by Frederick Weekes (fl. 1854-1893) remain in situ on either side of the *Romaunt of the Rose* chimneypiece.

The inspiration for the painted framework with the star shaped inlets is very likely derived from the Westminster Retable, with which Burges was familiar; he quoted it as one of the very few examples of medieval painted furniture remaining in England. An illustration also accompanied his article in G.G. Scott's *Gleanings from Westminster Abbey*, 1863.

M.A.

Exh *Victorian and Edwardian Decorative Arts* V.&A. 1952
Exh *Victorian and Edwardian Decorative Art* RA 1972, Bl4, 15
R.P. Pullan, *House of William Burges* (1885), Pl.19
E.W. Godwin, *AJ* (1886)
C. Handley-Read, *Burl. Mag.*, cv (1963), ill.

Lent by the Trustees of The Cecil Higgins Art Gallery, Bedford

B.23

B.24

B.23 Settle
Carved, painted and gilt wood
1869-71

Three painted panels by H. Stacy Marks (1829-1898) surround a Turkish embroidery to form the back of the 'Zodiac Settle'. A crenellated canopy is supported by spiralled pillars which adjoin the sturdy box-like seat. Marks remembered painting the figures onto the three panels of burnished gold, which he found rather glaring. The ideas were Burges's own; the amusing and detailed theme is typical of his love of colour, mythology and fun.'Sol is represented as seated on a throne; while on both sides of him are the signs of the Zodiac, engaged in dancing a breakdown. To his right may be seen Leo making love to Virgo; Cancer dancing vigorously, supported by the graceful Gemini; Taurus and Aries completing the figure. On his left Libra and Scorpio are footing it, followed by Sagittarius and Capricorn; then comes the most amusing group of Aquarius in the guise of a pump, administering the pledge to two flabby Pisces. Outside are the planets playing the dance music. St Cecilia and another female figure stand below under graceful foliage.'* On the underside of the canopy are gilt stars, cast in lead and covered by domes of glass or crystal.

The settle is another Buckingham Street piece which moved from Burges's six overcrowded rooms in the Strand to Tower House where with the painted aumbry doors — and a missing bobbined armchair — it enriched the drawing room, illuminating the theme 'Love, its Fortunes and Misfortunes'.   M.A.

R.I.B.A. Arc IV
W. Burges 'Own Furniture', R.I.B.A., Pl.18
*R.P. Pullan, *The House of William Burges* (1885), Pl.17
H.S. Marks, *Pen and Pencil Sketches* (1894), 220
R.A. Briggs, *R.I.B.A. Journal* (1916), 'The Art of William Burges'
E.W. Godwin, *A.J.* (1886)
C. Handley-Read, *Burl. Mag.* cv (1963), ill.

Lent by Auberon Waugh Esq.

B.24 Cabinet
Painted and gilded wood
h 7'10½" (240) w 4'2½" (128.4) d

In Burges's Estimate Book for January 1879 appears the note 'Own wardrobe painting — 9 birds @ 5/-. 14 flies, eggs et @ 2/- and decoration @ £2.0.0', for which less 10%, Campbell & Smith charged Burges £5.2.0.

The cabinet still exhibits influences of the Noyon armoire absorbed many years previously, in its use of articulated doors, metal straps and figure compositions within panels; the subjects of the latter being the domestic troubles of philosophers and literary men. The four philosophers figure on the doors while above them, from windows, lean the causes of their trouble: Zantippe pours water over the head of Socrates as he attempts to instruct a youth; Martin Luther is plagued by a devil-sent woman, but grasps an ink bottle to hurl at his assailant. Aristotle is disturbed from his revelry by his harridan of a wife who is also flirting with Alexander. Finally Diogenes lectures a youth while Lais encourages an urchin to disturb him. On either side appear the figures of Virgil and St. Paul fleeing the torments of matriarchy by climbing from windows by ropes. Beneath these scenes of discord, domestic animals play, and on the base (now removed) a crocodile used to bask.   M.A.

R.I.B.A. Arc IV
R.I.B.A. 'Own Furniture', Pl. 17
R.P. Pullan, *House of William Burges* (1885), Pl. 37
E.W. Godwin, *A.J.* (1886), 304, ill.
C. Handley-Read, *Burl. Mag.* cv (1963), ill.

Lent by Auberon Waugh Esq.

B.25 with B.26 and part of B.6 behind

B.25 Bedstead

Carved, painted and gilt mahogany and pine.
1879
h 5′5″ (165.1) w 5′3″ (160) l 7′8″ (243.8)

The head is inset with two large bevelled mirrors and ten smaller ones, as well as a painting in oil by Henry Holiday (1839-1927), 'The Judgement of Paris', with figures in 13th century costume. The side boards and posts are inset with vellum and textile fragments under glass and rock crystal, the latter also forms the knops of the posts. The foot is inscribed 'VITA NOVA' and the bedposts 'WILLIAM BURGES ME FIERI FECIT' (right) and 'ANNO DOMINI MDCCCLXXXIX' (left).

'The Golden Bed' was designed as the main feature of Burges's most gorgeous room, the Guest's Bedroom in Tower House. The entire room was 'made of fire and flowers', butterflies covered the ceiling and Eastern ceramics and coloured glass reflected the gold that covered furniture, walls and woodwork. The theme of the chamber was 'The Earth and its Productions', everywhere the decorations abounded with examples — 'the beams being decorated with comic illustrations of battles between those relentless enemies, the frogs and the mice'*; flowers and plants filled the frieze that lined the walls.

Burges's 'Estimate Book' has an entry for 25 June 1879, 'carving to Bedstead, Guest's room'. Nicholls was the craftsman and the price £15 5s. 0d. 'The Judgement' panel had been transferred from Buckingham Street and employed in the creation of the 'Golden Bed'. Burges's design combines features based on his own experiments, such as the medieval use of vellum under crystal, and references to medieval sources which may be derived from Viollet-le-Duc's *Mobilier*. But whatever its inspiration, Burges has united all the arts in creating a piece of furniture typical of his eclecticism: scholarly, massive and fantastic.

M.A.

Exh *Victorian and Edwardian Decorative Arts*, V.&A. 1952, J2
W. Burges, 'Own Furniture' R.I.B.A. Pl.30
*Mrs. Haweis, 'William Burges's House' in *The Queen* (1880), 481
E.W. Godwin, *A.J.* (1886), ill.
Tower House Sale Catalogue, 1933, Lot 107
C. Handley-Read, *Burl. Mag.* cv (1963), ill.

Victoria and Albert Museum

B.26 Wash-hand-stand

Carved, painted and gilt wood
1879-1880
h 5'3" (160) w 2'8" (81.2) d 1'10" (55.8)

The top, soap dishes, splashback and bowl are of marble, the latter inset with silver fishes and a butterfly; the taps and fittings of bronze. The back and tank are of wood embellished with painted decoration and several small bevelled mirrors. It is variously inscribed 'VENEZ LAVER' on the cold tap, 'VITA NOVA' on the back, on the left side 'WILLIAM BURGES', and on the right side 'ME FECIT MDCCCLXXX'.

A Victorian visitor to the house waxed ecstatic about the wash-hand-stand; '. . . here we have a gem fit to splash at all day in poetic enjoyment. It is of gold, with fragments of bright stones and shells inlaid; those called Venus's ears have been largely used. Every blank space is carved minutely in flowers, beautifully tinted, and we discern a lizard or two and some butterflies among them. Thick crystals enclose small shells, where a scent bottle, some hundreds of years old, and a toothpowder receptacle, some thousands, nestle and shine. Marble plates receive the soap. A fine bronze, which most of us would place on some table for ornament, here makes itself useful — a bull, from whose throat ajar the water pours into a Brescia basin, inlaid with silver fishes. How do you get the water in? See you that other bronze, a tortoise, which seems to creep beyond the bull's reach — it is a plug; twist him round and the bull fills the basin. Such is the use which Aladdin makes of bronzes, and I beg to add that the lapis and the amber and crystal and marble are not papier-mache and glazed chalk — they are the real thing.'*

This sparkling piece of furniture originally stood, with the 'Golden Bed', in the Guest bedroom at Tower House for which it was designed.   M.A.

Exh *Victorian and Edwardian Decorative Arts.*
V.&A. 1952, J3
BN. 23 April (1880), 497
*Mrs. Haweis, 'William Burges's House' in *The Queen* (1880), 481
E.W. Godwin *A.J.* (1886)
Tower House Sale Catalogue, 1933, Lot 109
C. Handley-Read, *Burl. Mag.,* cv (1973), ill.
C. Handley-Read, *C.L.,* CXXXIX (1966), 600-604

Victoria and Albert Museum

B.26 with B.22 above

(detail)

B.27 **Chair**

Painted and gilded wood, with the seat and back panel upholstered in Morris & Co. 'Utrecht velvet'
h 2′8″ (81.2) w 1′5″ (43) d 1′3″ (38)

A small upright chair with upholstered seat and panel in the back; the reverse of the back is decorated with a merman holding a club and shield and wearing a helmet of shell. One of a pair of such chairs, the other decorated with a mermaid, holding up tresses of her hair in one hand, with a mirror in the other. The framework of the chair is painted a deep red with bands of gilding on the legs and uprights. Both chairs were in use at Tower House, as is seen in the Pullan volume of photographs, another very similar pair is visible in the volume of photographs for Sir John Benson
M.A.

V.&A., P.&D., Album 93.E.8, sheets 27, 30
R.P. Pullan, *The House of William Burges* (1885), Pl.19
C. Handley-Read, *Burl. Mag.* cv (1963), 496-509, Pl.33
R. Watkinson, *William Morris as Designer* (1967), Pl.40

Lent by the William Morris Gallery, Walthamstow

B.28 **Design for a Chair and Design for a Sideboard**

Watercolour, pen and gold paint over pencil on paper
Page 27 of the 'Furniture' album
Front, side and back elevations of a small red chair, rush seated, with a tortoise monster on the reverse of the chair back and patterns on the front
3⅞″ (10)×7⅜″ (18.5)

This chair is a similar design to the small 'Merman chair' (B27), with the exception of the rush seat and the differing monster on the reverse. Merman and Mermaid sketches for the chairbacks may be found in the same album.

Front and side elevations of the 'Wines and Beers' cabinet
8″ (20)×11⅛″ (28.5)
Details for the central panels on flimsy paper pasted on.
M.A.

Victoria and Albert Museum

B.29

B.30

B.29 Chair
Steel with strapped leather seat
h 3′8″ (111.7) w 24½″ (62.2) d 20¾″ (52.7)

One of four steel chairs with finials in the form of pine cones or buds, and ball finials for the hand rests. The chairs have upright backs and circular legs held by leaf frond apron pieces. The seat is formed of a continuous leather strap wound across the supporting bars. The design follows exactly an illustration in Viollet-le-Duc's *Mobilier,* vol. i (1858), 50. Designed for Cardiff Castle.   M.A.

Lent by Cardiff City Council

B.30 Chair
Walnut inlaid with box and mother of pearl
h 3′6¾″ (108.5) w 1′5″ (43) d 1′5½″ (44.5)

One of six dining chairs with turned knobs, backs on square and turned supports, linked by a section of lattice work and a padded top rail. Square and turned legs are joined by stretchers and it is inlaid overall with stringing and mother of pearl in geometric patterns. The seat and back have been re-upholstered, and originally were probably adorned by a tasselled fringe. Several such chairs were made for Cardiff Castle, differing in the sorts of wood and inlay used. These upright chairs resemble in style those designed by Viollet-le-Duc and Edmond Duthoit for Château de Roquetaillade, near Bordeaux in the 1860s.   M.A.

Lent by Cardiff City Council

Catalogue C:
Ecclesiastical Architecture, Stained Glass, Metalwork and Decoration

Architectural Sculpture

Sculpture for Burges was the voice of architecture. He regarded figure-drawing as an indispensable part of any architect's equipment. And he considered the study of antique and medieval sculpture crucial to any architect's training. In his commitment to the integration of architecture and sculpture, Burges was an out-and-out Ruskinian. But he was well aware of the difficulty inherent in reviving what was virtually a lost art. Happily, his talent for sculptural design was given full rein in a series of extraordinary monuments and memorials. From Cardiff to Kensal Green, from Fleet and Canterbury to Skelton and Studley Royal, from Waltham Abbey to Tower House, Kensington—Burges's instinct for sculptural form is unmistakable. And the 1260 pieces of sculpture built into the fabric of Cork Cathedral—each one personally designed by Burges, each one modelled under his superintendence and carved under his direction—add up to a formidable justification of his artistic theory and practice.   J.M.C.

Painted decoration, stained glass, mosaic, etc

Burges revelled in the minutiae of decoration. His use of mosaic was based on a knowledge of medieval techniques unequalled in his generation. In the field of stained glass, as designer, patron and pundit, he was involved in the production of some of the finest windows of modern times. As a master of the totality of interior design, he was—quite literally—unique. Burges assimilated the 13th century, mingled its features with Renaissance, Pompeian, Japanese, Assyrian and Islamic work, added a touch of personal fantasy—and ended up, almost despite himself, with a New Style. Only Burges managed to combine the surface abstraction of Islamic art with the robust three-dimensionality of 13th century Gothic. In his work the calligraphic and sculptural elements of both traditions are fused in a new synthesis. The rooms of Cardiff Castle are not machines for living in. They are fantasy capsules, three-dimensional passports to fairy kingdoms and realms of gold. And at home in London—at Tower House, Melbury Rd., Kensington—Burges created his own dream-world: a multi-coloured fantasy, shimmering with stained glass, painted furniture and exotic metalwork, 'massive, learned, glittering, amazing'.   J.M.C.

Lille Cathedral

The Lille Cathedral competition was announced in December 1854. Burges and his partner, Henry Clutton (1819-93), employed their knowledge of the great Early French churches of Normandy and Picardy as a basis for their design. The competition specification allowed little room for manoeuvre and the cost was not to exceed £120,000. Burges and Pullan delivered the design on 28 February 1856; the results were announced on 13 April. Of the forty-one entries from seven countries, Burges and Clutton were first and G.E. Street (1824-81) second. Didron, one of the competition judges acknowledged 'England has indeed triumphed . . . .. The defeat is for us and on our soil: at Lille the architecture and archeology of France have met with their Agincourt'.*

Clutton was at that date the more experienced architect of the two, and it seems likely that he was largely responsible for the exterior design, but there is evidence to suggest that Burges was almost entirely responsible for the interior furnishings. Both the style and the complex interior iconography support this theory.

Burges and Clutton competed eagerly, but the 'Abstract' for 13 May 1856 records 'Row with Clutton': the subject of the argument is uncertain. The foundation stone was laid on 9 June, and the architects received their prize money— 6,000 Francs. The prize was to have been 10,000 Francs, but unfortunately their cathedral was not to be built. For reasons that are not entirely clear, the Commission did not stand by their jury's choice. Clearly they had hoped for a local winner, and the emergence of two foreign, Protestant victors must have been a disappointment. Still the final, and much criticised result was an unfortunate solution. One of the judges combined with one of the local defeated competitors to produce a design which was clearly an amalgamation of several of the competing schemes. M.A.

Eccl. xvii NS xiv (1856), 80-105, 209
Eccl. xix (1858), 42
B. xvi (1858), 13, 33
G. G. Evans and R.P. Pullan, *Photographs of Designs for Lille Cathedral* (Wimborne Minster, 1860)
G.G. Scott, *Personal and Professional recollections* (1879), 205-6
B.F.L. Clarke, *Church Builders of the Nineteenth Century* (1969 ed), 153

C.1

(detail)

C.1 Design for an Organ, Lille Cathedral

(a) Pencil and wash on paper; pencil on flimsy paper details pasted on.
29½"(74.9)×20¼"(51.5)
(b) Also pen and sepia ink over pencil on paper, seperate sheet.
8¾"(22.2)×20¼"(18.5)

Both sheets attached to page 67 of the *Lille Cathedral* album in the R.I.B.A.

Burges completed four or five drawings for the organ at Lille. One may be found among the competition designs in Lille, Pl.10, another in the V.&A., Prints and Drawings Department in the album *Sketches by E.W. Godwin*. Didron's article in the *Annales Archéologiques* of 1856 also contained an engraving of the organ, though this may have been taken from the drawing in the Godwin album; it shows the details of the iconography. C. Handley-Read suggests that the Lille organ case was probably the first iconographic scheme of Burges's invention.

The ornate structure towered, battlemented and painted is very archaic in nature, and it is interesting to note that this proposal predates Burges's first executed piece of painted furniture, the 'Yatman' cabinet of 1858. M.A.

Lent by the British Architectural Library/R.I.B.A.

C.2 Design for a Lectern, Lille Cathedral

Pen and ink and wash on paper with details on flimsy paper pasted on.
18"(45.5)×16½"(42)

Front and side elevations for a lectern, detailing incomplete. The sheet comes from page 71 of the *Lille Album* in the R.I.B.A. C. Handley-Read notes that this design appears, very little modified, as that executed by Jones and Willis in 1878 for St. Fin Bar's Cathedral, Cork. They also sent the design to the Paris Exhibition of 1878. M.A.

Lent by the British Architectural Library/R.I.B.A.

The Crimea Memorial Church, Constantinople

The competition for the design of an anglican church to stand in Constantinople as a memorial to the English dead of the Crimea was announced in June 1856. The cost was to be £20,000, the land to be supplied by the Sultan and the funds raised by The Society for the Propagation of the Gospel. Of the forty-six entries submitted by January 1857, thirty-nine were English. Burges took first place and the prize of £100, and Street, as at Lille, came second. The following year a site was found and the foundation stone was laid in October with Burges present. Within months a combination of Turkish inflation and English parsimony forced him to make continuous reductions in size and materials; by 1863 the nave had been reduced from six bays to two and the portals from three to one; the ambulatory, flying buttresses and south transept had also been removed. Finally the Committee requested the removal of the stone vaulting. Burges would compromise his design no further, and Street took over.

Burges claimed to have based his competition scheme upon the church of St. Andrea at Vercelli, supposedly built by English workmen and English money. In essence the design was a combination of Early French and Italian, but bowing to its Eastern locality in its use of materials. Some praised this synthesis, others found Burges's attempt to unite elements of Turkish and Western architecture an afront to the 'Englishness' of the memorial. It was further criticized for 'horizontality', 'orientalism' and even for appearing 'Romanesque'. As at Lille bureaucratic uncertainty and continual attenuation of the funds eventually resulted in the construction of a church pale in comparison to the polychromatic building with aisled nave, monumental apse and optional campanile that Burges had first envisioned.   M.A.

R.P. Pullan, 'The Works of the Late William Burges, ARA'. *R.I.B.A. Trans* (1881-2), 17-30, Obituary

C.3 Sections through the Crimea Memorial Church

Pen and wash on Whatman paper
20¼″(51.5)×29″(73.5)
Inscribed 'Section thro' Transepts' 'Looking East'. and 'Section thro' Nave' 'Looking West'.

Two sections from the 'No. 1 Set' of competition drawings for the Crimea Memorial Church. (Sets numbered 1, 3, 4, 5 are in the possession of the Society for the Propagation of the Gospel.)

Lent through the British Architectural Library/ R.I.B.A.

C.4 Ground Plan for the Crimea Memorial Church

Ink on Whatman paper
20½″(52)×29″(73.5)
Inscribed 'Plan' 'Church at Constantinople'.

From the 'No. 1 Set' of competition drawings for the Crimea Memorial Church.

Lent through the British Architectural Library/ R.I.B.A.

C.5 Two Elevations for the Crimea Memorial Church

Pen and wash on Whatman paper
20½″(52)×29¼″(74.5)
Inscribed 'West Elevation' and 'East Elevation', 'Church at Constantinople',

From the 'No. 1 Set' of competition drawings for the Crimea Memorial Church.

Lent through the British Architectural Library/ R.I.B.A.

C.6 Elevation for the Crimea Memorial Church

Pen and wash on Whatman paper
20½″(52)×29¼″(74.5)
Inscribed 'South Elevation', 'Church at Constantinople', 'this elevation applies equally to the North Side'.

This elevation for the South Side of the church has a campanile on a detachable flap; the estimated cost for this tower was an extra £3,000. From the 'No. 1 Set' of competition drawings for the Crimea Memorial Church.

Lent through the British Architectural Library/ R.I.B.A.

C.7 Section through the Crimea Memorial Church

Pen and wash on Whatman paper
20½″(52)×20″(73.5)
Inscribed 'Longitudinal section'

From the 'No. 1 Set' of competition drawings for the Crimea Memorial Church.

Lent through the British Architectural Library/ R.I.B.A.

C.5

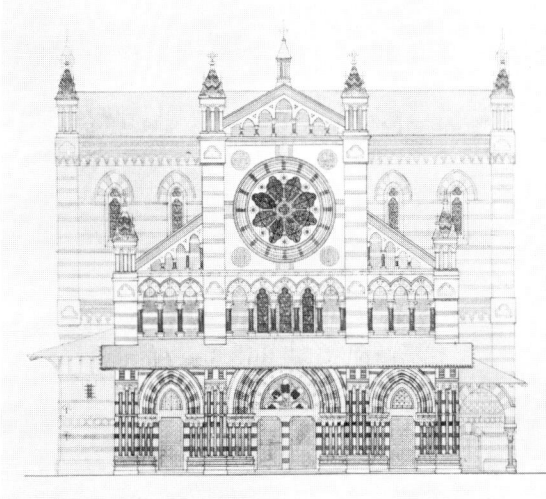

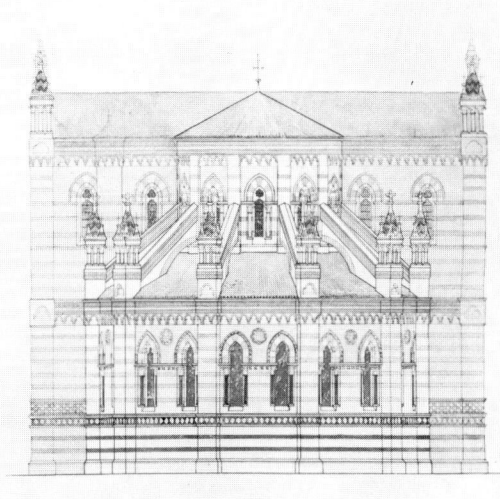

CHURCH AT
CONSTANTINOPLE
WEST ELEVATION
EAST ELEVATION

(detail)

C.7

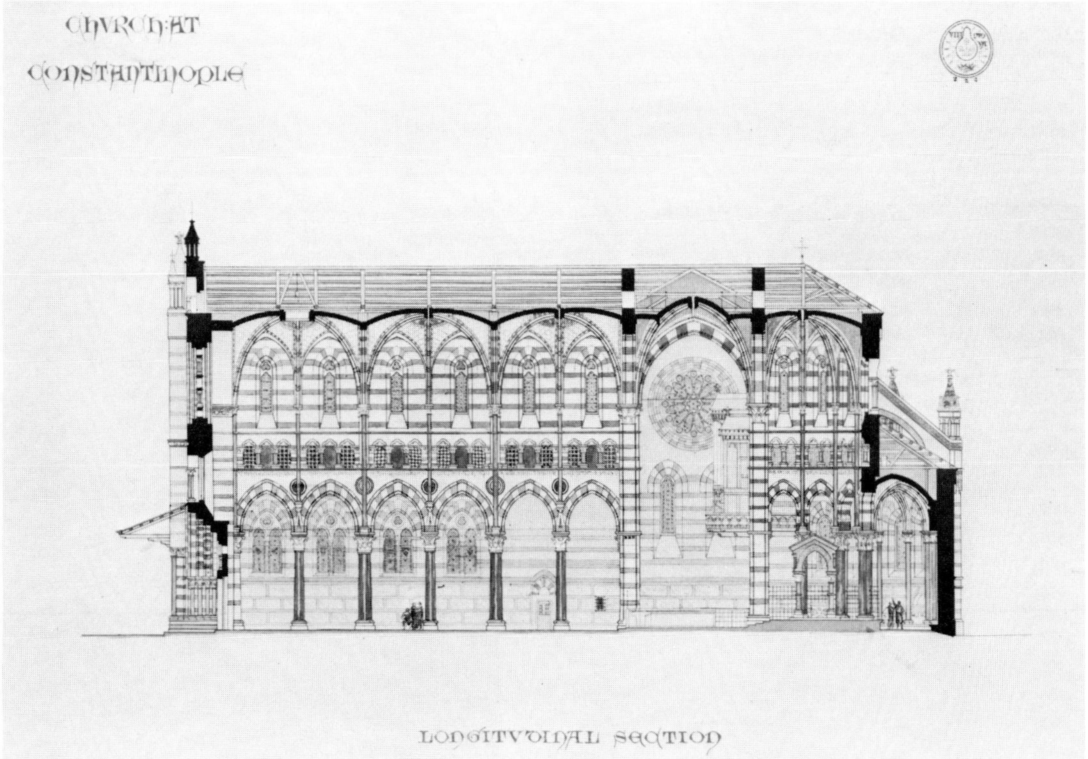
CHURCH AT
CONSTANTINOPLE
LONGITUDINAL SECTION

(detail)

St Fin Barre's Cathedral, Cork

The competition for the new cathedral of St Fin Barre was announced in April 1862; of the sixty-eight competitors many were not of the stature required, and Burges emerged an easy winner, receiving the £100 winner's prize in 1863. The new cathedral was his first major commission destined to reach completion. There were grumblings that Burges had not played fair, for the cost was to be £15,000 and he had submitted a design which he admitted would cost twice that sum. The fund raising machinery of the committee and the powerful local bishop, Bishop Gregg, began to gather money, and as they collected, Burges enhanced his designs with greater size and richness of materials. In size the new cathedral was little larger than a church, being 162 feet in length, but the grandeur of the three spires, the expense of the decoration and the profusion of exterior ornament gave it a quality rarely seen in Victorian church building. Again turning to Early French for inspiration, Burges used splayed portals adorned with sculpture on a scale almost comparable with the transepts of Chartres. Of the 1,260 pieces of sculpture in the cathedral's fabric, every one was designed by Burges and modelled by Nicholls. Burges felt that 'The Western front of Cork Cathedral should be a specimen of the best architectural sculpture the age can produce'. The local masons employed were entirely sensible of their task, as is proven by the outstanding combination of architecture and sculpture; the West front sculpture alone took ten years to complete. In the decoration Burges chose finer craftsmanship and better materials, regardless of cost. When he died in 1881, there was still work in progress; Chapple and Pullan supervised the decoration, and though the polychromatic interior remained incomplete, the cathedral remains a masterpiece of strength and colour. It cost finally over £100,000.

M.A.

R. Caulfield, *Hand-Book of the Cathedral Church of St. Fin Barre Cork* (1881)
R.P. Pullan, 'The Works of the Late William Burges ARA' *R.I.B.A. Trans* (1881-2), 183-219
A. i (1869), 36-7. 179 and ii (1870), 147-8
R.P. Pullan, *Architectural Designs of William Burges* (1883)
BN. xxvi (1874), 421

St. Fin Barre's Cathedral, Cork — a watercolour view from the East End

St. Fin Barre's Cathedral, Cork — the West Front

C.8 **Longitudinal Section—Cork Cathedral No. V**

Pen and wash on tracing paper
20″(50.8)×29½″(75)

One of the early designs, before Burges managed to introduce the towers and spires, showing the three-story interior elevation in the 'French' style and the apsed east end.
Inscribed 'note: The Blue tint shows the second contract'
      'Referred to in Contract'
      Signed 'Robert Walker Junr'
      'W. BURGES ARCHT 15
      BUCKINGHAM STREET. W.C.'
On the original drawing the west front and the first three bays of the nave are washed in pale blue.
                              V.G.

Lent by the Dean and Chapter of St. Fin Barre's Cathedral, Cork

C.9 **Through Transepts, Through Choir—Cork Cathedral No. VI**

Pen and wash on tracing paper
20″(50.8)×29½″(75)

Another early design, before Burges managed to introduce the towers and spires. These sections show the three storey interior elevation and the distribution of the windows in the transepts and around the apse.
Inscribed 'Referred to in Contract'
      'Robert Walker Junr'
      'W BURGES ARC^{HT}/15
      BUCKINGHAM STREET W.C.'

Lent by the Dean and Chapter of St. Fin Barre's Cathedral, Cork

C.10 **West Elevation, East Elevation—Cork Cathedral No. IX**

Pen, pencil and wash on Whatman paper
19″(48.3)×27⅞″(65.9)

The original towerless design. The west elevation is entirely tinted blue with four great Evangelist Symbols and one of the side portals sketched in in pencil. As built the apse was of course crowned by the beautiful figure of a gilded angel.
Inscribed 'note: The Blue tint shows the second contract'
      'Referred to in Contract'

Signed by Norman Cockburn, Gilbert Cockburn and Robert Walker Jun.   V.G.

Lent by the Dean and Chapter of St. Fin Barre's Cathedral, Cork

C.11 **West Elevation—Cork Cathedral**

Pen and wash on tracing paper
26⅜″(67.2)×16¼″(41.3)

The west front, more or less as executed with twin towers and spires and three gabled portals. The wealth of sculpture is not indicated.
Inscribed 'note: For new work compare this drawing with original West Front'.
                              V.G.

Lent by the Dean and Chapter of St. Fin Barre's Cathedral, Cork

St. Fin Barre's Cathedral, Cork—the Nicholls models as abandoned in the finished building

A detail of Cork Cathedral Furniture *as traced for the* West Front Estimates for the Carving

The finished carving on St. Fin Barre's Cathedral by MacLeod from the Nicholls model C.14

C.12 **Cork Cathedral—West Front Estimates for the Carving**

Pen and ink on writing paper, pen tracings pasted on
12¾"(32.5)×8"(20.5)

There are two copies of the book, this bound version dated '1 May 1878'. There are fifty-eight blue pages, 1-24 headed 'Nicholls', 25-48 headed 'MacLeod', 49-57 headed 'Burke' and 58 showing a summary of the expenses. On page 1 the conditions are laid out respecting materials, models, the fact that the estimates are to be inclusive, that some stone has already been furnished and is in position, sizes, the mosaic grounds and the use of the scaffolding by the mosaicist. The book was prepared in black ink on blue paper and the prices added by the artists in red. Designs in ink on tracing paper, taken from the presentation album 'Cork Cathedral Furniture' were pasted on to show precisely what was required; some tinted with ochre and brown.

The summary of costs at the end showed what an expensive exercise it was to be—

Nicholls	models for centre portal and gable	£884.10.0
	models for north and south doorways	£885.10.0
	use of cases	£10.00.0
	5 journeys to Cork	£100.00.0
	carriage of models	£60.00.0
MacLeod	for the carving	£5153.00.0
Burke	mosaic and journeys	£427.10.0
Burges	10% on the models 5% on carriage, carving and mosaic 8 journeys at £20	
Contingencies	say	£150.00.0
Hinges and doorwork		£151. 5.0 £291.10.0

The grand total was to be £8743.5.0

Here open at page 7 of Nicholls' estimates, for the great gargoyles of the west front, where the sculptor has inserted in red '4 at £20 each model—80.0.0 '

V.G.

Lent by the Dean and Chapter of St. Fin Barre's Cathedral, Cork

C.13 **Building the portals of St. Fin Barre's Cathedral**

Early photograph

Taken from a watercolour in Cork Cathedral, possibly by Burges himself this shows sketchy figures in medieval dress erecting the sculpture on the west front. The watercolour pre-dates the detailed design of the statues as photographs of it were pasted into 'Cork Cathedral Furniture' opposite to the sculpture designs with the exact locations of the pieces marked in red ink. V.G.

National Museum of Wales

C.14 **Model for the Bear of the Vision of Daniel**

Plaster
13"(33)×28½"(72.4)×15"(38.2)

Thomas Nicholls' model for the South East corbel under the central tower. There are four of these representing the Four Beasts of Daniel's Vision. Another version appears in the stained glass, see (C.23)

V.G.

Lent by the Dean and Chapter of St. Fin Barre's Cathedral, Cork

C.15 **Model for a Winged Monster**

Plaster
15¼"(38.7)×25½"(64.7)×10"(25.4)

Thomas Nicholls' model for the gryphon attacking a man on the South Tower of the West Front, at parapet level.
Inscribed "This ground to be.........up"

V.G.

Lent by the Dean and Chapter of St. Fin Barre's Cathedral, Cork

The finished carving on St. Fin Barre's Cathedral by MacLeod from the Nicholls model C.15

C.16 **Model for the Head of a Man**
Plaster
15″(38.2)×12⅝″(32)×6¾″(17.3)

Thomas Nicholls' model for a handsome bearded head, for the upper corner of the main West Door. The model was to cost £2.00 and the carving by McLeod £7.0.0 according to 'Cork Cathedral—West Front Estimates for the Carving.' V.G.

Lent by the Dean and Chapter of St. Finn Barre's Cathedral, Cork

C.17 **Stained Glass Windows—Cork Cathedral**
Pen, pencil, watercolour and printing, on Whatman paper
22½″(57)×25¾″(65.6)

A presentation album bound in red leatherette, with estimated prices and designs for all the windows in the church. A small printed plan is pasted on each page with the particular window located in red ink. A list of the final prices is given at the beginning of the book. Beside each design is a label with its number, position, subject and the original estimated cost. In every case this had risen by the time the glass came to be made and the final prices are inserted in red. The designs are initialled and in some cases signed by Burges himself and by H.W. Lonsdale.
Open here to show the four lancets of the North Transept illustrating the lives of the Prophets Job, Elijah, Jonah and Zechariah, all by H.W. Lonsdale. For the full size cartoon of the top of the right hand light see C22. V.G.

Lent by the Dean and Chapter of St. Fin Barre's Cathedral, Cork

C.18 **Stained Glass Design**
Pencil, pen and watercolour
14″(35.6)×5⅝″(14.5)

Detached from leaf no. 10 of the album. 'Stained Glass Windows—Cork Cathedral'. Set into an elaborately tile patterned field is a panel of Adam and Eve with a standing angel. Labelled in the book 'No. of Window-32. Position-South Aisle of Nave. Subject-Adam and Eve working. Cost-£44.10.0 (deleted) £47.15.3 (inserted in red)'.
Signed 'H.W.L' Dated 'May 11th 69'
Inscribed 'Approved by the Cathedral Select
　　　　　Vestry/Robert S Gregg^{Dd}/
　　　　　Dean/Chairman/Oct. 17.1874'
　　　　　'Approved John Cork/Oct. 17th 1874'
The design itself bears the text
'GOD:SAID:IN:THE:SWEAT:OF:THY:
FACE:SHALT:THOUGH:EAT:BREAD:'' and the dedication ''IN:MEMORY:OF:JOHN:MOLYNEU SOMETIME:LORD:LIEUTENANT:OF:THE: COUNTY/DIED:MAY:186(?)'
The actual window is dedicated to Montgomery Blair Robinson, 1841-1853.
'Mr. Robinson' has been written in pencil on the design.
　　　　　　　　　　　　　　　V.G.

Lent by the Dean and Chapter of St. Fin Barre's Cathedral, Cork

C.19 **Stained Glass Design**
Pencil, pen and watercolour
14″(35.6)×5⅝″(14.5)

Detached from leaf no. 13 of the album. 'Stained Glass Windows—Cork Cathedral'. Set into a field of inter-locking cusped quatrefoils is a panel of three figures, one with a hammer and chisel. Labelled in the book 'No. of window—48. Position—South aisle of nave. Subject—Nehemiah rebuilds the walls of Jerusalem. Cost £44.10.0 (deleted) £47.15.3 (inserted in red)'.
Signed 'H.W.L.' Dated 'May 11th /69'
Inscribed 'Approved by/Cathedral Select
　　　　　Vestry/Sep 9th 1873/
　　　　　Approved /John Cork/Oct 3rd 1873'.
The design itself bears the text
'SO:BUILD:WE:THE:WALL:AND:ALL:THE: WALL:WAS:JOINED:TOGETHER' and the dedication 'THIS WINDOW/WAS GIVEN/TO THE CHOIR/BY FRANCIS/DONAN(!)ESQ./AD MDCCCLIX.'

The actual window is to the memory of Richard Sainthill 1787—1869 and his wife Catherine, died 1859. V.G.

Lent by the Dean and Chapter of St. Fin Barre's Cathedral, Cork

C.20

C.20 **Stained Glass Cartoon—Leo**
Ink and wash on Whatman paper
14½″(37)×13″(33)

A golden lion passant spangled with stars, against a blue ground. Inscribed 'EO'
From the eastern most window in the north clerestorey of the nave, design no. 6 ('Signs of the Zodiac, Leo and Virgo') in 'Stained Glass Windows—Cork Cathedral', which is signed W.B. and dated 'May 11th/69'. Approval was given on August 6th, 1877. The windows cost £32.11.6. The main ground of the lancet is filled with a lattice pattern in pale green with the two coloured panels in the centre. V.G.

Lent by the Dean and Chapter of St. Fin Barre's Cathedral, Cork

C.21

C.22

C.21 Stained Glass Cartoon—the Creation of the Birds of the Air and the Fish of the Sea

Ink and wash on Whatman paper
31″(78.6) diameter

A roundel with a vulture, a peacock, a parakeet and other birds in the branches of a tree above grey waves, where a pelican is fishing among spiny fish and an eel.
Inscribed on the reverse 'Messrs Saunders and Co'. One of the nine roundels for the great west rose window. The design for this is no. 1 in 'Stained Glass Windows—Cork Cathedral' and is signed by Burges himself. It shows God the Father in the centre surrounded by eight scenes of the Creation in the radiating lobes. Among the inscriptions are 'approved /John Cork/ Jan 13th. 1876' and 'Note: It will be seen that/the cost of the window is /rather greater if the parts/are executed separately,/than if the whole is/carried out at once'. Each lobe containing a roundel like this was originally to cost £23. The whole finished window in fact cost £240.18.0, and these cartoons were £5.10.0 each, while the cartoon for the great central window was £12.10.0.   V.G.

Lent by the Dean and Chapter of St. Fin Barre's Cathedral, Cork

C.22 Stained Glass Cartoon—Fountain in New Jerusalem

Ink and wash on cartridge paper
39″(99) to apex×34¾″(88.2)

A lancet top with two standing figures, an angel with a red mantle and ochre robe and a prophet with a bluish green cloak over a purple gown. Between them is a characteristically Burgesian fountain in two tiers with three crouching lions spouting water above and one leopard head gushing below.
From the head of the eastern lancet in the north transept, design no. 52 in 'Stained Glass Windows—Cork Cathedral', which is signed 'H.W.L.' and dated 'May 11th/69'. Approval was given on Jan. 6th 1879. The other three scenes which fill the lancet are from the top, 'The Crucified Prophet', 'Measures Jerusalem' and 'Zechariah's Vision of a horseman'. The window was erected 'To the Glory of God and in loving memory of John Gregg DD Bishop of Cork, Cloyne and Ross'. Presented by his widow and younger children MDCCCLXXIX. It cost £111.13.0.   V.G.

Lent by the Dean and Chapter of St. Fin Barre's Cathedral, Cork

C.23

C.23 **Stained Glass Cartoon—The Vision of the Four Beasts.**
Ink and wash on Whatman paper
38½"(98) to apex×35"(89)

A lancet top showing the sleeping prophet seated at one side in a blue mantle and red robe, while the Four Beasts appear in a great arc of formalised clouds and turquoise waves. The text illustrated is Daniel VII 4-7:—

4. 'The first was like a lion, and had eagle's wings: I beheld till the wings thereof were plucked, and it was lifted up from the earth, and made stand upon the feet as a man, and a man's heart was given to it.
5. And behold another beast, a second, like to a bear, and it raised up itself on one side, and it had three ribs in the mouth of it between the teeth of it: and they said thus unto it, Arise, devour much flesh.
6. After this I beheld, and lo another, like a leopard, which had upon the back of it four wings of a fowl; the beast had also four heads; and dominion was given to it.
7. After this I saw in the night visions, and behold a fourth beast, dreadful and terrible, and strong exceedingly; and it had great iron teeth: it devoured and brake in pieces, and stamped the residue with the feet of it: and it was diverse from all the beasts that were before it; and it had ten horns'.

From the head of the western lancet in the south transept, design no. 53 in 'Stained Glass Windows—Cork Cathedral', which is signed 'H.W.L.' and dated 'May 11th /69'. Approval was given on March 19th. 1880.
The other three scenes which fill the lancet are from the top 'In the lions den', 'Interprets the writing on the Wall' and 'Daniel interprets Nebuchadnezzan's dream'. The window was erected in memory of Brigadier General Ernest A.B. Travers of the Madras Army, died 1879. It cost £111.13.0. V.G.

Lent by the Dean and Chapter of St. Fin Barre's Cathedral, Cork

C.24 **Stained Glass Cartoon—St. Stephen**
Ink and wash on Whatman paper
12½"(31.8) diameter

A roundel showing a profile head and shoulders of the saint in red vestments holding the stones of his martyrdom, with a red halo against a deep blue ground.
The full window design appears as design no. 18 in the album 'Stained Glass Windows—Cork Cathedral' and is signed and dated 'H.W.L. May 11th/69'. It is a clerestorey window in the south transept. Approved in October 1876, it also contains a roundel of St. James, the Martyr. The whole window cost £32.11.6. V.G.

Lent by the Dean and Chapter of St. Fin Barre's Cathedral, Cork

C.25 **Stained Glass Cartoon—St. Luke**
Ink and wash on Whatman paper.
12½"(31.8) diameter

A roundel showing the head and shoulders of St. Luke drawing, in a green cloak over a blue robe and wearing a yellow cap; his halo is blue against a deep red ground. The full window design appears as number 13 in the album 'Stained Glass Windows—Cork Cathedral' and is signed and dated 'W.B. May 11th /69'. It is a clerestorey window in the north transept, which also contains a roundel of St. Mark. The whole window cost £32.11.6.
V.G.

Lent by the Dean and Chapter of St. Fin Barre's Cathedral, Cork

C.26 **Stained Glass Cartoon—St. Titus**
Ink and wash on Whatman paper
12½"(31.8) diameter

A roundel showing the head and shoulders of St. Titus wearing a green mitre and purple vestments and holding a gold crozier; with a red halo against a deep blue ground. The full window design appears as number 20 in the album 'Stained Glass Windows—Cork Cathedral' and is signed and dated 'W.B. May 11th /69'. It is a clerestorey window in the south transept, which also contains a roundel of St. Timothy. Burges originally labelled this figure St. Peter on the design, but amended it to Titus in the margin. The whole window cost £32.11.6.
V.G.

Lent by the Dean and Chapter of St. Fin Barre's Cathedral, Cork

The nave and choir of St. Fin Barre's Cathedral, Cork

The lectern at St. Fin Barre's Cathedral, Cork

C.27 **The Bishop's Throne**
Watercolour on thick cartridge paper
36⅜″(91.8)×21″(53)
Signed 'A.H. Haig./1877'

A perspective watercolour showing the Bishop's throne in situ in the Cathedral at Cork. The throne is 46 feet high and was erected in 1878 at a cost of £1,463. The carving, of symbolic birds and beasts, and representations of bishops from St. Fin Barre to Bishop Gregg is by Walden, in solid oak. It was executed from models by Thomas Nicholls.

M.A.

R.I.B.A., Arc IV
Furniture Designs 16, Cork Archive
Exh RA. (1877), No. 1,065
Exh Paris Universal International Exhibition, 1878, Cat. of British section, part i, class 4, No. 33
B. xxxv (1877), 442
A. xvii (1877), 306 and xxvii (1882), 251
R. Caulfield, *Handbook of the Cathedral Church of St. Fin Barre* (1881) Pl.2.

Lent by the British Architectural Library/R.I.B.A.

C.28 **Design for a Church at Brighton**
Pencil, pen and wash on flimsy paper pasted on cartridge paper
21¼"(54)×19"(48.5)
Inscribed 'Proposed Church/at Brighton'.
      'W.Burges/archt/15 Buckingham Street
      W.C./adelphi'.

North and west elevations, plan, transverse and longitudinal sections for temporary church for Fr. Arthur Wagner, the celebrated Anglo-Catholicist. Burges notes in his diary for 1863, 'Wagner's church, to be used hereafter as a hall'. The design is typical of Burges's cheaper churches, small and Early French in style, combining features such as high-pitched gable, plate-traceried lancets and cartwheel window.   M.A.

Victoria and Albert Museum

St. Mary's Cathedral, Edinburgh

In 1873 Burges entered a limited competition for St. Mary's Episcopal Cathedral, Edinburgh. The other competitors were Lessels of Edinburgh; Peddie and Kinnear; Alexander Ross of Inverness; G.G. Scott and G.E. Street. If the London Law Courts competition marked the climax of Gothic eclecticism in the secular sphere, then the Edinburgh competition might be said to hold much the same position in ecclesiastical design. Scott proved to be the winner, but his design lacked altogether the flair of Burges's scheme.   J.M.C.

C.29 **Competition perspective for St. Mary's Cathedral, Edinburgh**
Pen and wash on paper
26"(66)×22"(55.9)
Unsigned. By A. H. Haig.

R.P. Pullan and Ewan Christian thought this the finest of Burges's ecclesiastical designs. For his spires Burges went to Noyon; for his *flèche* to Amiens; for his transept gables to Ely; for his plan to Sens and Langres, Dijon and Lisieux—a plan he had already used before at Cork and Constantinople.   J.M.C.

Exh., R.A. 1873, No. 1133
R.I.B.A., Arc. IV
R.P. Pullan, *Architectural Designs of William Burges* (1883), 17-18

Lent by J. Mordaunt Crook

C.29

Christ the Consoler, Skelton-on-Ure, Yorkshire—from the south.

Christ the Consoler, Skelton-on-Ure, Yorkshire—the organ and crossing.

Christ the Consoler, Skelton-on-Ure, Yorkshire

The church of Christ the Consoler stands in the grounds of Newby Hall; it was built by Lady Mary Vyner in memory of her son, Frederick Grantham Vyner, who had been murdered by Greek bandits. Commissioned in 1870, begun in 1871 and consecrated in 1876, at a cost of around £25,000, the church at Skelton shared with that at Studley Royal a common cause for construction and a common builder in J. Thompson of Peterborough. Both churches are also similar in plan and scale, having a short nave and equal aisles with a rectangular chancel and single tower and spire. Pevsner describes the decoration as of 'determined originality' and 'great opulence, even if of a somewhat elephantine calibre'. Marble shafting of various colours frames the chancel, a large rose window adorns the West end and a huge organ blocks one of the bays. Lonsdale and Weekes were cartoonists for the very fine stained glass, executed by Saunders & Co, and the mass of carving in both the structure and the decoration is the work of Thomas Nicholls. The glowing decorative scheme, 13th century in appearance, and the complex iconography of the windows and carving are representative of the fact that all was carefully supervised by Burges, resulting in 'one of the most remarkable churches of the 19th century, and to my thinking one of the most beautiful'.*

M.A.

*H.S. Goodhart-Rendel Index, National Monuments Record.
B. xxxvi (1878), 63, 65.
N. Pevsner, *Yorkshire, West Riding* (1967), 59, 477

C.30 **Skelton Church, Yorkshire.**
Album of architectural drawings, designs for stained glass etc., mostly signed H.W.L(onsdale).

Burges began the preparation of designs in 1870; buildings commenced in 1871; and consecration followed in 1876. The bill was reported to be £25,000. Burges employed his favourite team: Nicholls for sculpture; Lonsdale for sketches and Weekes for cartoons; Saunders for stained glass; Barkentin and Hart for metalwork; Walden for woodwork; Campbell for painted decoration.

The album consists of detailed designs, mostly in Lonsdale's hand. At Skelton, Lonsdale was employed in drawing small sketches for stained glass from Burges's instructions. These were then turned into cartoons, probably by Weekes. Then the windows were manufactured by Saunders and Co. Although not quite comparable with the superb stained glass at Studley Royal, the Skelton windows are excellent examples of the stained glass produced under Burges's direction during the 1870s.

Lent by Mr. and Mrs. Robin Compton (Newby Hall)

St. Mary's Studley Royal

C.31

St. Mary's, Studley Royal, Yorkshire

As with Skelton, commissioned in 1870 and begun in 1871, the church at Studley Royal was a memorial to the death of Frederick Grantham Vyner. It was built by his brother-in-law, Lord Ripon, though the motivating force was Lady Ripon who laid the foundation stone; the church was completed in 1878. Both churches were of a similar design and of the same stone, both also tended to English rather than Continental sources, though there are undeniable influences of Early French architecture. The original estimate was £15,000 but the final cost must have been nearer £50,000, much of the increased expenditure being attributable to the lavish and glittering decoration. Lonsdale and Weekes again collaborated with Burges to produce stained glass designs for Saunders & Co, their subjects scenes from the Book of Revelation, Life of the Virgin, Bible history and the Angelic Hierarchy as well as a profusion of beasts and monsters. Black marble forms the pillars of the nave, and varicoloured Egyptian alabaster the walls of the chancel. Floors of mosaic, steps of porphyry, frescoes in window surrounds and carving in wood by Nicholls are all linked by an elaborate iconography of Burgesian intricacy on the theme 'Paradise Lost and Paradise Regained'. Pevsner describes Studley Royal as 'a dream of Early English glory', an 'ecclesiastical masterpiece'.   M.A.

N. Pevsner, *Yorkshire, West Riding* (1967) 218, 625
R.P. Pullan, 'The Works of the Late William Burges, ARA', *R.I.B.A. Trans* (1881-82), 183-219

C.31 **Interior View of Studley Royal**
Watercolour on Whatman paper
17″(43.2)×13¼″(33.8)
Unsigned. By A.H. Haig

A perspective watercolour of the interior of Studley Royal, looking towards the East end, with small figures in the foreground.

Exh *RA* 1872, No. 1242
A. xi (1874), 346 and xxvii (1882), 235

Lent by the British Architectural Library/R.I.B.A.

St. Paul's Cathedral

By the time that Burges was appointed Architect to the Dean and Chapter in August 1872, the appeal for funds for the decoration of St. Paul's, and the arguments as to how they were to be spent, had been raging for many years. The feeling that the decoration of St. Paul's required completion was not at issue, the question was, in what style should it be done, and most importantly, by whom? Burges was a strange choice; undoubtably a genius, and the favourite of the ecclesiologists who wanted a system of polychromy and Christian symbolism, but also an avowed anti-Wrenite and a 'Goth'.

Burges submitted his preliminary report in February 1871. Having travelled extensively in Italy, he contributed models for one bay of the nave and the choir in 1873 and '74. After considerable inter-committee disagreement, these designs were accepted in May 1874. The model was exhibited in the RA in 1874. Pullan recalled that it 'brought forth a string of criticism... High Churchmen, Low Churchmen, no Churchmen filled the columns of the daily papers and the reviews with their opinions for and against his scheme'. Burges's scheme was unfairly labelled 'Mediaevalist'. His decoration was certainly High Church in nature, a mass of ornate gilding and painting illustrating scenes from the Old Testament, the New Testament, Christ in Majesty above the altar, Heavenly Jerusalem and the Apocalypse in the dome, and the Cardinal and Theological virtues in the chapels. But its style was basically cinquecento.

Knowledge of Wren's original intention for the decoration, upon which the Committee agreed the design should preferably be based, was virtually nil. Burges was therefore instructed to fall back on Wren's sources of inspiration, but the nature of these sources was open to doubt, and aesthetic doubts were compounded by ecclesiological and theological disputation. The result for Burges was the burial of his scheme in bureacratic and public wrangling. All work was suspended in November 1874; Burges received £1,175 for his work and recorded in his diary of 11 June 1877 'Dismissed from St. Paul's'. M.A.

R.P. Pullan. '*The Decoration of the Dome of St. Paul's Cathedral*', in *Trans R.I.B.A.* (1882-3), 33
W. Burges, *A Description of Mr Burges' Models for the Adornment of St. Paul's now exhibited at the Royal Academy* (1874).

C.32 **Design for the Decoration of the Eastern Part of St. Paul's Cathedral**
Watercolour on paper
41"(104)×26"(66)
Signed and dated 'A.H. Haig 1874'

This view shows the proposed interior decoration for the East end. With two other Haig watercolours, it was shown at the Royal Academy in 1875; since the models had been exhibited the previous year, the watercolours provoked further discussion in the press about Burges's proposals. 'We have ... coloured drawings which are intended to show what the pictorial effect of Mr. Burges's scheme would be. The first thought which will occur to many minds is that a clever artist will make a pleasing picture out of the most unpromising materials, by toning down a crude effect here, and throwing an awkward feature into obscurity there, and introducing arbitrary effect of light and shade and colour everywhere. If anyone could, while giving the architectural features correctly, throw this kind of glamour over them, it is Mr. Haig, who is one of our most experienced and most artistic architectural draughtsmen and colourists. We happen to be in a position to say that Mr Haig endeavoured to represent as truthfully as possible what the actual effects of St. Paul's decorated on Mr. Burges's plans would be to the eye of the spectator, and he believes that these drawings are honest representations of those effects from their various points of view.' (*Church Builder*, 1875, 86-8) M.A.

Exh R.A. 1875, No. 995

Lent from St. Paul's Cathedral

C.33 **Design for the Decoration of the Dome of St. Paul's Cathedral**
Watercolour on paper
39½"(100.3)×29"(73.6)
Unsigned. By A.H. Haig

A view of the dome area for Burges's proposed decoration scheme for St. Paul's; one of three watercolours by Haig exhibited at the Royal Academy in 1875. (See C32).

Exh R.A. 1875, No. 952

Lent from St. Paul's Cathedral

Metalwork and jewellery

Burges's genius as a designer is expressed to perfection in his jewellery and metalwork: the crystal Cat Cup; the Elephant Inkstand; jewelled decanters, gem-studded chalices, reliquaries, crosses, flagons and patens; soup-plates, knives and forks, bracelets, brooches, tea-pots, dog-collars, scent-bottles and pins. Such range, variety and originality is unique among 19th-century designers. Motifs and materials are widely disparate, skimming the centuries in search of style. Byzantine, Romanesque, Chinese, Japanese, Assyrian; medieval Gothic—English, French and Italian; bronze, jade and glass, antique coins, crystal, ivory, silver, gold and a bewildering variety of jewels and gems. Here is eclecticism in fantastic vein, and scholarship too. In the history of 19th-century metalwork, Burges is the link between the early and late Victorian periods; between the precise medievalism of Pugin and the febrile experiments of *art nouveau*. The result is unforgettable. **J.M.C.**

C.34 **Study of a Candlestick for Lord Leighton's 'Cimabue's Madonna Carried in Procession Through the Streets of Florence'**
Pencil and wash on Whatman paper
14¾"(37.5)×10½"(27)

An elevation and some details for a candlestick c. 1853 for Leighton's 'Cimabue' (now at Buckingham Palace.) M.A.

Exh *George Aitchison, Lord Leighton's Architect*, R.I.B.A., 1980

Victoria & Albert Museum

C.35 **Pectoral Cross and Chain**
Gold, set with gem stones
Height 3⅝"(9.3)
c1860

A gold cross on a gold chain. The cross Neo-Gothic in style with pierced ornament forming the inscription: 'PER CRUCEM AD LUCEM', and set with a central ruby, sapphires and emeralds. The cross was designed by Burges, and appears, exactly as made, among a page of designs for Neo Gothic crosses in his 'Jewellery' album in the V&A. Burges himself had no strong religious leanings, and it is uncertain for whom the cross was created. M.A.

V&A, P&D, 93.E.9
H Tait and C Gore, *The Jewellers Art* (1978) Pl. xii

Lent by The British Museum

C.36 **Beanlands Chalice, from St. Michael and All Angels, Brighton**
Silver and semi-precious stones
h 6¾"(17)
1862

The chalice has a conical bowl set in an applied leaf-shaped calyx. The knop is a spherical crystal held in serrated straps set with cabochon gems. On the foot are engraved scenes representing the Four Rivers of Paradise, the Tree of Life and the Tree of Knowledge.

Inscribed 'URBS.BEATA.HIERUSALEM. DICTA.PACIS.VISIO.QUAE.CONSTRUITOR. IN.COELIS.VIVIS.EX.LAPIDIBUS'.

Makers' mark of John Hardman and Co., Birmingham 1862.
The church of St. Michael and All Angels, Brighton was designed by Bodley and consecrated in 1862 by the Rev. Charles Beanlands. Burges designed a number of fittings for the building. For most of this work he used Hart as a manufacturer. When he came to have the specimen for the dossal made up however, he chose to employ Barkentin (C40). The first scheme for enlarging Bodley's church was produced by Burges in 1868, but the raising of the necessary funds was not complete by his death. However, the present structure in which Bodley's nave has become a mere south aisle is certainly much as Burges intended. V.G.

Exh *Copy or Creation*, Goldsmiths Hall, 1967, C15
Victorian Church Art V.&A. 1971, D3
Birmingham Gold and Silver 1773-1973 City Museums and Art Gallery, Birmingham, 1973, C28

Lent from The Church of St. Michael and All Angels, Brighton

C.37 **Flagon for St. Michael and All Angels, Brighton**
Silver, formerly gilt, with agates
h 10″(25.4)
1862

Pear shaped body, the neck decorated with mouldings and engraving. The base is stepped and circular with an imbrecated design, the spout curving, and the handle strapped and set with agates. The hinged, domed cover has an acorn finial. The flagon is engraved with the inscription 'DAVID:MALACHI:ABEL:NOAH EGO SUM VITIS VERA ET PATER AGRICOLA EST EGO SUM VITIS VOS PALMITES'.

The design of the flagon is similar to that designed for All Saints' Church, Selsley, Gloucestershire.

Maker's mark of Charles Hart of Hart & Son, London 1862.   M.A.

R.I.B.A. 'Orfevrerie Ecclesiastique', 34
Exh *Copy or Creation*, Worshipful Company of Goldsmiths and the Victorian Society, 1967, C15.

Lent from The Church of St. Michael and All Angels, Brighton

C.38 **Chalice from St. Michael and All Angels, Brighton**
Silver, enamel, malachite, cornelian and rock crystal, studded with gem stones
1864

This chalice is much less architectural than the Beanlands chalice and is studded with gems in a lush profusion more characteristic of commercial High Victorian taste than of Burges's usual more recherché selection of materials. The bowl is hexagonal, enamelled with flowerets in black and green; a stem of malachite and cornelian, with a crystal knop held in filigree, gem studded straps joins it to a circular foot. The foot has ogee arched niello panels of Christ and the archangels Gabriel, Michael and Raphael.

Inscribed 'HIC CALIX IN NON ECCLESIAE SANCTI MICHAELIS IN CIVITATE BRIGHTON FABRICATUS EST MDCCCLXIV'.

Makers' mark of John Hardman and Co., Birmingham 1864. Sketches for this chalice appear in the R.I.B.A. album 'Orfevrerie Ecclesiastique', pages 15-16.   V.G.

Lent from The Church of St. Michael and All Angels, Brighton

C.39 **Design for a Specimen Dossal for St. Michael and All Angels, Brighton**
Pencil and wash on paper
6¾″(17.1)×10″(25.4)
Signed 'W. Burges Aug. 4 1865'

Design for the whole dossal, of which a part was made up Barkentin. (C.40)

Victoria and Albert Museum

C.39

C.40

C.40 Specimen panel for Dossal
Copper gilt, enamel and semi-precious stones, on a wood backing
15¾"(40)×13¼"(33)
1866

Part of a reredos designed for St. Michael and All Angels, Brighton in 1865. In very close imitation of a late 12th century Mosan reliquary chest the top border resembles the die-stamped mouldings to be found, for example, on the Shrine of St. Serviatus at Maastricht; while the alternating panels of filigree, enamels and gems are to be found in the metalwork attributed to Nicholas of Verdun (fl. 1181) and carried on into the 13th century by craftsmen like Hugo d'Oignies (fl.1230s).

The Ecclesiologist reported that at a committee meeting on Monday Dec 3, 1866, 'Mr. Burges . . . showed a specimen of a metal dossal intended for St. Michael's, Brighton. The enamels and filigrees by Mr. Barkentin were exquisitely wrought'.

V.G.

Victoria and Albert Museum

C.41

C.41 Photograph of the Dunedin Crozier
Early photograph by Francis Bedford; the crozier itself is made of ivory, silver, precious and semi-precious stones
1866-7

The crozier is in the form of a dragon curled back on itself to make the crook, with a maiden bound to the staff below its claws. A knight in armour grasps the jaws of the monster and thrusts his sword into its mouth. The staff and the figures are carved and painted ivory; the whole is in a crocketted silver mount. The arrangement of the figures is based on a medieval prototype, where an angel figure takes the place of the maiden in this case. There are silver gilt examples at Cologne and at Città di Castello which Burges almost certainly knew. He drew croziers in the Cluny Museum and the Louvre and in England, but mainly plainer Limoges types. It is very probable that he decided on ivory as a material having seen the early examples in the Treasury of Siena Cathedral. The iconography, however, belongs entirely to Burges and to the 19th century. He described it as follows: 'The delivery of the virtuous from the power of the Evil One, through the instrumentality of the Champion of the Church, symbolised by the combat of St. George and the Dragon'. The crozier was made for presentation to the Rev. H.L. Jenner (1820-98) on the occasion of his appointment as first bishop of Dunedin, New Zealand. It was given to him by the Ecclesiological Society of which he had been Secretary. The maker was Barkentin, who as a result was appointed official goldsmith to the Society. A preparatory model was made and shown to the committee for approval then Bedford's photographs were included in the Architectural Photographic Exhibition. Burges re-drew this design in his Vellum Sketchbook with the arch annotation: 'This is the staff of the Lord Bishop of the isles where they eat one another'. In 1875 he pulled a trick on posterity by publishing it as a 13th century original in a French periodical called *L'Art Pour Tous*. V.G.

E. xxviii, n.s. xxv, (1867), 124, 252
B. xxv, (1867), 467 and xxvi, (1868), 333 No. 401
R.P. Pullan, *Designs of William Burges* (1885) Pl.14

National Museum of Wales

C.42

C.42 **Chalice made for St. Andrew's, Wells St**
Silver, enamels, semi-precious stones and stained glass
h 8⅜″(21)
1868

A wide bowl set in a double calyx, the lower tier with projecting filigree foliage and the upper with arcading surrounded by engraved fillets and set with enamel. Every alternate panel is decorated with stiff-leaf foliage, and the others with animal symbols of Christ—the Agnus Dei, the Pelican, the Lion, the Eagle, the Antelope, the Phoenix, the Ox and the Swan. The large knop is decorated with applied filigree set with six enamel bosses of the Church, the Synagogue and the Four Rivers of Paradise. The stem is made of polished stones, the foot also is embellished with filigree and gems and six cusped quatrefoils; five contain enamels of the Angel of the Annunciation, the Virgin, the Crucifixion, St. John the Evangelist and St. Andrew. The sixth contains a fragment of Early Christian glass donated by Burges himself.

Inscribed 'MEMENTO:DOMINE:JOHANNIS: BAKER:GABB:ET:MARIAE:UXORIS:EIUS: QUI:HUNC:CALICAM:IN:USUM:ECCLESIAE: S.ANDREAE:DE:WELLS:STREET: DEDERUNT:ANNO:SALUTIS: MDCCCLXVII'.

The chalice was presented by John Baker Gabb, Superintendant of the Alliance Marine Insurance Company and his wife. The church itself was removed to Kingsbury, Middlesex in 1933.

There are annotated sketches and an early photograph of this chalice in the R.I.B.A. Album 'Orfevrerie Ecclésiastique'. Its iconography was exhaustively discussed in *The Ecclesiologist* in the year of its manufacture.

Maker's mark of Jes Barkentin, of Barkentin and Krall, London 1868

Exh *Festival Exhibition of Church Plate and Vestments* Usher Art Gallery, Lincoln, 1951, No. 142
Victorian and Edwardian Decorative Arts V.&A. 1952, O8
Copy or Creation Goldsmiths' Hall, 1967, C16
Victorian Church Art V.&A., 1971, D5
E. xxix, (1868), 372   V.G.

Lent from St. Andrew's Church, Kingsbury, Middlesex

C.43 **Crucifix, made for St. Andrew's, Wells Street**
Silver-gilt set with enamel and crystal
1875

The crucifix is decorated with an image of St. Andrew, accompanied by four sacrificial emblems: Abel, Abraham, Melchisedec and Esca Angelorum. Burges also designed for the church a chalice, two vases, two candlesticks, the memorial to James Murray, and the litany desk (B18). With the exception of the chalice, the plate was all presented to the church by W.R. Cusack-Smith (1832-87), a London barrister, and made by Barkentin and Krall. Burges's 'Estimate Book' for 28 December 1875 notes that the cost of the crucifix was £340. The crucifix resembles one made for Lord Bute in 1871. M.A.

Lent from St. Andrew's Church, Kingsbury, Middlesex

C.44 **Goblet**
Silver, semi-precious stones and enamel
h 4¾"(12.1) d 4¼"(10.8)
1863

A partial gilt silver cup, with applied ornament, set with stones and enamelled. The foot is flat chased with panels on diaper grounds; the knop is a polished stone held by eight straps of linked silver trefoils; round the cup is a deep band in high relief of applied silver foliage tendrils and stones in high serrated settings.

Inscribed with a quotation from the 'Pange Lingua': 'OMNIS.MUNDI.CREATURA QUASI. LIBER.ET.PICTURA.NOBIS.EST.ET. SPECULUM/I.N.MAA ANO DNI MDCCCLXIII/ NOSTRAE.VITAE.NOSTRAE.MORTIS. NOSTRI.STATUS.NOSTRAE.SORTIS.FIDELE. SIGNALCULUM'.

Made by Joseph Hart and Son.

Like Nicholson's decanter (C47) this is a variation on a piece made in 1862 for Burges himself—the cup photographed with the two decanters (C45 and C46). In Burges's own version of the cup, the inscriptions naturally differed, the foot was plain except for four jewels and the bowl lacked the extra gems set into the lower part here.

James Nicholson (d.1894) was a prosperous lead merchant and friend of the Burges family. V.G.

Exh *Victorian and Edwardian Arts*, V.&A. 1952, J7
P. Wardle, *Victorian Silver* (1963), Pl. 48

Victoria and Albert Museum

C.45 **Decanter**
Glass, silver, jade, lapis lazuli, mother-of-pearl, Persian seals, antique coins, intaglio gems and semi-precious stones
h 11⅛"(28) w 7¾"(19)
1865

A glass bottle in a fantastic mount of silver, chased and partial gilt set with semi-precious stones, Persian seals, intaglio gems and Greek and Roman coins. The handle of the decanter is a winged monster with claw feet (apparently inspired by an Assyrian ivory dagger pommel of the 8th-7th century B.C., which Burges presented to the British Museum in 1864), its head carved out of mother-of-pearl; the spout is a stylised goat's head, the horns curling back on to the neck of the vessel, the stopper rammed into its open mouth and secured by a chain. On the lid a woven palisade surrounds a Chinese jade group of two horses and a monkey, under a silver loop with a dangling ball ornament.

Inscribed 'WILLIELMUS BURGES EX HON(O)ARIIS LITERARIIS MDCCCLXV'.

Makers' marks of George Angell and J.M., London 1864-65. It can be assumed from the inscription that Burges had this piece made for himself with the proceeds of *Art Applied to Industry* published in 1865. The earliest versions of this design are in the R.I.B.A. Album 'Orfévrèrie Domestique' and date from 1858. It was photographed for Burges along with its companion piece (C46) and his drinking cup. The pieces were published four times as a group, Pullan eulogising, 'It is impossible to praise too highly these splendid vessels which are triumphs in the way of medieval design'.

Exh *Victorian and Edwardian Decorative Art* R.A. 1972, B87

BN. xxvi (1874), 418
B. liii (1887), 100
R.P. Pullan, *Architectural Designs of William Burges*, Pl. 17
R.P. Pullan, *The House of William Burges*, Pl. 35
V.G.

Cecil Higgins Art Gallery, Bedford
Regrettably this item was not available for exhibition

C.45 and C.46 with Burges's drinking cup — early Bedford photograph

C.46 **Decanter**
Glass, silver, malachite, rock crystal, ivory, coral, antique coins, cloisonné enamels and semi-precious stones
h 10⅝"(26) w 7½"(19)
1865

Designed *en suite* with C45, the head of the animal on the handle is carved ivory here and a Chinese lion in rock crystal is imprisoned behind the palisade on the lid.

Inscribed 'WILLIELMUS BVRGES ME FIERI FECIT ANNO DI MDCCCLXV (indistinct) . . . . . VEX NON SAECULAE CONSTANTINOPOLITANAE (MD) CCCLXV'.

Maker's marks of J.M. and George Angell, London 1865.

This was also made for Burges himself and again the inscription refers to a particular source of funds. In this case it was the drawings for the Crimea Memorial church in Constantinople. Although the building was not executed Burges had charged a handsome fee for producing the proposals. The design closest to this version of the decanter is dated 1864 in 'Orfevrerie Domestique'.
V.G.

Exh *Victorian and Edwardian Decorative Art* R.A. 1972, B88

BN. xxvi (1874), 418
B. iii (1887), 100
R.P. Pullan, *Architectural Designs of William Burges*, Pl. 17
R.P. Pullan, *The House of William Burges*, Pl. 35

Lent by the Fitzwilliam Museum

C.47 **Decanter**
Glass, silver, amethysts, opals, other semi-precious stones and antique coins
h 11"(27.9) d 7"(17.8)
1865

Another glass bottle mounted in silver, richly decorated and set with coins and stones. The design is very similar to Burges's own two decanters with minor differences. The silver loop over the lid has been omitted, and within the palisade on the cresting is a square architectural feature pierced with quadrilobes, chased with fictive masonry coursing and topped with battlements. The finial is a crystal carving of a crouching animal.

Inscribed 'JAMES NICHOLSON ANNO DOMINI MDCCCLXV'.

Maker's mark of Richard Green, London 1865-66.
V.G.

Exh *Victorian and Edwardian Decorative Arts* V.&A. 1952, J6.

P. Wardle, *Victorian Silver* (1963), Pl. 49.

Victoria and Albert Museum

C.48 **The Cat Cup**
Silver, enamel, crystal, pearls and semi-precious stones
8⅛″(20.6)×3⅜″(8.6)
1867

The piece chosen by Lady Bute from Burges's own collection after his death. It is a Chinese crystal beaker, scored with hieroglyphics and carved with mimosa fronds mounted in silver gilt. The base is set with pearls and opals; the foot has an inscription, with Burges's personal devices on shields among tree roots in a band above. The upper rim also has an inscribed band, then a circle of six chased running mice among large cabochons; above is a fleur-de-lis border with alternating pearls and a battlemented cresting around the edge of the cover. The cover is set with two rows of large polished crystal hemispheres with a chased enamelled figure of an emerald-eyed cat sitting upright, wearing a collar set with emeralds and sapphires and playing with a coral ball. Inside the lid is an enamelled roundel of a cat in boots standing upright holding a dead fox in one paw and a chicken in the other. The interior of the rim is also decorated with grotesques and formalised foliage, telling the story of Puss in Boots.

Inscribed 'WILLIAM:BURGES:IN: REMEMBRANCE:OF:THE:LAW:COURTS: COMPETITION:AD:MDCCCLXVII'.

Maker's mark of J. Barkentin, London 1867. The style of this piece owes someting to 17th century Nuremburg, something to 12th century France. Its technical virtuosity sets standards for the finest metalwork of the Arts and Crafts phase. But the overall conception, the range of materials, the ingenuity, the inventiveness, the sheer gusto of the design, is peculiarly, triumphantly Burgesian.
J.M.C.

R.P. Pullan, *Designs of William Burges* (1885), Pl.18

Lent anonymously

C.49 **Design for a Crystal Vase and Cover**
Pencil and wash on Whatman paper
10⅛″(23.5)×15¼″(38.5)
1867

Front and side elevations, top, section and details of a crystal cup and cover mounted in silver gilt. The cup has elephant head handles, with rings suspended through their trunks; the cover is surmounted by a small crouching lion. The mount is a very light one by Burges's standards, composed only of a shallow enamelled foot, a neckrim set with plain cabochons and a border of fleur-de-lis to the cover. This piece was made up in this form and appears in the photographs of Buckingham Street (see C60).

Page 6 of the album 'Jewellery'. V.G.

Victoria and Albert Museum

C.48

C.50 **Two Designs for Crystal Bowls**
Pencil and wash on Whatman paper
(a) 11⅜″(29)×8½″(21.5)
(b) 9¼″(23.5)×9⅝″(24.5)
(a) 1867

Two designs for crystal bowls mounted in silver gilt: (a) consists of a section, plan and details of a gilt support in the shape of legs and clasps formed of serpents.

Inscribed 'W. Burges July 5. 1867/order given Aug 15-1867/Brought back Feb 29-1868'.

(b) is a section and plan with various written instructions for materials and execution for a circular crystal dish to be mounted between gilt lions' heads and raised on paw feet.

Page 16 of the album 'Jewellery'. V.G.

Victoria and Albert Museum

C.51 **Design for a Silver Mounted Jar and Cover**
Pencil and wash on Whatman paper
20¼″(26)×15⅜″(39)
1867

A section, elevation and details of a blue ceramic (?) jar mounted in silver gilt straps set with red and green stones. The hinged lid was to have been formed by an inverted Chinese cloisonné enamel bowl, also held by a silver gilt cage with curling crockets.
Inscribed 'William Burges July 9-1867. Observe that the 5 jewels ABCDE/are all on the same level so/as to allow the lid to stand steady/when reversed'.

Page 1 of the album 'Jewellery'. V.G.

Victoria and Albert Museum

C.52 **Design for a Cruet Holder**
Pencil and wash on Whatman paper
11″(28)×15½″(39.5)

Elevations, plan and section of a cruet in the form of a stoppered bottle, carried in a ship with an animal prow on silver gilt and blue enamel formalised 'waves'. The bottle (there were to be others not shown on this drawing) was to be of crystal, with a green stopper and all the silver parts were to be gilt.

Page 9 of the album 'Jewellery'. V.G.

Victoria and Albert Museum

C.53 **Design for a 'Sang de Boeuf' scent bottle**
Pencil and wash on Whatman paper
9¾″(24.7)×11½″(29)
1867

A section, elevation and details of a bottle and cover in red ceramic, mounted in silver gilt set with enamels and cabochon jewels. A 'cage' design similar to that for the sang de boeuf decanter (C55); with a spider for a knop, the body formed of a polished stone on silver gilt legs. There is a partially decipherable inscription 'William Burges . . .' around the foot. This appears to be the design for the piece shown in the National Museum of Wales album of photographs of Burges's collection and interiors at Buckingham Street.

Inscribed 'W. Burges/July 14/1867'. At this time Burges was much taken up with this particular theme. A design in the album *Orfevrerie Domestique* in the R.I.B.A. which is very close to the sang de boeuf decanter (the necking deeper in the finished object, the gothic shapes having been added, and the fleur de lis band of the design was replaced with naturalistic foliage), is dated July 2 1867.

Page 3 of the album 'Jewellery'. V.G.

Victoria and Albert Museum

C.52

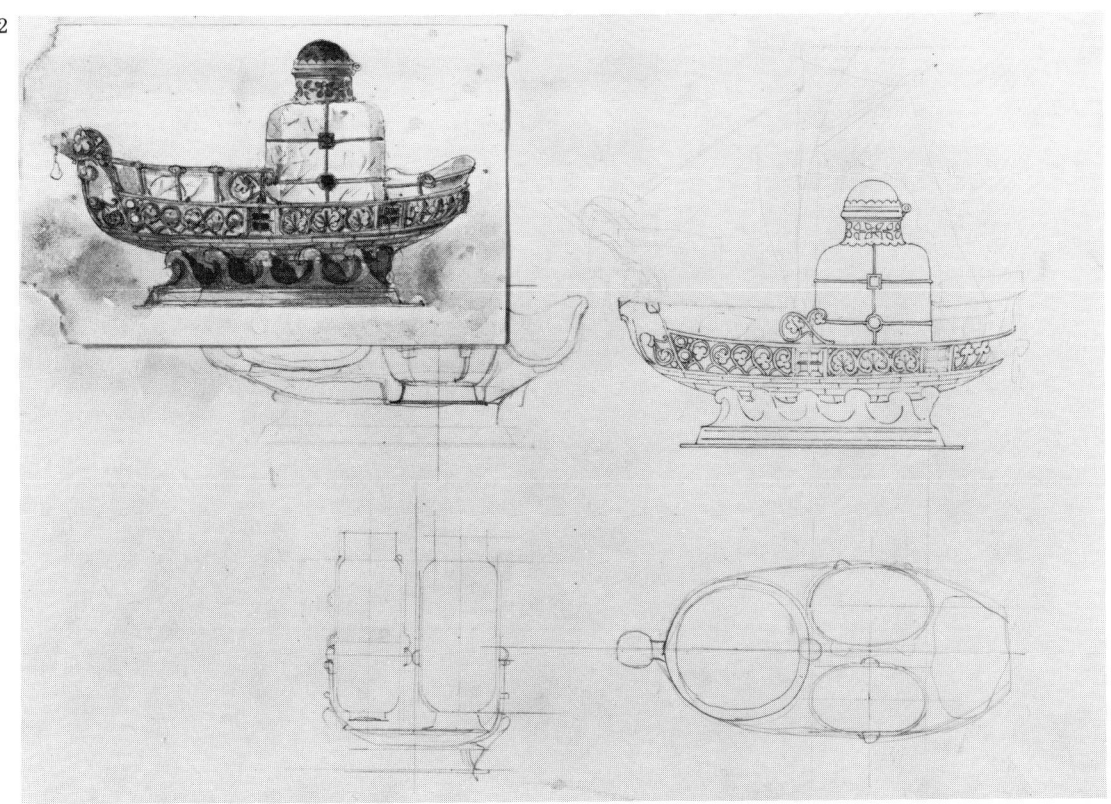

C.54

C.55

C.54 Photograph of a 'Sang de Boeuf' Scent Bottle.
Early photograph

One of the pieces photographed while Burges lived at Buckingham Street. It was executed almost exactly according to the design (C53). V.G.

National Museum of Wales

C.55 'Sang de Boeuf' Decanter
Porcelain, silver gilt, enamel and semi-precious stones
h 11⅛"(28) d 5½"(14)
1870

A Chinese 'sang de boeuf' vase mounted in silver-gilt with filigree, enamel and semiprecious stones. The mounting is in two parts; the foot is beaded and carries the inscription 'WILLIELMUS: BVRGES:EX:LIBRO:SUO:ANO:DNI: MDCCCLXX' reserved on blue and green enamel; the necking is pierced in gothic shapes and hinged to a lid which has a silver gilt rim with applied scrolls and is surmounted by a carving in coral of a sphinx and a female face. Inside the lid is an enamelled grotesque. These two parts are joined by a cage of silver gilt straps enclosing the vase, set with carved Chinese jade and other stones. Burges's collection contained numerous Chinese monochrome porcelain pieces in both light and dark colours, some with whimsical or richly medievalising mounts of his own design. A scent bottle labelled 'liver colored china and opals' and very similar in design to this piece is known from the early photograph albums. The inscription on this decanter refers to the publication of *Architectural Drawings* in 1870. In his will Burges directed that Lord and Lady Bute should each select one item from his own metalwork: this was the piece chosen by Lord Bute. V.G

Exh *Victorian and Edwardian Decorative Art* R.A. 1972, B89.
R.P. Pullan, *Architectural Designs of William Burges*, Pl.19.

Victoria and Albert Museum

C.56 Photograph of the Elephant Inkstand
Early photograph
Present location unknown

Burges's detailed drawings for this ingenious invention are in the R.I.B.A. album 'Orfevrerie Domestique'. In his 'Abstract of Diaries' for 1862-63 he noted: 'Elephant Inkstand... Elephant made up' The elephant is a Chinese bronze incense-burner; the lid is a Chinese cloisonné bowl; the finial is a Japanese ivory carving. In one drawing he specified all these details, showing an Eastern lady with her fan. He also noted that the round bead ornaments were to be, from the top down, agate, cornelian, amber, brown enamel and green enamel. The cylindrical neck was a 'Green China Pot'. There are receptacles for matches, red ink and black ink; seals and rings are attached by chains. There is a note on the drawing to the effect that, conveniently, a 'Square hole for inkstand is already cut in his back'. Burges designed another elephant inkstand for Garnett of Bingley, Yorkshire, in 1867. It probably remained unexecuted.

This inkstand—which commemorated literary labours of 1862—sat on Burges's writing table at the window in the Sitting Room at 15 Buckingham Street (see D26), and later in the drawing room at Tower House, Kensington. 'Observe the power of adaptation: the things (Burges) is dealing with are Chinese and Japanese, but the whole is 13th century—Burgesesque. A few pieces of metal in his favourite style to unite them, and lo! This strange group of Eastern things fall into their places as if they had originally been designed for the purpose' (E.W. Godwin).

Burges's Elephant Inkstand is not only a paradigm of the eclectic process. It is the very epitome of its creator's special genius. J.M.C.
V.G.

R.P. Pullan, *Designs of William Burges* (1885), 20.
A.J. (1886), 180.

National Museum of Wales

C.57 Ring
Gold, decorated with applied ornament and set with a cabochon sapphire.
d ¾"(2.1) h (with stone) 1"(2.5)
c.1870
Unmarked, maker unknown

The design is a plain gold hoop, the shoulders decorated with applied trefoils, three large and four small, rising from a double band of moulding. The vertically set cabochon sapphire is held by a serrated bezel. A similar ring design exists on page 15 of the 'Jewellery' album (93.E.9) in the V.&A. Prints and Drawings Department, inscribed 'No 5' and 'opal'. Its design is slightly similar, with the stone set horizontally, and may be for a woman's ring.
M.A.

Victoria and Albert Museum

C.56

C.58 A Set of Six Knives and Forks
Silver, steel and ivory
Length of knives 9⅛"(23)
Length of forks 8⅜"(21)
1871

The handles are carved ivory representing symbolically the meats and vegetables—veal, venison, onion, pea &c.; the blades of the knives were once engraved but have been severely worn and replated; the forks are decorated with lion masks and scrolling foliage in gilt.

Inscribed on the ivory handles 'WIL M S BURGES/AD:MDCCCLXXI'.

Silver mounts with maker's mark of Jes. Barkentin for Barkentin and Krall, London 1870.

These too were made for Burges's own use and amusement. Thomas Nicholls almost certainly carved the ivory handles. Again there are numerous drawings dating from the two years before the making of the set in 'Orfévrèrie Domestique'.
V.G.

Lent by The Trustees of The Cecil Higgins Art Gallery, Bedford

C.59 **Designs for Scent Bottles**
Pen, pencil and wash on Whatman paper
(a) 6¼″(16)×5¾″(14.5)
(b) 6⅝″(17)×6″(15)
1875

Two sketches for scent bottles pasted to a sheet of cartridge paper. (a) is a crystal bottle in a gilt mount set with jewels, and a gilt lid secured by a chain; shown in elevation and section with details including a roundel with one of Burges's personal devices. (b) is an irregularly shaped crystal mounted as a standing bird. The claws are silver gilt, as is the jewelled band around the body; the head is also silver, with a red enamelled beak, crimson stones for the eyes, and rows of blue beads round the neck. The finished article is shown in one of the Buckingham Street photographs (C60). Burges devoted great care to its design, showing in detail here how it was to hinge, giving a horizontal section and a detail of a claw foot. Inscribed 'W. Burges, Sep 18/75'.

The ultimate source for this design is presumably Suger's famous eagle vase in the Louvre made from an antique porphyry vase to which the twelfth century goldsmith added silver gilt head, feet and wings—although it was a very much larger scale vessel. Burges's drawing of it in the R.I.B.A. album 'Metalwork' is inscribed: 'This is Suger's workmanship/the vase appears to have been a relick'.

Page 5 of the album 'Jewellery'. V.G.

Victoria and Albert Museum

C.60 **A Collection of Scent Bottles made for William Burges**
Early photograph

Six curiously shaped and carved crystal or hardstone vessels, apparently oriental, and a spoon, mounted in silver gilt and gems to designs by Burges. C59 is on the extreme left-hand side and C49 is the design for the cup and cover with elephant head handles. V.G.

National Museum of Wales

C.61 **A Table at Buckingham Street with a Collection of Burges's Metalwork**
Early photograph

For tables to this design see B3. Among the objects grouped on top are Burges's decanters (C45 and C46), the Cat Cup (C48) and the ewer from the Summer Palace in Peking (D27). V.G.

National Museum of Wales

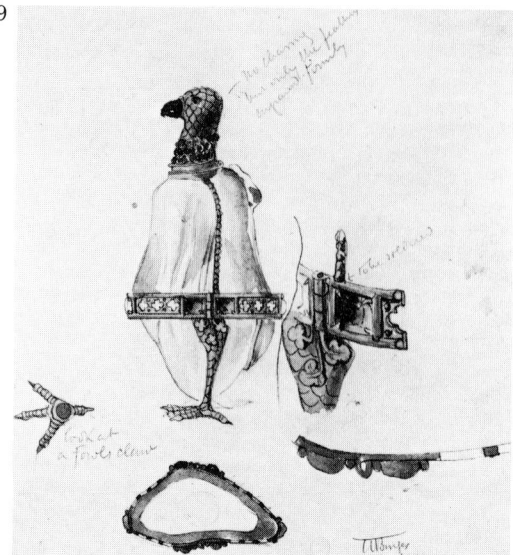

C.59

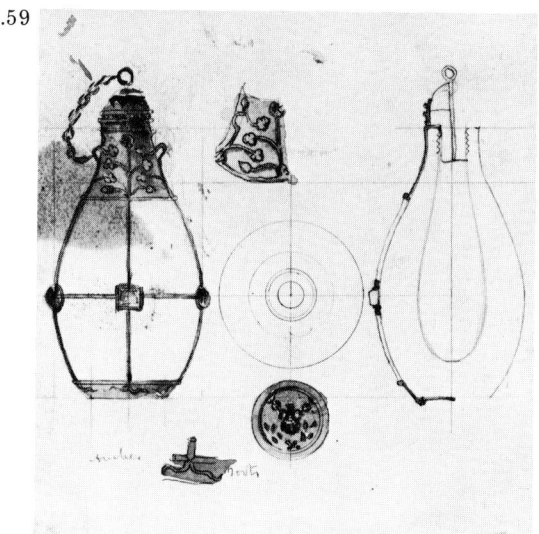

C.59

C.62 **Dish**

Gilt brass, with silver and niello decoration
h 3¼"(8) d 12¾"(32)
1875

A shallow bowl with eight rings for hanging. Inside there is a silver mermaid with golden hair outlined in niello as a central motif, surrounded by the inscription 'WHO:WOULD:BE:A:MERMAID: FAIR:SINGING:ALONE:COMBING:HER: HAIR:UNDER:THE:SEA:IN:A:GOLDEN:CURL: WITH:A:COMB:OF:PEARL'. There is then a border of formalised waves and round the rim is a series of round-headed stone arches with monstrous fish swimming behind them. Inscribed on the underside 'WILLIAM:BURGES:MARCH: MDCCCLXXV'. There are a number of drawings for this dish in 'Orfévrèrie Domestique' and a version of it was shown by the manufacturers, Hart and Son, at the Paris Universal Exhibition in 1867. The quotation is, of course, from Tennyson's poem 'The Mermaid' and that poet was obviously an inspiration to Burges (see D33). Mermaids as a motif appear frequently in his work—on the head of his own bed (with fighting sea monsters behind arches on the mural frieze above), in the Vellum Sketchbook, and in a design very similar to this in the pottery basin for Lord Bute's private bathroom at Cardiff Castle (A63). V.G.

Exh *Victorian and Edwardian Decorative Art, R.A.* 1972, B102.
R.P. Pullan *The Designs of William Burges,* Pl.22.

Victoria and Albert Museum

C.63 **'The Mermaid Bowl designed by the late Wm. Burges, A.R.A.'**

Newspaper reproduction on paper
1887

A plate from *The Building News,* Jan. 7, 1887, inscribed 'Maurice B. Adams Del! from sketches and photographs lent by Mr. R.P. Pullan F.S.A.'. Burges himself drew the bowl in this form with the segments flattened out, and it was probably one of those drawings which Pullan supplied to the printers. V.G.

National Museum of Wales

C.64 **Claret Jug**

Glass, silver gilt, enamel, turquoise, pearls and amethysts
h 12¼"(31.1) base d 4⅝"(11.7)
1869

A glass bottle mounted in silver gilt as a decanter; the round foot is chased and enamelled with the arms of the Crichton Stuart family; the body is held by straps with applied filigree of vine branches, studded with pearls and cabochon gems; on the four round bosses on the body of the vessel and around the necking are engraved and enamelled scenes of the legendary career of Dionysus. The spout is a male human mask, the handle a gnarled tree trunk with a leopard stalking towards the lid. On the cover inside a gallery pierced with quadrilobes are cast figures in medieval dress, enamelled in *ronde bosse.*

Inscribed 'JHS:PATS:CRICHT:STUART: MARCH:DE:BUTE:ME:F:F:MDCCCLXX.'

Maker's mark of Barkentin, London 1869-70. V.G.

Lent anonymously

C.63

C.64

C.65 Design for Lord Bute's Claret Jug
Pencil and wash on paper

A side elevation of the decanter as executed. Signed 'W. Burges, Arch!.' V.G.

Lent anonymously

C.66 Photograph of the Bute Reliquary
Early photograph
Present location unknown.

Firmly based on an amalgam of medieval reliquaries seen by Burges including those in Aachen, Paris and Assisi the reliquary consists of a two bay gothic aedicule with traceried lancets, crocketed gables, a fleur-de-lis cresting and an angel finial. The actual relic was to be contained in the central crystal tube around which three dimensional figures of Christ bound and wearing the Crown of Thorns, Herod, a soldier and a torturer represent the Flagellation. It is mounted on a high foot and a stem like a monstrance, decorated with cabochons set among applied beaded wires and scrolls. The tendency to allow the relic itself to be seen and the representation of associated scenes with realistic statuettes in this manner was characteristic of reliquary design in Northern Europe from the beginning of the 14th century onwards. V.G.

Lent by the British Architectural Library/R.I.B.A.

C.67 Design for the Bute Reliquary
Pen, pencil and wash
Six sheets of paper pasted together, various sizes
1870

Front and side elevations, with constructional details, and five smaller drawings for the figures and inscriptions, one of which was to read 'IOHANNES CRICHTON STVART/ME F F MDCCCLXX'. The reliquary was carried out almost exactly to the design, with few variations. V.G.

Lent anonymously

C.68 Lady Bute's Jewel
Enamelled gold set with gems and pearls
1872

The body of the brooch is in the form of a crowned Gothic 'G' with three pendant shields. The reverse of the brooch is inscribed 'XVI AP MDCCCLXXII AMABILIS UT RACHEL SAPIENS UT REBEKAH FIDELIS UT SARAH'. The reverse of the two outer pendant shields are inscribed J.P.C.S., for John Patrick Crichton Stuart, and the central one, G.M.A.H., for Gwendolen Mary Anne Howard; the reverse of the shield in the centre of the brooch is inscribed G.M.A.B. for Lady Bute's married name. The brooch was intended for Lady Bute's marriage, sketches for it appear in the R.I.B.A. small note book for 1871, while one of the drawings is dated April 1872, however, Burges did not present it to Lady Bute until 1873. In a letter to her sister of September 1873, Lady Bute remarks 'He (Burges) gave me a most beautiful brooch the other day. I have drawn it as well as I can but my best is bad. It really is quite beautiful'. (From a letter in the Mount Stuart archive.)

There are also designs for a tiara in the small note book of April/May, 1874, and for a coronet for Lord Bute in the note book of September 1873/January 1874, though it is uncertain whether either of these was manufactured. M.A.

C. Gere, *Victorian Jewellery* (1972), Pl.20a

Lent by the Marchioness of Bute

C.69 Design for Lady Bute's Jewel
Pen, pencil and wash on paper
1872

Three sheets mounted together, showing:
(a) The front of the jewel complete, the jewel without decoration and the reverse of the jewel with inscription.

(b) The front and reverse of the three pendant shields, with the first part of the jewel's inscription.

(c) The front and reverse of the central shield, and the last part of the inscription.

The monograms and inscription are exactly as in the finished jewel (C68). M.A.

C. Gere, *Victorian Jewellery* (1972), Pl.19a

Lent by the Marchioness of Bute

C.70 Lord Bute's Cameo Stand
Silver set with twenty semi-precious stones
5½"(14)×4⅝"(11.7)
1869

The Sacred Heart miniature was presented to Bute by Pope Pius IX, after Bute's papal confirmation in Rome in 1869. The cameo stand to hold it, however, was presumably designed subsequently by Burges, perhaps on the occasion of Bute's marriage in 1872, when Pio Nono sent the bridal pair a cameo brooch. The stand is gilt and all the stones polished cabochons.

Inscribed 'HANC SANCTAM SACRATISSIMI CRODIS IESU ICONEM DONO DEDIT JOHANNI PATRICCIO MARIE MARCHIONI DE BUTA:SANCTISSIMUS DOMINUS NOSTER PIUS DIVINA PROVIDENTIA PAPA NONUS POST SACRAMENTUM CONFIRMATIONIS EI A PONTIFICE IPSO COLLATUM ROMAE DIE XI MENSIS FEBRUARII MDCCCLXIX'.

Makers' mark of John Hardman & Co., Birmingham 1869.   J.M.C.

Lent anonymously

C.71 Cup and Cover
Silver, gilt, enamel, lapis lazuli and gems
h 7¼"(18.4) d 4³⁄₁₆"(10.6)
1875

A cup and cover *en suite* with the claret jug (C64), which has the same foot design and gallery to the lid. The cup itself is reminiscent of Burges's own cup and the similar version created for James Nicholson, with a broad band of gem-set filigree round the bowl. The shallow domed lid is engraved with grotesque monsters and heraldry, matching the upper rim of the claret jug. The finial is a crystal sphere mounted on a leafy stalk.

Inscribed 'IOANNI: PATRICIO: CRICHTON: STUART: MARCHIONI: DE: BUTE: UXORIS: DONUM: PRIDIE: ID: SEPTEMB: NATALI: DIE: MDCCCLXXV'. The piece was a birthday present to Lord Bute from his wife. Maker's mark of J. Barkentin, London, 1875.   V.G.

Lent anonymously

C.72 **Design for Lord Bute's Cup and Cover**
Pen, pencil and wash on paper
1875

An elevation, section and details of the decoration of the cup and cover. There are copious written notes on the materials to be used and three suggested versions of the inscription, of which a translation is given as 'To J.P.C. Stuart—Marquess of Bute/a birthday gift from his wife'.
V.G.

Lent anonymously

C.73
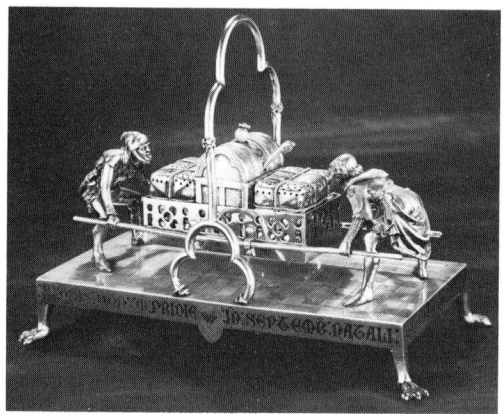

C.73 **Cruet**
Silver, gilt, enamel, gems and coral
1877

A comical cruet in the form of two figures in medieval garb, struggling to hold up the heavy burden of the salt, pepper and mustard pots on poles. Over the top is a silver gilt trefoil arch, on the base are enamel tile patterns and around the edge is the inscription. It stands on four paw feet. There are ten detachable sections including the mustard spoon in the shape of a tiny claw. Inscribed 'IOHANNI: PATRICIO: CRICHTON: STVART/MARCHIONI: DE: BVTE/VXORIS: DONUM: PRIDIE: ID: SEPTEMB: NATALI: DIE. MDCCCLXXVII'. Small 'J.S.' monograms appear enameled on the mustard casket, the sleeves of the figures and elsewhere. Also a birthday present from Lady to Lord Bute. Maker's mark (probably Barkentin), 1877. The cruet is made up of ten detachable sections. Burges's notebooks indicate that before choosing the present figures, he toyed with the idea of knights and clerics as supporters.
V.G.

Lent anonymously

C.74 **Design for Lord Bute's Cruet**
Pen, pencil and wash
1877

Side and end elevations of the cruet, with details and written notes for the decoration. Signed 'William Burges/Aug 6 1877'.

There are other drawings for this cruet in 'Orfévrèrie Domestique' and the small notebooks at the R.I.B.A., datable to 1876-77.
V.G.

Lent anonymously

C.75 **Two Soup Dishes and Two Fish Plates**
Silver
1868 (soup dishes)
1878 (fish plates)

Four pieces from a set of twenty-four dishes and eighteen fish plates designed by Burges for Lord Bute. Each is partial gilt and engraved with a visual pun in an eight-pointed star—here we have Smelt (a fishmonger holding his nose); Perch (a winged fish upon a branch); Scotch Broth (a sheep dressed as a Highlander); and Turtle (a city gent wearing his chain of office). The drawings for these characters are in the Bute archive and the making of the fish plates is recorded in the V.&A. Estimate Book.

Inscribed 'JOANNES PATRICIUS CRICHTON STUART MARCHIO DE BUTA ME FIERI FECIT MDCCCLXVIII/MDCCCLXXIX'.

Makers' mark (soup dishes) John Hardman & Co., Birmingham 1868; (fish plates) R. Garrard, London 1878.

Both sets may have been designed in 1867-68, but the fish plates were made up only in 1878 and engraved in 1879.
V.G.

Lent anonymously

C.76 **Lord Bute's Water Bottle**
Glass, silver, enamel, amethyst and other gems
h 10¼" (26) d 4¾" (12.1)
1880

A clear glass bottle encased in silver gilt; above a plain moulded foot there is an inverted fleur-de-lis frieze, below the band carrying the inscription. The upper part of the body is moulded around openwork foiled ogee shapes, containing saw-pierced motifs of leaping fish, with small gems set into their eyes. The neck is divided by plain moulded rings into four bands, two undecorated, one filled with gem-set foliage tendrils and one with swimming fishes and armorial devices in translucent enamel. The domed lid is enamelled in scale pattern and has an elaborated acorn finial set with a cabochon jewel.

Inscribed 'IOHANNI:PATRICIO:CRIC/HTON:STUART:MARCHIO/NI:DE:BUTE:UXORIS:DONU/M:NATALI:DIE:MDCCCLXXX'. Also a birthday present to Lord Bute from his wife. Maker's mark of Barkentin, London 1880.
V.G.

Lent by the Marquess of Bute

C.77

C.76

C.77 **Design for Lord Bute's Water Bottle**
Pen, pencil and wash on paper
1880

An elevation, section and details of the arms to be used and the translucent enamel fishes. There are also thumbnail sketches showing how the bottle was to be lifted away, leaving the lower part of the silver mount to act as a cup. Three written estimates are given for the piece including a plate box. The decoration is almost as carried out, except that in this design the inscription runs to two lines, not the single line as executed. Signed 'W. Burges/July 1880/15 Buckingham St. Strand'.
V.G.

Lent by the Marquess of Bute

C.78

C.78 **Epergne, Rose-water Dish, Flagon and Two Spoons**
Silver, enamel, agate and lapis lazuli
Various sizes
1880

Five pieces from the Sneyd dessert service which altogether comprises twenty-five pieces, including a dozen spoons. The style is a much soberer approximation to late gothic design than most of the objects Burges had made for himself or for Lord Bute. The lobed and cusped shapes of the silver gilt bowls, the beaded and enamelled central bosses of the rose-water dishes in tazza form and the quatrefoil profile of the foot of the epergne are all based closely on 15th century prototypes, of which Burges had collected many in the R.I.B.A. album 'Metalwork'. This service was commissioned from Burges by Lord Bute as a wedding present for G.E. Sneyd, Bute's lifelong friend and secretary, with exception of the spoons which were from Burges himself, and are inscribed 'G.E.S. from W.B.'. There are preliminary designs and sketches in 'Orfévrèrie Domestique' and the small notebooks for 1880 in the R.I.B.A. The original cost of the whole set was £359. Makers' mark of Barkentin and Krall, London 1880-81.   V.G.

Victoria and Albert Museum

C.79 **Lady Bute's Pearl Shell Bottle**
Silver, shell and mother of pearl
1880

A pearl shell, mounted in silver and faced with mother of pearl, carved with low reliefs of the Last Supper and Nativity. Silver mount with paired trefoils and rings. The bottle is inscribed 'JOHANNES MARCHIO BOTHAE HIC ROSOLYMIS ACQUISIVIT ET UXORI DONO DEDIT AD MDCCCLXXX'. Burges's Diary and Estimate Book record that his very last work was this 'Pearl Shell Bottle for Lady Bute'.

Maker's mark of Jes Barkentin of Barkentin & Krall.   J.M.C.

Lent anonymously

William Burges as a Medievalist
by Virginia Glenn

On May 5, 1881 in his capacity as President, Lord Talbot de Malahide expressed the regret of the Archaeological Institute at the death of William Burges 'for many years a valued and faithful friend and supporter'. Following complimentary references to his principal architectural works, the President added, 'his contributions to the *Journal* showed how thoroughly he had mastered the details of medieval art of all kinds'. This was an appropriate accolade which would have pleased Burges, coming as it did from one of the more serious antiquarian bodies of his day, which had published seven of his major historical articles and at whose meetings he had taken a leading part in the discussions and 'exhibited' a bewildering variety of ancient and exotic objects.

There is no doubt that Burges took the Middle Ages seriously. From the age of eighteen he travelled extensively first in Britain and then in Europe. Everywhere he went it was principally the medieval architecture, wallpainting and manuscripts along with the early metalwork in the church treasuries which he recorded meticulously with notes and sketches. He was broadminded enough also to make a careful coloured drawing of how the Parthenon must have looked in its original painted state, to record the Renaissance architecture of France in a book written in conjunction with Clutton, and to include in the 'Vellum Sketchbook' a fountain by 'Verochio' which he had seen in Florence. However it was the 13th century tracery of France and the 14th century enamelling of Italy which filled him with real enthusiasm. By the end of the 1860s his knowledge of what was to be seen in both those countries was exhaustive and he had also made forays into Belgium and Germany. Of the material studied by modern medievalists, only that in Spain and Eastern Europe eluded him.

He wrote copiously both in the guise of a straightforward historian and as an advocate of medieval studies as the only proper foundation of any architectural training. Most of his historical articles are concerned with the decorative aspects of medieval building such as sculpture and wall-painting, or with the minor arts, but on embarking on his one great book on the subject, *Architectural Drawings* (1870), he declared that he had set himself 'to write a sort of grammar of thirteenth-century architecture'. Unfortunately, he felt obliged to abandon that scheme when Viollet-le-Duc made it redundant by publishing his *Dictionnaire* and it remains a charming but slightly inconsequential collection of assorted details which had taken Burges's fancy.

On the subject of medieval architecture as the only valid source of inspiration for his contemporaries Burges was adamant. He lectured in 1860 at the Architectural Photographic Exhibition, demonstrating the only possible principles of church portal design to be enshrined in the buildings of 13th century France; citing exemplars from the Romanesque St. Trophime at Arles (St. Trophonius to Burges), to the Portail de la Calande at Rouen, built as he put it 'when art began to wane in the fourteenth century'. He had sternly advised architectural students, speaking at the R.I.B.A. the previous year, to copy 13th century conventional carved foliage for architectural ornament as being very adaptable to any part of a structure, large or small. Particularly, he told them that suitable motifs could be found in manuscript illuminations of the period, and added that 'an order to draw from the illuminated manuscripts in the British Museum is not very difficult to obtain, while nothing can exceed the courtesy of the present officers and attendants'.

Burges also read widely, keeping abreast of contemporary publications on antiquarian subjects in both English and French. In his own country he had a high regard for Rickman, who as he justly says in 'Art and Religion' 'was the first to reduce things to order' in the field of English medieval architectural history. He does, however describe as grotesque the terms 'Norman, Early English, Decorated and Perpendicular' by which Rickman first distinguished our native styles of architecture. Pugin was something of a hero to Burges although perhaps more as an architect than a scholar; Ruskin he treated with considerable respect and the two were on sufficiently good terms for Burges to get permission to photograph Ruskin's own plaster casts of the capitals of the Doge's Palace to illustrate an article which he published in *Annales Archéologiques* in 1857. Robert Willis, a fellow contributor to *Gleanings from Westminster Abbey,* also received his due tribute from Burges: 'Few men, either in or out of the Profession, have greater claims upon the confraternity of architects than the Jacksonian Professor at Cambridge. Every paper from his pen has been a step gained in the upward progress of the art'. Dean Stanley, on the other hand, rhetorical and eloquent in his *Memorials of Westminster Abbey,* he regards with some disfavour. Numerous other English writers on all kinds of subjects were an inspiration to Burges, for example Sabine Baring-Gould whose *Myths of the Middle Ages* he quotes in 'Art and Religion' and another of whose works is prominently displayed on the bookcase in the photographs of the architect's own house. Baring-Gould's great series of volumes on Celtic saints was published between 1872 and 1877 and must have been a useful iconographic source to Burges particularly for the glass and some of the murals at Castell Coch.

About French scholarship his feelings were more mixed. To some extent he shared the hearty chauvinism of his companons at the R.I.B.A. On March 9, 1861 a long formal debate there involving among others Seddon, Street and Prof. Donaldson condemned the evils of restoration, particularly as carried out in France. Among the contributions 'Mr. Burges said that, in point of fact, no such edifice as the Abbey of St. Denis now existed. It was utterly spoiled many years since. Some years ago an attempt had been made to restore the tombs to their original positions. In Louis Philippe's time a terrible restoration took place in the sculpture, and Blessed Virgins were metamorphosed into apostles and apostles into Blessed Virgins'. (Saint-Denis had been virtually wrecked during the French Revolution and very clumsily restored by Debret in 1839-40. At the date of this discussion, Viollet-le-Duc was directing the restoration of architecture, sculpture and painted decoration there—a campaign which lasted from 1851 to 1879). Again, in *The Gentleman's Magazine* of 1863 Burges is pleased to dismiss an article by one M. le Docteur Cattois in a recent issue of *Annales Archéologiques* in round terms; 'as in most French writing there is a vast amount of "bunkum" to be waded through before one gets to the real matter'. M.le Docteur's crime had been to bewail the fact that a reliquary had been sold from the 'Sultykoff' Collection to the South Kensington Museum and was consequently lost to the citizens of France forever.

On the other hand, arguably the most important scholarly influence on Burges was a Frenchman, Adolphe-Napoléon Didron. Didron aîné (his nephew Edouard-Aimé Didron took on many of his business interests and his publications after Adolphe-Napoléon's death) was himself a very remarkable man. Trained in Paris in law, letters and medicine he became a friend of Victor Hugo and by 1835 had become Secretary of the Comité des Arts et Monuments. At the vitally important period when most early ecclesiastical French buildings were finally being restored after the ravages of the Revolution, he and Arcisse de Caumont virtually invented the scientific study of medieval archaeology and made a determined and sometimes very unpopular stand against over-restoration in that country. Didron's most positive contribution was to found *Annales Archéologiques,* which he directed until his death in 1867. A man of wide interests, he wrote about architecture and the decorative arts, but his abiding passion was for iconography. His *Iconographie Chrétienne* of 1843 was one of the earliest handbooks on the subject; and it was iconography in particular which he discussed with Burges, to whom he transmitted some of his ideas on the subject. They collaborated on *Venise: Iconographie des Chapiteaux du Palais Ducale* in 1857, not always agreeing, and on occasions both getting it wrong. Clearly, Burges liked and admired Didron and they had much in common. Although the

Frenchman was never a practising architect, he had a highly successful stained glass works and glazed buildings as prestigious as Notre Dame and St. Eustache in Paris. In 1858 he added a bronze foundry to his enterprises, which made at least one major reliquary dedicated to Saints Cyr and Juliette in Nantes Cathedral. Twenty years older than his English associate he must have had much useful advice to give him. On January 10, 1868, Burges wrote in the *Building News*: 'To write the biography of a departed friend can hardly be accounted either a pleasant or desirable occupation and it is with no small grief in the present case that I am called upon to record the acts of one to whom both architecture and archaeology owe so much, and who was so comparatively little known in this country. Yet there were some few of our countrymen to whom a visit to the Rue St. Dominique and an interview with M. Didron were as much a duty (whenever they found themselves in Paris) as an inspection of the last treasures added to the Louvre or to the Hotel de Cluny'.

About the celebrated Viollet-le-Duc, Burges's opinions fluctuated. In 1863 giving almost unstinting praise to the massive *Dictionnaire Raisonné de l'Architecture Francaise du XI au XVI Siècle,* then published up to the letter 'M', he cheerfully declares 'one rises from the examination of the work with the conviction, that if M. Viollet-le-Duc had not got three heads and three pairs of hands at least he ought to have them'. He was particularly impressed by the quality of the illustrations, and found much to interest him in the entries headed *Hôtel de Ville, Hôtel Dieu, Maison* and *Manoir.* Burges, like all architects of his period working in the Neo-Gothic style, was constantly faced with the problem of carrying out secular commissions in a style originally applied mainly to church building, and of finding suitably domestic ornament in an historical area where virtually none survived. One can see the importance to him of those specific items by Viollet. Carcassone, one of the best known and most attractive of Viollet-le-Duc's restorations, came under critical attack at another R.I.B.A. meeting in 1866 when C.F. Hayward described it as a waste of money to restore such an isolated structure and one which was valueless as a historic monument. Burges sprang to the defence: 'It was one of those things which would bear restoration, because there was no art to destroy. It had been restored in the most perfect manner, and afforded a good idea of the military architecture of the Middle Ages, and in that respect he thought M. le Duc deserved immense credit. It was valuable inasmuch as it was a page for them to learn from'. (It was almost certainly a page which Burges at least referred to when he came to carry out an even more drastic reconstruction at Castell Coch.) By 1860 Burges had rather changed his tune. During a discussion following a lecture on The Chateau of Pierrefonds and its restoration by M. Viollet-le-Duc, delivered by Phené Spiers, there was the following outburst: 'Mr. Burges confessed that the works of M. Viollet-le-Duc had bitterly disappointed him; he agreed with others that, as an artist, he excelled, but he (Mr. Burges) parted company with him on architecture. They all owed him, he was of opinion, a great deal for his numerous works, his letters and writings being well received; but he could not allow him to be considered a great architect'.

All the other predictable French writers are quoted from time to time by Burges—Caumont, Darcel, Labarte, Charles de Linas—but he was also familiar with earlier publications. The *Voyage Littéraire de Deux Bénédictins* (1717-30) and Félibien's *Histoire de St. Denis,* both comparatively rare books, are quoted by him. His knowledge of early texts, for example the *Speculum of Vincent de Beauvais,* the basis of so many medieval French sculptural programmes, I suspect he derived from Didron.

Burges's own library was clearly very large, but it was not catalogued until it was sold as late as 1918, by which time it was very evidently no longer complete. It does tell us, however, of his collection of books on medieval costume; his large collection of guide books and of the many source works he owned in translation—among them Vasari, William of Malmesbury and the Greek and Latin classics. Dante, too, he frequently used when he wished to humanise some piece of Italian medieval art or architecture.

When we come to examine Burges's own studies and writings we discover that his architectural interests were, if not exactly limited, certainly closely channelled. When he drew a medieval building it was for its decorative details. If he studied the construction at all it was the timbering and not the stonework. Screens, choir stalls, niche work and delicate *flèches* attracted him. In *Architectural Drawings* the building of which we are shown the most complete sections and elevations is Beauvais Cathedral, which Burges in fact drew and measured jointly with Frederick Warren, and even there the vaults are only indicated very summarily. Plate X, of Troyes Cathedral, is called 'section through upper part of choir made during the repairs in 1854', but only shows the pattern of the flying buttresses and their fancy finials, stopping short at an abbreviated indication of the springing of the high vault.

In the 1830s and 1840s, the construction and the basic principles of medieval architectural design were being studied scientifically for the first time by scholars like Anderson, Whittington, Saunders, Gunn, Whewell and above all Robert Willis. Burges himself says of Willis 'he was one of the first to tell us how the wonderous vaults of the middle ages were constructed; how the intricacies of impenetration were to be referred to a few simple members, co-existing in the same space; and by what names our ancestors designated their mouldings'. If these writers were explorers in comparatively uncharted territory, Burges was a tourist following in their wake. This was, however, entirely consistent with his professional principles as firmly stated in a lecture to the Architectural Association in 1871. Burges expatiated at length on the functions of the 'art-architect' as he preferred to see himself and contrasted them with the job of the 'surveyor'. He said it was 'useless to attempt to be architects and surveyors at the same time. The practice of the surveyor . . . was quite incompatible with the pursuit of architecture, which demanded the whole thoughts of the student, and could not be successfully carried out if he bothered himself with dilapidations, measuring and quantities'. When it came to medieval buildings his reasoning was the same. The manner in which they had been erected, their systems of support, were of only secondary significance; to a creative artist in search of stimulus they were mundane matters. Cork Cathedral for all its sturdy round piers, its shafting and its carefully 'correct' carved detail is a characteristic piece of High Victorian 'art-architecture': its appearance—
ironically like that of most Renaissance and Neo-Classical buildings—is imposed artificially on a purely supportive structure. Never could it be taken for a contemporary of Noyon, Laon or Senlis, the buildings to which its style owes so much. Their soaring proportions the dynamism and the tension of their designs, are so marked because the architectural effects are dictated by, and created from, the necessities of construction by the technical and imaginative skills of the medieval architects (who were mainly 'surveyors') courageous enough to push those structural constraints to their limits.

It is perhaps fair to say that while the written works of Prof. Willis, particularly on Canterbury, have for the most part still not been superceded, when he attempted to design a building the result was the profoundly dull King's Walk Cemetary Chapel in Wisbech. The same is true of almost the only building designed by Willis's Cambridge colleague Dr. W. Whewell. The last word on this subject should be given to Burges himself. Speaking again of Viollet-le-Duc, he remarked tartly that 'a knowledge of antiquarianism and archaeology did not make an architect'.

What Burges did examine with an extremely penetrating eye were the applied arts of the Middle Ages. He knew, and frequently based his arguments on, *De Diversis Artibus*; a volume of practical instructions mainly for gold—and silversmiths by a 12th century monk called Theophilus. Enamelling especially fascinated him, and he made particularly painstaking drawings in the treasuries at Mainz, Perugia and Aachen. At the first two he minutely sketched not only the decoration, but also the construction of the elaborate 14th century chalices and at Aachen he paid special attention to a similar base for a monstrance, noting tiny features which were to reappear completely transmogrified in his own chalice designs. He was also fortunate enough to gain access to the Sacro Corporale at Orvieto, no easy matter even today, as it contains an unusually sacred relic from the miraculous mass at Bolsena. In the brief article which he wrote on it for the *Archaeological Journal* in 1879 Burges gives a typically ebullient account of how he effected an entry to the holy of holies where Du Sommerard, Labarte and Didron had failed. 'In the month of April last I found myself at Orvieto, in company with Mr. R.P. Pullan, the well-known architect, and of course our first question was to the possibility of seeing the Corporale. I need scarcely say that we expected a repetition of the old story, but to our intense surprise we were told that there was a chance, inasmuch as a German nobleman had just arrived in the city who was the bearer of the requisite order. Whether the production of the four keys is still demanded, I do not know; but, at all events, on the next day (Sunday) we had the pleasure of seeing the hitherto invisible reliquary'.

The Reliquario del Sacro Corporale is a silver gilt polyptych 4 feet 6¾ inches high and 2 feet 1 inch wide signed and dated 1338. It is covered with enamel scenes of the story of the miracle at Bolsena and of the Passion of Christ. It rests on eight cast silver gilt figures of prophets, and has three crocketed gables between buttresses set at 45 degrees with tall spires and angel finials. It is the most elaborately decorated piece of early 14th century enamelled silver in existence. Burges's mission was to establish the precise technique employed for producing the 'painted' scenes, which he duly did—confirming that they were indeed *basse taille*. Having admitted the beauty of the enamels, he had little else to say in favour of the Sacro Corporale, declaring its architectural framing 'nothing particular'. Strangely enough he did not comment at all on the feature most striking to modern eyes—the transmission into miniature form of a narrative cycle closely linked to Duccio's *Maestà*, many figures directly indebted to Ambrogio Lorenzetti and even borrowings from Florentine painting of the early 14th century. Perhaps a little remiss in a man who had enunciated that, to advance ecclesiastical art, the first requirement was to establish 'A Professor of Fine Arts (monumentally considered) in either University. By this I mean that he should not only instruct his pupils to distinguish between a Raphael and a Rembrandt, but he should tell them something about the principles of Wall Painting, as practised by Giotto and his followers . . . It would be a question whether attendances at these lectures should not, in certain instances, be compulsory'. However, by 1879, Burges's eyesight really was very bad and in spite of the intervention of the German nobleman he may not have been able to get all that close to the reliquary.

Catalogue D:
Scholarship Sources and Collections

Ely Cathedral

This was one of the first medieval buildings which Burges examined in detail. He first spent three months there sketching in 1848, the occasion on which he met George Gilbert Scott. In 1852 he returned to take measured drawings. It remained a favourite monument, details of Bishop Alcock's Chapel appearing in *Architectural Drawings* in 1870. As late as 1874, when Burges prepared a printed report angling for the commission to restore King's College Chapel, Cambridge, he had the following to say: 'I have endeavoured to steer a middle course between the pure perpendicular of the Chapel and the equally pure renaissance rood-screen. Happily we are not without examples of this 'via media' in England, and we are specially fortunate in having a most excellent one not far from Cambridge, in Bishop West's Chapel in Ely Cathedral'. V.G.

D.1 Sketch inscribed 'Prior Crawden's Chapel, Ely Cathedral'
Watercolour and gouache on Whatman paper
13⅞"(35.2)×8⅝"(21.9)

A very early drawing, made before Burges's grasp of perspective was invariably equal to such a complicated subject. Highly coloured in red, emerald green, royal blue, white and gilt; it is a study of the windows and nichework below in this small late medieval chamber. There are traces of colour remaining on much of the Ely stonework, which being in many cases soft local clunch, absorbed the pigments and retained them in spite of the vandalism of the Reformation and the cleaning campaigns of later centuries. The use of colour in the decoration of medieval buildings remained a major interest of Burges's; publications by him on the subject appeared in 1857, 1862 and 1864. Writing in *The Building News* in May, 1862 he mentions Ely a number of times in the course of an article entitled 'The various systems of coloured decoration in the Middle Ages', the main contention of which is that historiated schemes like those of the Painted Chamber at Westminster and Giotto's Arena chapel are lively and exciting, while mainly non-figurative patterning of the type that ornaments the Sainte Chapelle in Paris is fussy and meaningless and detracts from the beauties of the architecture itself. V.G.

Lent by the British Architectural Library/R.I.B.A.

D.2 Study of a Niche in Prior Crauden's Chapel, Ely Cathedral
Pencil and wash on Whatman paper
13"(33)×9½"(24.2)

A more finished drawing, and much more assured, of a detail of D1. This is a very careful record of the foliate finials and crockets and elaborately interlocking ogee curves of one niche with its miniature vault. V.G.

Lent by the British Architectural Library/R.I.B.A.

D.3 View of Ely Cathedral
Pencil and wash on grey paper
20¾"(53)×7½"(19)

An elevation of one window bay, showing the brightly coloured stonework of the niches below and the patterned vault above.

In his 1862 article on medieval polychromy Burges said that 'the Lady Chapel at Ely . . . is simply coloured and powdered with gold ornaments. The spandrels of the arcades were generally filled with sculptured groups; these were highly coloured and gilt, i.e., a good deal of gold and a good deal of white, tinted and powdered with other colours, was used to detach them from the ground, which was a simple and rather dark colour, such as blue or red . . . At Ely there were a series of niches left white, but with coloured figures and coloured backgrounds. . . . At Ely the vault is powdered with red roses'. V.G.

Victoria and Albert Museum

D.2

(detail)

The Long Journey 1853-54

Burges made his first foreign excursion in 1849, when he was only twenty-one. He visited Normandy and Paris, penetrating a little further in 1850 to Belgium and Germany. In the two following years and early 1853 he explored Paris more thoroughly and went to Beaune, Troyes, Bourges, Nevers, Blois, Amboise and Lille.

His 'Long Jurney' began in April 1853. This time he revisited Normandy and finally got as far as Italy. In addition to a thoroughgoing knowledge of French and Italian applied arts, he had now acquired a complete familiarity with the architecture of late 12th and early 13th century France. In spite of the advice of acquaintances like Lord Leighton and the careful adherence to Murray's guidebooks, in 1870 Burges was to complain apropos his early travels in France, in the preface to *Architectural Drawings*: 'The excellent Dictionary of M. Viollet-le-Duc was not then published, nor indeed was it even begun, and it was therefore not very easy to ascertain where the best examples of thirteenth-century architecture were to be found'.

Nevertheless by his return in November 1854, there was very little that he had missed.　　V.G.

D.4 **Study of the apse of Beauvais Cathedral**
Pencil, pen and wash, on twelve pieces of pasted down cartridge paper
Original measurements lost

A partial section with details of the elevation in the apse; annotated with a printed plan attached and lists of the principal chapels and monuments. This drawing first appeared in published form in *Building News,* v (1859), later it was the basis of Plates V and VI in *Architectural Drawings,* and Beauvais is discussed at some length in the introductory text. Burges regarded the building as an effort to improve on Amiens and speculates on the disastrous collapse of the original vault of the 1230s—a catastrophe still not fully explicable—before he goes on to explain how he and Frederick Warren obtained the heights of the more accessible parts of the aisle vaults by dropping tapes over the iron tie-bars, inserted during the 1284 rebuild, and measuring them. A careful drawing of the roof timbers forms Plate XLV of the same publication.　　V.G.

Victoria and Albert Museum

D.5 **Study of the nave buttressing at Châlons-sur-Marne**
Pencil and pen on Whatman paper, with an alteration pasted on
16½″(42)×10¾″(27.5)

An elevation and perspective of the buttresses, with written notes. This also appeared in *Architectural Drawings* forming the basis of Plate IX. Signed with the monogram 'WB'. Châlons-sur-Marne was one of the group of French buildings of the earliest Gothic phase which so much influenced Burges's own design.　　V.G.

Victoria and Albert Museum

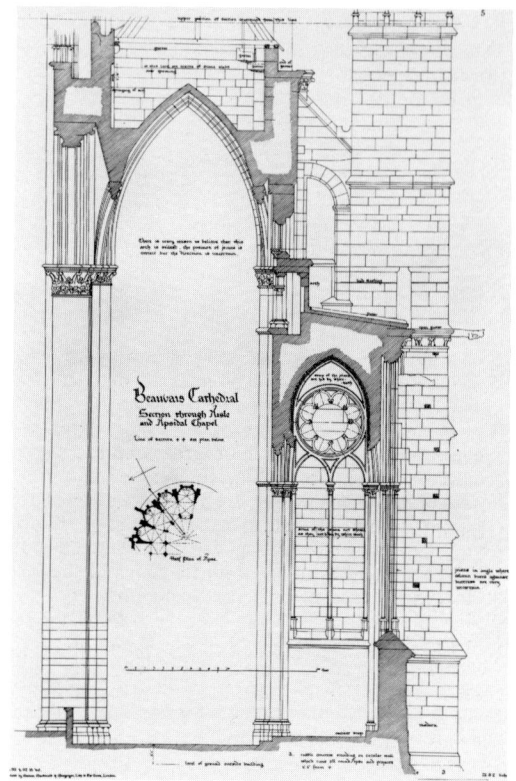

Architectural Drawings, plate v

D.6 **Perspective drawing of the East End of Waltham Abbey**
Pencil and wash on paper
15¼"(38.7)×9½"(24.2)

A highly finished watercolour of the interior of the east end of the choir, with a heavy rose window in the Transitional French style in the gable wall—which was rebuilt by Burges—and the three-story 12th century elevation at either side. The flat ceiling is patterned with painted lozenge-shaped panels. The reredos, the Annunciation to the Magi, has white figures on a gold ground. Signed 'E.S. Cole'.

To pre-empt adverse criticism of his activities at Waltham, Burges published a booklet in 1860, *The Legend of Waltham Abbey and the History of the Church founded by King Harold*, which contains an account of the work then in progress and the architect's reasons for taking the somewhat drastic steps which he did. He gives a fairly highly coloured account of the history of the founding and building of Waltham Abbey, up to the destruction of the east end during the Reformation and the 'unfortunate' repairs in the 17th and 18th centuries. Then he describes his own policy: 'The roof being in good repair, although by no means of the original pitch, has been retained, but the plaster ceiling has of course been removed and its place supplied by boarding painted in imitation of the only contemporary ceiling remaining, viz., that at Peterborough. The centres, however, represent signs of the zodiac, the labors of the year, and the elements. The execution of these figures is due to Mr. Poynter the son of the architect.
A new east end in the style of the early half of the 13th century is now in progress, and stained glass of the very best description has been ordered for the lower lancets.' Of the exterior he also says that most of the work is necessary to remove the effects of earlier restoration in inferior or unsuitable materials.

The debate about the original dates of the various building campaigns at Waltham carried on for years, cropping up in the discussion following a paper on 'Romanesque' at the Architectural Association in May 1861 and at the R.I.B.A. the following year. In another discussion Burges was reported as putting forward the following rather individual views about Norman vaulting: 'At Waltham, also, and in most of the Norman churches, they might call the pillar which runs from the ground to the wall plate a vaulting shaft, but it was partly to divide the bays, and partly to act as an extra support to the tie beam, and thus diminish the span by a couple of feet. If we could be transported to Norman times, he doubted whether we should ever see an open roof in a church, or even a coved roof, or indeed any other than a flat ceiling. Most Norman churches he had seen had flat roofs, or the collar might be put a little way above the wall plate. Mr. Burges concluded by saying that he believed the Norman architects did not vault their clerestories because they were unable to do so.'

In 1876 Burges returned to the subject, publishing with J.A. Reeve, 'Notes on the Dates of Waltham Abbey' in *The Architect*. V.G.

Lent by the British Architectural Library/R.I.B.A.

D.6

The Sketchbook of Villard de Honnecourt *folio 30v interior of one of the apse chapels at Reims.*

D.7 'Fac-Simile of the Sketch Book of Wilars de Honecourt an architect of the thirteenth century', by R. Willis
1859

Villard's sketchbook is one of the most intriguing documents of the medieval period. Architectural drawings are virtually unknown for 13th century buildings, but this album contains numerous plans, sections and elevations; directions for timber structures, architectural, military and purely utilitarian; studies of sculpture and tombs and directions for the construction of church fittings as various as pew ends and a mechanical Eucharistic dove. To 20th century eyes it is more probably a collection of samples made by some kind of travelling consultant passing from one great *chantier* to another, amassing ideas from other masters' works to pass on to his clients across Europe: not any kind of corpus of original designs. There is however, one plan which bears the inscription '*Istud bresbiterium invenerunt Ulardus de Hunecort et Petrus de Corbeia*' much discussed by Burges *et al.* To Victorian architects, 'Wilars' appeared to be precisely one of themselves, going around as they did designing; seeking inspiration in all he saw. Burges knew the book already and had made a careful study of it, in what was then the Bibliothèque Royale in Paris. It was published, with a preamble on French 19th century art at the beginning and a glossary at the end, in 1858 by Quicherat (who had rediscovered the manuscript), Alfred Darcel and J.B.A. Lassus (one of the architects who had worked on the recent restoration of the Sainte Chapelle). Willis translated it and greatly expanded the explanatory text the following year. Where possible actual examples of the material recorded by Villard are supplied as they survived in the 19th century. In this case the book is open to show Plate LIX (Villard's interior of one of the apse chapels at Reims); on the opposite page 205 is an illustration of the same subject by Cullamot Jeune from Viollet-le-Duc's *Dictionnaire*. Burges enthusiastically reviewed the French edition in *The Builder* in 1858 and Willis's edition in *The Building News* in the year of its publication. Later in 1859 he added his own ideas in an article on Villard's plans in *The Ecclesiologist*, attributing Cambrai to him and remarking on the 'menagerie, Pagan sculpture, Hungarian pavement plans . . . built or excogitated by Wilars'

V.G.

Victoria and Albert Museum

D.8 William Burges's 'Vellum Sketchbook'
Pencil and pen on vellum
1861 (dated on folio 9 recto)
9½"(23.5)×6½"(16.5).

This is not a working sketchbook like the multitude of others which survive from Burges's hand containing notes, studies and reminders of material made on the spot during his travels, interspersed with original design ideas. This is a *jeu d'esprit* deliberately imitating Villard. Each page is designed to create an attractive composition and many have small blocks of inscription in a pseudo-13th century hand, some with word contractions in the medieval manner. The subjects are mainly from Burges's favourite French and Italian buildings, including the major Florentine Gothic churches, Carcassonne and Poitiers. In contrast to Villard, the only plan he includes is a small one of the Hall in the latter building. Armour, pottery, tombs, metalworkers' recipes and textiles (including the Opus Anglicanum Clare Chasuble now in the V.&A.) are also included. Not based on the medieval original, are some beautifully drawn and naturalistically observed animals, flowers and decorative maidens in the Pre-Raphaelite taste.

Open here at folios 9 verso and 10 recto to show a collection of medieval fountains, from sources in Switzerland and north Italy.

Inscribed 'BALE/brass' 'top too long'. 'This is Saturn/green red and Gold/The general Color is black/with lots of gilding and some silver/BERN/ slate colour'. 'This is the Serpent of/brass made by Moles/I know what is now/to be seen in the chu/rch of S.Ambrose/at Milan/porphyry'. 'Baile/Berne/ Bern'.

Burges wrote a letter anonymously to the *Building News* in 1867 headed 'Medieval Fountains' and had designed a number himself including the Sabrina Fountain for Gloucester (c.1856) and the bronze centrepiece for the Cardiff Castle Roof Garden.

V.G.

Lent by the British Architectural Library/R.I.B.A.

D.8

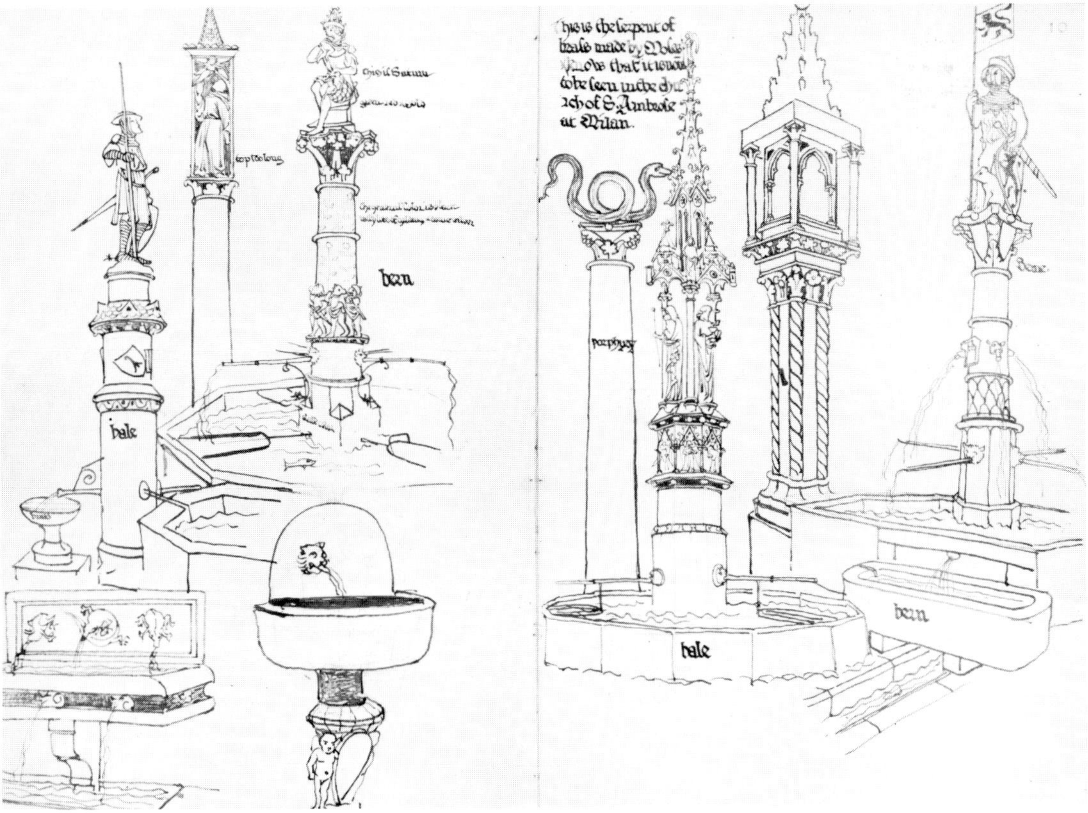

D.9 'Architectural Drawings' by William Burges
1870

A collection of plates, prefaced by explanatory notes prepared by Burges from detailed measured drawings made on his European travels and in England and Wales. Again the reference to Villard is obvious in the inscriptions and the layout of the pages. The drawing style shows a certain influence too; in the *Building News* of 1859 Burges had said of Villard's sketchbook: 'How different this stern style of drawing is to our fashionable method of etching everything up with a free pen! We take immense trouble; we put imaginary lichens on the roof, and imaginary weather stains on the stonework, showing each individual stone as possessing some amount of light and shade; until the whole affair looks most charming. However, somehow or other, when the building is erected, it looks very different to the drawing ... Of course, I do not by any means, infer that we should give up our perspective and color, &c., and draw architecture as Wilars drew it. I only mean that we may learn one or two very useful lessons from him, such as to draw bolder, with thicker lines, and to leave out or simplify unimportant parts'.

Plate XXII open here to show details of timbering etc. in the Château de Chillon, Lake Geneva, on which Burges drew heavily as a source for both Cardiff Castle and Castell Coch.   V.G.

Victoria and Albert Museum

D.9

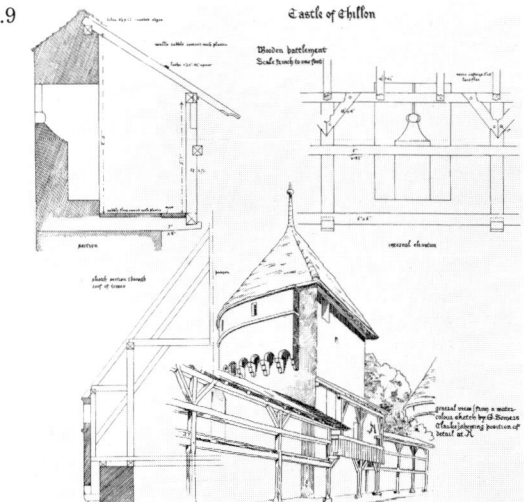

(detail) plate XXII

Westminster Abbey

By the beginning of the last century the state of the mainly mid-13th century church of Westminster Abbey was already giving cause for alarm and comment in informed circles. Not gravely damaged in the Reformation or the Civil War, nonetheless by the early 18th century natural weathering had reduced the exterior of the structure to such a decayed condition that there was concern for its safety. Sir Christopher Wren, 'chief director' of works there from 1697 until his death, supervised extensive repairs to the north transept, had the east end and south side largely recased and began plans to finish the west front left incomplete at the Dissolution. This was finally undertaken by Hawksmoor and his successors in the same practice. The chapter house had by 1340 been pressed into service for parliamentary meetings and by the end of Edward VI's reign housed the Public Record Office. For this latter purpose a mezzanine floor and storage shelving were inserted, the windows were converted to round-headed clear apertures allowing the requisite amount of light to enter; finally (with some assistance) the vault collapsed in 1740.

In 1793 a major campaign of repairs to the roof was set in hand and when the scale of the task was realised James Wyatt was called in. As a result of further negotiations in 1807 a government grant of £2,000 was raised towards the restoration of the building. Altogether £42,000 of public money had been spent on Westminster Abbey by 1830, and further distinguished architects became involved— for example Blore who rebuilt the eastern walk of the cloisters about 1835.

None of this was satisfactory to Burges or his contemporaries, particularly Sir George Gilbert Scott who wanted, and eventually got, the job of refurbishing all the Abbey buildings according to 'correct' Neo-Gothic taste. In both editions of *Gleanings* Scott described in detail how the chapter house should be reconstructed, as finally it was under his guidance. Burges added his weight to the argument in speeches and publications. In 1864 he thundered to the Ecclesiological Society: 'In these days of restoration is it not a crying shame that the beautiful North Portal which Sir Christopher Wren spoiled should remain in the condition in which it does? It is a disgrace to London. The pediment is made into an ogee, the whole of the centre sculpture is gone and the twelve apostles have disappeared'.

Gleanings represented something of a tract in the agitation for the restoration of the church. When the rebuilding was at last carried out, it too was harshly criticised by the next generation of architects. W.R. Lethaby in *Westminster Abbey and the King's Craftsman* (1906) admitted: 'The exterior of the church has been subjected to such a series of injuries and 'improvements' that hardly one stone of it remains upon another. The original form of the once so beautiful North Transept with its three great portals, had to a large extent disappeared under a layer of alterations even before the great restoration (1875-90) which made all false. The Westminster transepts were of such extraordinary interest as showing the progress of London building in the middle of the thirteenth century, that it is worth some trouble to gather up the evidence as to their original form before they were made over in the 'Early English' of today'.

Wistfully Lethaby said of Wren's north transept 'The smile of the old work shone as it were through an ungraceful veil and the whole front still preserved a certain lightness and spring'. Altogether he shared the scorn of discerning early 20th century critics: 'Such is scientific restoration; but let me not be misunderstood. Now it is done don't alter it; I would not meddle even with the restorations of a restorer. The north gable as it stands has already more than a dozen years of antiquity ('Early English' they call it!). It is now the nearest we can have to the original work'.

Three decades before, Burges had shown no such lack of confidence in his approach to his predecessors' work. 'Unfortunately Mr. Essex (certainly the most distinguished Gothic architect of his day) was not satisfied with his own additions to the furniture but set to work to improve the architecture by cutting two large niches in the space between the angles of the building and the jambs of the eastern windows. It is useless for me to describe this modern alteration; suffice it to say that any restoration, however conservative, would demand in the very first instance the removal of the woodwork in question as well as the obliteration of the niches'. (*Report on the Condition of the Eastern Part of King's College Chapel*, 1874).

It was in this spirit of certainty that Burges and his friends advocated the return of Westminster to what they had absolutely no doubt was its medieval form.

V.G.

D.10 'Reconstruction of the Feretory of Edward the Confessor, Westminster Abbey'

Watercolour on light card
26½"(67.3)×18¾"(47.5)

A very highly coloured and imaginative perspective view of the high altar of Westminster Abbey with the Shrine of the Confessor towering above. Tonsured priests and acolytes are celebrating mass in the foreground.

There is some evidence, both archaeological and documentary, to serve as a guide to the liturgical arrangements installed in the Abbey by Henry III. Having rebuilt it as a royal mausoleum, with the tombs of his family surrounding the great shrine of their canonised ancestor, Henry lavished funds and jewels on the *châsse* which held the relics of St. Edward and its surrounding fittings. Much of this, and all the precious metalwork were destroyed at the Dissolution in the 1530s, but its royal connections saved Westminster from the wholesale wreckage which was the fate of so many other Abbey foundations.

The Cosmati shrine base with its twisted columns, which is visible here has survived largely intact and *in situ*. The outer ciborium to the gilded *châsse*, which could be raised and lowered, now exists only in a form reinstated during Queen Mary's reign, but Burges has taken that to be a reasonable approximation to its 13th century predecessor. Burges discusses the Confessor's shrine at very great length in the second edition of *Gleanings*. Among the sources he quotes and one which he illustrates is a mid-13th century manuscript *Life of St. Edward* in Cambridge University Library. This shows a group of kneeling supplicants, the foremost crawling into the hole in the shrine base to get as near as possible to the sacred relics. On either side of the shrine are figures of the Confessor and the Pilgrim raised on columns. The actual reliquary in the manuscript looks like a generalised view of some Mosan prototype or combination of prototypes from about 1200. Similarly, Burges has concocted a large gilt and enamel *châsse* in the watercolour, which owes something to the Three Kings Shrine in Cologne, something to the Shrine of Charlemagne at Aachen and a little to the arm reliquary of the latter in the Louvre. All three were certainly known to him. What is surprising is that Burges chose a style and type of *châsse* which would have been distinctly archaic at the date of the Confessor's translation, 1269. By then the influence of objects whose designs were based on architectural motifs, such as miniature buildings like the Shrine of St. Taurin (D14), would have certainly been making itself felt at the fashion concious English Court as well as St. Louis' Court in Paris.

This was one of Burges's first drawings to be exhibited and what was considered its 'Popish' treatment of the subject caused a considerable furore. V.G.

Exh. R.A., 1852, No.1220
Lent by the British Architectural Library/R.I.B.A.

D.11 Drawing Inscribed 'Portion of central composition of the Retabulum Westminster Abbey—Full size'

Pencil and wash on Whatman paper
17¾"(45)×10¾"(27.4)

The Westminster Retable occupies a uniquely important position in the history of European painting, in that it is the only known panel painting of anything like its date—now assumed to be the late 13th century—surviving from England or France. Manuscript and wall paintings of the period are reasonably plentiful, but for northern Europe there is nothing comparable in the way of wooden altarpieces until over a century later. Even in Italy, panel painting was still comparatively unsophisticated, but the Retable, which on stylistic grounds must be associated with either the English or the French court is of the very highest quality. Indeed, the only works with which it can be convincingly compared are the Douce Apocalypse in the Bodleian Library and the great wall-paintings of St. Christopher and Doubting Thomas in the South Transept of Westminster Abbey, both also recognised masterpieces of their time.

The Retable was noticed by George Vertue about 1725, when it had been pressed into service as the top of a cupboard. Although Vertue called it 'a most curious piece of painted carved gilded work, finely embellished' it was not until 1827 that it was rediscovered by Blore, its importance recognised and efforts made for its preservation and display.

Burges devotes eight pages to it in the second edition of *Gleanings,* with four illustrations. Naturally, he contests Viollet-le-Duc's suggestion that it might be French. There then follows a long and careful analysis of the processes by which the moulded gesso framing with its fictive jewels was produced.

The pattern of compartments shaped as eight pointed stars which fills the right and left wings was one which he was to use repeatedly in his own work, for example on the cupboard doors now in the Cecil Higgins Museum at Bedford (B22). V.G.

Victoria and Albert Museum

D.12

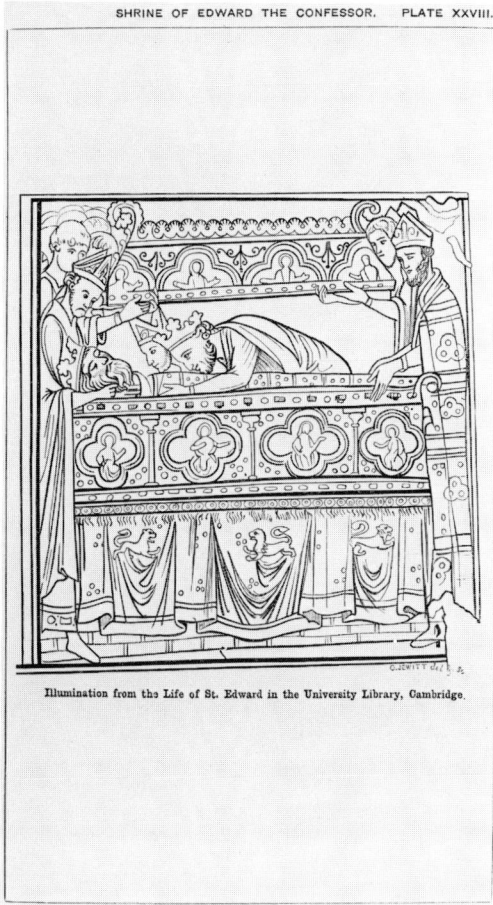

D.12

(detail) — plate xxiii

D.12 'Gleanings from Westminster Abbey', the Second Edition, Considerably Enlarged
1863

This is a set of essays on the fabric and history of the Abbey by Burges; Joseph Burtt, Assistant Keeper of the Public Records; eight fellows of the Society of Antiquaries including J.H. Parker; and Professor Robert Willis—all appended to the main article on the building by George Gilbert Scott. The first edition had come out in 1861 and Scott sums up the activities of the two years which separate the publications in his foreword, 'The rapid sale of the first edition of this work makes no apology necessary for the publication of a second edition; rather perhaps, some explanation is required of the long delay which has occurred in producing it. This has arisen from the time required by the engravers for the number of new illustrations; and full advantage has been taken of this for the elaborate researches of Mr. Burges in the new and admirable papers which he has added to the volume. These have indeed required more time than was expected, but the reader will be well satisfied with the result, and the inconvenience of a few months' delay has been cheaply purchased by the addition of so much valuable matter. The papers added to the present edition are those on the Metal-work, the Mosaic Pavements, the Retabulum, the Sedilia, the Coronation Chair, the Shrine, and the Tombs'.

In other words, Burges had painstakingly catalogued and recorded all those aspects of the Abbey, which most interested him—the applied arts. Perhaps, subdued by his august fellow authors, he produced in *Gleanings* some of his most carefully considered historical writing, larded with learned sources and seldom purely speculative.

Open here at Plate xxvii showing the Shrine of Edward the Confessor from the Life of St. Edward in the University Library at Cambridge.

V.G.

Victoria and Albert Museum

Metalwork and Floors

Burges made more notes and studies of medieval metalwork than almost anything else. Early pieces like the Treasure of the Empress Theodolinda at Monza and the Crown of Queen Costanza from Palermo, the many pieces of gothic silver and enamel which influenced his own work and the iron grilles over the tombs in Westminster Abbey were all grist to his mill.

One of his earliest long articles in *The Ecclesiologist* in 1855 was devoted to another major interest, and one prominent in his own architectural designs, appropriate floor decoration. In it he traced the history and iconography of incised and inlaid floors from Arras and St. Omer, to Canterbury Cathedral, the Baptistry at Florence and the Duomo at Siena. He regarded these as infinitely preferable to the commercial ecclesiastical products of his own day, particularly for the central areas of church building such as the sanctuary. V.G.

D.13 'Metal-Work and Its Artistic Design', by M. Digby Wyatt
1852

A collection of fifty chromolithograph plates of medieval fittings and renaissance metalwork, some bronze, some functional fittings in iron and other base metals, but mostly silver or silver gilt and enamel. The plates are from drawings by a number of hands, including Wyatt himself and Burges. Burges had, of course, entered Wyatt's office as an 'improver' in 1849 and many of his ideas for his own travels and studies in Europe must have been formed while this book was in preparation with its entries on objects in England, France, Italy and Sicily, Germany and Flanders. For example, Wyatt and his artists had preceded Burges at Florence, Siena, Verona and Bologna, Wyatt himself had drawn one of the more spectacular reliquaries at Pistoia, and items from Venice included a very exact representation of the 'Double Reliquary' in the Treasury of St. Mark's by E. Willison. Burges contributed 'Door Handles and Lock Escutcheons' from Germany, Lincoln and St. John's College, Cambridge; keys and locks from the Cluny Museum in Paris, from Blickling Church in Norfolk and from various English private collections; five spectacular pieces of precious metalwork from the Louvre and the Cluny Museum, some from Suger's St. Denis; details of the doorway of the hall of Merton College, Oxford; sections from the screen of Edward IV's tomb at Windsor; from the Gothic metalwork in the Treasury of the Cathedral and the church of St. Ursula at Cologne, and finally the plate here displayed.

The book is here open at Plate 49, 'a group of church plate, of which the most remarkable specimens are the celebrated enamelled challice and paten preserved in the treasury at Mayence'. To make up the composition, a book cover from Siena and a processional cross from Randazzo in Sicily (sketched by Edward Falkener) have been drawn in behind. The original study of the Mainz chalice and paten and for the Suger metalwork in the Louvre are in the album entitled *Metalwork* in the R.I.B.A. drawings collection. V.G.

Lent by Michael Darby Esq.

The Shrine of St. Taurin at Evreux

D.14 Drawing of the Shrine of St. Taurin, Evreux
Pencil, pen and wash on flimsy and cartridge paper
44″(1m 11.8)×26″(66)

A detailed drawing of part of one of the most important extant 13th century French metalwork shrines known either to Burges or to modern scholars. Closely datable to between 1248 and 1255 it is the only surviving large scale (70×100.5 ×45) piece of goldsmiths' work from the ambience of the Paris of St. Louis. Heavily restored in 1830, it was possibly known to Burges from A. le Prévost, *Notice sur la Châsse de Saint Taurin à Evreux* (1829).

Inscribed 'Chasse of St. Thaurin, Evereux/Full size'. V.G.

Victoria and Albert Museum

D.15 Drawing of the Shrine of St. Romain, Rouen
Pencil, pen and wash
22¾″(57.8)×18¾″(47.6)

A part of the late 13th century metalwork shrine in highly architectural form, preserved in the Treasury of Rouen Cathedral. It has very delicate miniature buttresses and finials with spires; under elegantly crocketed gables are figures of the Virgin and Child and Apostles in a refined, almost affected Court Style. The *châsse* was largely reconstructed in 1776 and not returned to approximately its original form until 1869, so it was presumably while it served as the *fierte* of the cathedral during this period that it was seen by Burges. It was described by H. Langlois in *Remarques sur la châsse de Saint Romain* (1833). Inscribed 'Half of the Chasse of St Romanus/Real size'. V.G.

Victoria and Albert Museum

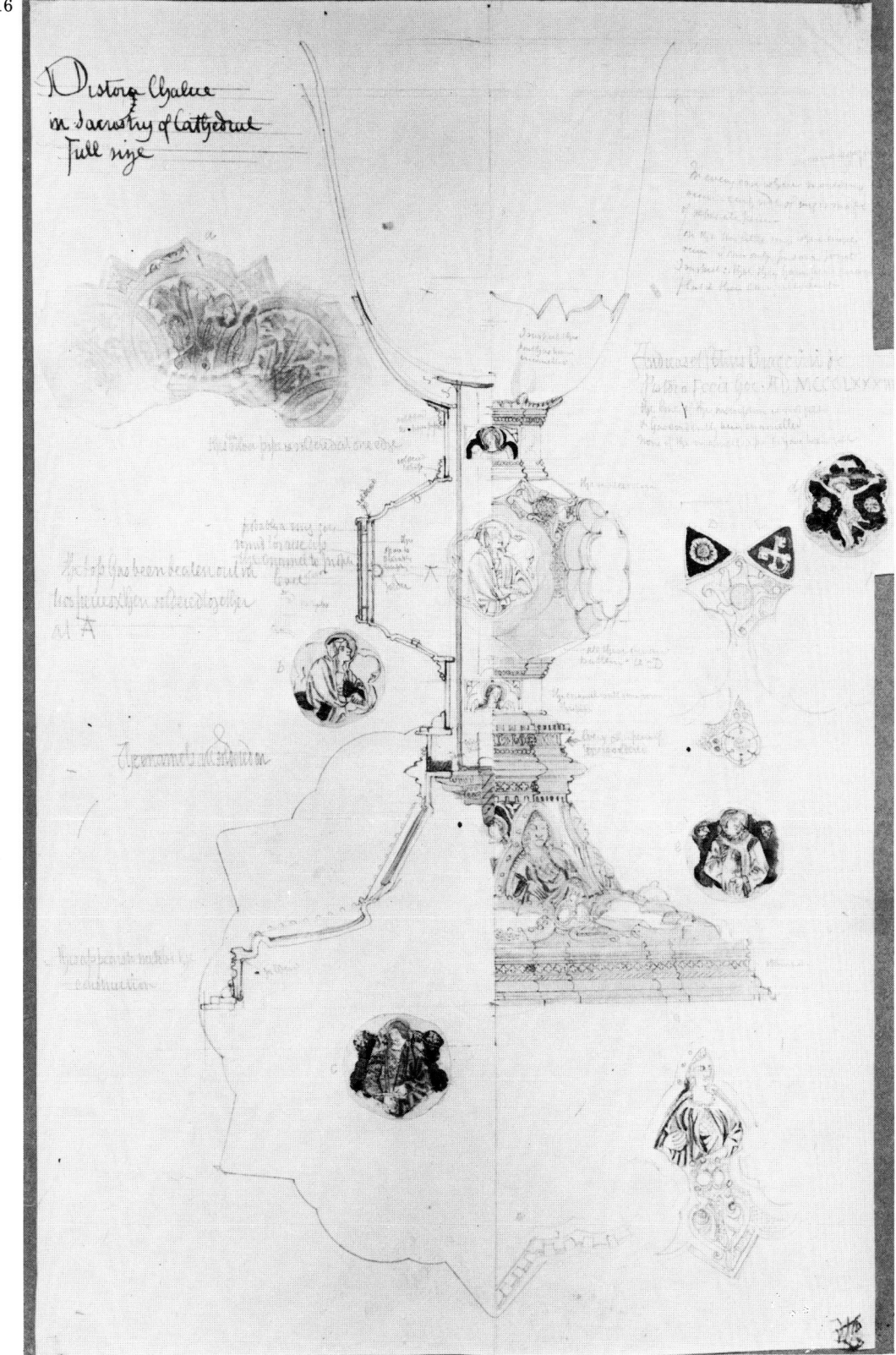

D.16 **'Pistoia, Chalice in Sacristy of Cathedral—Full size'**
Pencil and wash on cartridge paper; pencil rubbing on flimsy and four details of enamel medallions on parchment pasted on
12¼"(31.1)×8"(20.3)

A very careful record of the construction and details; there are sections of the knop, foot and bowl, the outline of the foot itself has been traced on to the paper round the actual chalice. There are laborious written notes of all the techniques involved such as enamelling, stamping and soldering. The inscription has also been recorded 'ANDREAS ET PETRUS BRACCINI de Pistoio Fecis hoc AD MCCCLXXXIIIII'. This with its painstaking examination and recording including rubbings of the relief decoration, is characteristic of the manner in which Burges approached Gothic metalwork, which of course so strongly affected his own designs, particularly for ecclesiastical plate.

A number of other pieces from the Pistoia Treasury had already been published by M. Digby Wyatt in 1852, none drawn by Burges.   V.G.

Lent by the British Architectural Library/R.I.B.A.

D.17 **'Iron hands, Musee Correr, Venice'**
Pen and wash over pencil on thick Whatman paper
13⅞"(35.5)×21⅛"(25)

A study of the workings of a mechanical iron hand; Burges brought this specimen to the notice of the Archaeological Institute in 1857. Under 'Antiquities and Works of Art Exhibited' is the entry, 'MR.W.BURGES—A drawing of an iron arm, intended to supply the loss of a right hand. The original is preserved in the Museo Correi at Venice. A similar piece of mechanism, in the Hon. Robert Curzon's Armory, has been figured in this Journal . . .'   V.G.

Victoria and Albert Museum

D.18 **Three Drawings Inscribed 'Antwerp—Matsys' Well'**
A set of pen drawings on cartridge and flimsy pasted together
Original measurements lost

The principal drawing is an elaborate perspective view of the intricate ironwork cover of the well in Antwerp's Handschoenmarkt. The painter Quentin Massys came from a family of blacksmiths and there is a tradition that he too was apprenticed to the craft, but abandoned it for painting in his twenties. A romantic tale of a love affair with a girl who could only be impressed by this more genteel calling was duly attached to the story. The figure on the well cover is Silvius Brabo one of the legendary founders of Antwerp.   V.G.

Victoria and Albert Museum

D.18

D.19 **'Mosaic traced from the floor of the Ziza, near Palermo'**
Wash over pencil on transparent flimsy
8½"(21.7)×12¾"(32.3)

Studies like this one of the Sicilian 'House of Delights' were part of the basis of Burges's inspiration for the Arab Room at Cardiff Castle. Signed with the monogram 'WM'.   V.G.

Victoria and Albert Museum

D.20 **Drawing of tiles 'From the Abbey of St. Catherine du mont Rouen'**
Wash over pencil and pen on cartridge paper
18¾"(46.5)×12⅛"(31)
'May 26/53'

A record of late medieval encaustic tiles and their technique.

Inscribed 'These have been two types of the animal as at a & b/& I strongly suspect that they are made of white clay/and the red applied afterwards—the last process was the/yellow glaze—the ◊ tile has more red in it so as to contrast/with the semi circles which have more yellow . . . the effect is red black and yellow'.

Burges was at all stages interested in tile decoration and used it to great effect in his own interior designs both ecclesiastical like Cork Cathedral and secular like Cardiff Castle.   V.G.

Victoria and Albert Museum

One of the Chertsey tiles as illustrated by Henry Shaw in 1858

D.21 **A Tile from Chertsey Abbey**
Fired clay
16¼″(41.5)×16″(40)

A roundel with a scene from the story of Tristram and Isolde, showing Tristram presented to Mark; set within four spandrel tiles decorated with stiff leaf foliage and grotesques in red and yellow.

The Chertsey tiles are close in style and date to those in Westminster Abbey Chapter House, which G.G. Scott had written up in *Gleanings*, Eds. 1 and 2. When the Architectural Museum first acquired their collection of tiles from Chertsey Abbey, Burges wrote an enthusiastic article about them in *The Builder*, July 24, 1858. At the same time he attacked the British Museum for not securing the whole set for the nation, 'I think a good deal is to be alleged on the part of the trustees when they are blamed for not purchasing this or that object or collection. They and the elder officers regard the functions of the Museum in a very different light to what the rising generation do. With us the Museum is a depository of things for the purposes of study: with them it is simply a collection of curiosities, such as stuffed birds, beasts and fishes; Elgin marbles, and New Zealand coalscuttle bonnets made out of tortoiseshell. The consequence was, that having got some few specimens of the Chertsey tiles presented to them, enough was done to satisfy curiosity, and they very consistently declined to purchase the collection'. (In the end, however, the Architectural Museum collection was reunited with that in the British Museum).

After giving a brief history of the abbey, Burges speculated on the secular subject matter of the tiles; and then described their technique, which he regarded as virtually identical to that noticed at St. Catherine's Rouen (D20).

They had been previously published by Henry Shaw, *Tile Pavements from Chertsey Abbey* (1857).
V.G.

Lent by the British Museum

D.22

D.22 **A Vitrine in the Aachen Cathedral Treasury in 1864**
From a contemporary photograph

Burges first went to Belgium and Germany in 1850. He recalled being shown round the Treasury at Aachen by the Sacristan in an article in *The Archaeological Journal* in 1859 and he spent enough time there to make a number of detailed drawings of, for example, Frederick Barbarossa's chandelier (1165-70) hanging in the centre of the octagonal Carolingian chapel; the ivory 'Horn of Charlemagne' (circa 1000 A.D.): a monstrance (14th century); and small details of various Gothic pieces. Surprisingly he does not seem to have recorded the large openwork architectural reliquaries, the two Aachen examples of which, dating from the second half of the 14th century would surely have been a fruitful source of ideas to him; in addition to the fact that at 1 metre 25 cms and 93.5 cms high respectively they are in themselves very striking concoctions of silver gilt. The Aachen Treasury underwent various rearrangement in the course of the 19th century. The case shown in this photograph was one of a set given by Canon Franz Bock in the mid-19th century. Consequently they may have been actually in course of installation when Burges made his first visit. The Gothic details which he drew come in some cases from the row of small monstrances and reliquaries at the front on the top shelf. The large *châsse* behind is the Shrine of Charlemagne (circa 1165-1215) and the Marienschrein (1220-1238) is on the shelf below. Both are rather what Burges had in mind when he invented his *châsse* for Edward the Confessor (D10).
V.G.

Medieval Painting and Manuscripts

Both wall painting and illumination were important to Burges and he drew on his knowledge of both for his mural schemes, his glass designs, his furniture decoration and even for motifs for his full scale architecture. Although he knew, for example, the frescoes of Giotto, it was English medieval polychromy which really interested him. He tried to describe the techniques employed in his opinion at Charlwood Church in Surrey, where a 13th century painted cycle had been discovered in 1858 and saw the scenes also as closely related to the Queen Mary Psalter. In these investigations he must have been helped by Edward Crocker who had made copies of the Westminster Painted Chamber before the 1834 fire. Crocker's daughters were close friends of Burges and he had portraits of them painted for his own dressing table (B14).

Matthew Digby Wyatt may have encouraged Burges in the systematic study of manuscripts. Wyatt read a paper at the R.I.B.A. in 1860, which was a fairly decent summary of the history of the illuminated book from the Early Christian Vatican Vergil to the invention of printing. Burges's contribution to the discussion afterwards was characteristic—he quoted recipes from Theophilus for madder and gilding and suggested that the art form should be revived for the production of cathedral service books. On his travels Burges saw and noted a number of foreign manuscripts, referring later to the iconography of the *Ovid Moralisé* in Rouen and the riches of Siena Cathedral library then, as now, displayed in the sacristy.

D.23 'Noyon—detail of figure on cupboard—full size'
Pencil and wash on Whatman paper
18¾"(47.5)×12"(30.5)

A copy of one figure, an unidentified standing female saint wearing the habit of a religious order; from the bottom left hand side of the left door of the Noyon armoire. A plate showing the whole door including this figure was originally published in Viollet-le-Duc's *Mobilier*, tome I, under the entry headed 'Armoire'. The influence of this piece of furniture on Burges's own designs has been discussed in the Furniture section of this catalogue under entries B1, and B6.   V.G.

Victoria and Albert Museum

D.24 'The Illustrations of Old Testament History in Queen Mary's Psalter' (MS.Reg.2 B.vii 'MUSEI BRITANNICI') by N.J.H. Westlake and W. Purdue, Architect
1864

The early 14th century English manuscript best known as the Queen Mary Psalter had always appealed to Burges. In 1859 he quoted it extensively when discussing the iconography of the Genesis cycle carved on the spandrels in Salisbury Chapter House. He opens his review of this edition in *The Gentleman's Magazine,* August 1865, with the words 'It is a curious fact that of all the many illuminated manuscripts contained in the rich collection of the British Museum, this is the one most frequently asked for by students'. As well as the exquisite figure drawing he drew attention to the military and civil costume, the plate armour and chain mail and the architecture, 'spherical triangles and ogee cuspings'. In fact, when Burges produced the Castell Coch Album for Lord Bute, it contained four tracings of turrets and gables from the Psalter, pasted to page 7, as examplars of a suitable medieval architectural style for castle building.

Open here to illustrate the story of Joseph and Potiphar's wife. Burges noticed this same subject at Salisbury and argued that the lady who tempted Joseph was in fact Pharaoh's wife. He remarked on very close links between the peculiarities of the two narrative cycles. He was much interested in the apochryphal sources for the extra non-Biblical scenes in the life of Joseph and obviously the more human and colourful aspects of these tales as 13th and 14th century painters had been before him. In the review he picks out for special notice 'the drawing where Samson shews Delilah to his father, and his father asks her to be wife to his son Samson, is a most beautiful and charming design; the figure and expression of the young girl being almost perfect'.   V.G.

Lent by the Society of Antiquaries of London

The Noyon Armoire as illustrated in Annales Archéologiques, *iv, 1846*

A detail of Queen Mary's Psalter *as traced in the Castell Coch Album (A84)*

A detail of Queen Mary's Psalter *as traced in the Castell Coch Album (A.84)*

D.25 'Vetusta Monumenta', vi, 'A Memoir on the Painted Chamber in the Palace at Westminster'
1842

The former Painted Chamber of the Palace of Westminster was destroyed by fire in 1834. Until then it had been one of the most remarkable medieval interiors in England. The walls were covered with murals of hectic and colourful narrative scenes designed to amuse and delight the English Court. Work had been carried out on them every twenty years or so from 1236 until nearly the end of the 13th century. Fortunately, copies were made of them by Charles Alfred Stothard and Edward Crocker in 1819. These copies are now in the Society of Antiquaries, the Ashmolean Museum and the Victoria and Albert Museum. The Stothard drawings were published in this edition of *Vetusta Monumenta*, but the Crocker drawings have never been published in full. They are accompanied in this volume by a historical essay by John Gage Rokewood.

This too was a medieval source of inspiration often mentioned by Burges; a tracing of it is attached to the same page in the Castell Coch Album as the details from the Queen Mary Psalter, chosen presumably for the elaborate architectural arcading under which the figure scenes are depicted.

Open here at Plate xxxii showing The Story of Hezehiah

V.G.

Lent by the Society of Antiquaries of London

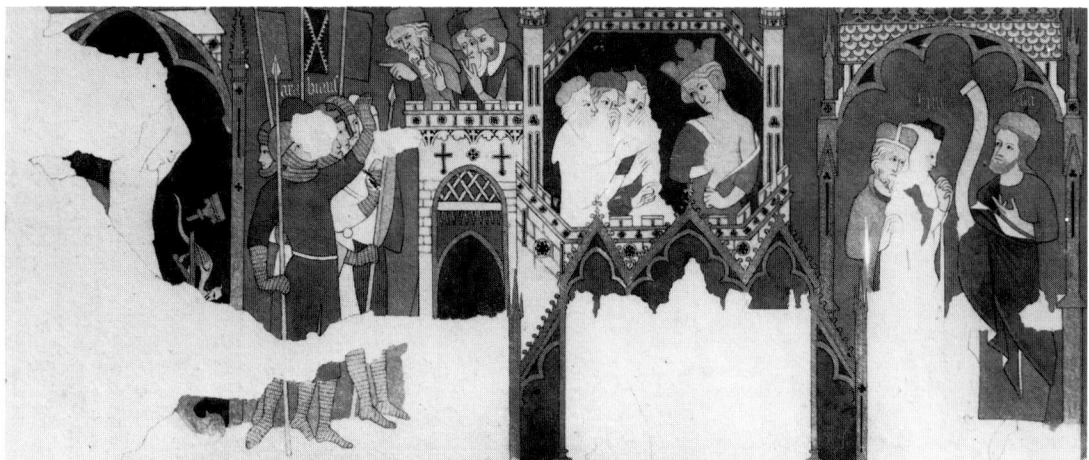

The Story of Hezekiah from the Painted Chamber at Westminster by C.A. Stothard—watercolour.

Tracing from one of the illustrations to Vetusta Monumenta *from the Castell Coch Album (A.84)*

Burges's Own Collection

It is only necessary to look through the photograph albums of Burges's rooms, first in Buckingham Street and then in Tower House to see how omnivorously he collected and how very various were his interests. Objects of his own design, exotic vessels mounted by him, contemporary bric-a-brac, medieval treasures and orientalia form a bewildering mixture.

On his death, the then Director, A.F. Franks, made a selection from Burges's collection for the British Museum. They were acquaintances from the Archaeological Institute and Franks must have known many of the pieces of old. Altogether he chose sixteen medieval manuscripts and seven ivories; five examples of oriental metalwork, four 'Saracenic' and one Chinese; some Classical, Byzantine and other oddments and one hundred and fifty three specimens for the department of arms and armour.

Widely travelled and never poor, Burges was able to indulge his magpie inclinations. He did not have the resources of a Rothschild, a Calland or a Spitzer, nor did he have the systematic approach of a historian collecting items to illustrate points or fill chronological gaps. However, among the treasure trove amassed by him were some charming and interesting things, although to Burges, collecting was hobby not a way of life.

V.G.

D.26 **Sitting Room, 15 Buckingham Street**
Early photograph

This view gives some idea of the profusion of objects with which Burges chose to surround himself in his antiquarian bachelor household. On the table is the famous elephant inkstand (C56) and on the mantlepiece two prototypes of Lord Bute's Summer Smoking Room Vase (A53); everywhere is a litter of books, figurines and Japanese lacquer boxes. The diptych by the window looks rather like part of the spoils from his travels in Italy or Belgium—possibly 'portions of a triptych, which had been attributed to Mabuse. It consisted of the two outer leaves, which had been joined together. The painting had evidently been retouched', which he exhibited to the Archaeological Institute in 1867.

V.G.

National Museum of Wales

D.26

D.27

D27 A Collection of Oriental Metalwork at Buckingham Street
Early photograph

When mounted in their original album these pieces were labelled from left to right 'Slop basin', 'Teaspoon', 'Tea Caddy/Sugar Basin', 'Coffee Pot from Summer Place'. These are in fact traditional Chinese bronze vessels for ritual use, decorated with cloisonné enamel. Very large numbers of objects of all kinds were attributed to the Summer Palace in Peking, after it was sacked during the 'Arrow' War in 1860, when as part of the general hostilities of the Opium Wars, British and French troops attacked the old city.
Early in 1863 at the Archaeological Institute, among the 'Antiquities and Works of Arts Exhibited— by Mr. W. BURGES.—[was] An ewer of Chinese work, enriched with *cloisonné* enamel'.

Burges became interested also in Western Medieval cloisonné enamels, on which he contributed an article to the *Gentleman's Magazine* in December 1865. V.G.

National Museum of Wales

D.28 A Japanese Cabinet on Stand from Burges's Album
Early photograph

An elaborate miniature cabinet with doors and drawers, made of ivory inlaid and painted with figures, plants and seascapes; sitting on a lacquered wood stand gilded in geometric patterns. Both cabinet and stand would have been of recent date when photographed for Burges. He was one of the first 19th century English collectors to take an interest in Japanese as opposed to Chinese art. In 1862 he published 'The Japanese Court' in the *Gentleman's Magazine*. V.G.

National Museum of Wales

D.29 Samples of Japanese Decorative Papers Collected by Burges
Two large pieces approximately 7½"(19.1)×10½"(26.7)

These are mounted in the Burges Album entitled 'polychromy'. The two larger pieces served as book wrappers, one has a leaf motif, the other a butterfly. The five small specimens are embossed in imitation of leatherwork. V.G.

Victoria and Albert Museum

D.30

D.31

D.30 Psalter
Painting on vellum
5¾"(14.5)×6"(15.3).

A psalter with Canticles, Athanasian Creed and other additions. Datable to before 1311, it has only a little decorative illumination. Its condition is imperfect in that an initial has been torn out of folio 99 and it has been brutally trimmed, changing its format from upright to horizontal. This was possibly done when it was rebound in royal blue velvet, with gilt brass clasps and bosses bearing Burges's personal emblems.

Burges began collecting manuscripts early in his career, for example the beautiful Angevin miniature bible (BM Additional Manuscript 31830) has one of his bookplates reading 'MDCCCLIII'—the year of the 'Long Journey' of which it may be a souvenir. The interest continued and he made at least one purchase (BM Additional Manuscript 31832) from the sale of William Bragge in 1876.   V.G.

BM Additional Manuscript 31833

Lent by The British Library

D.31 The Books of Samuel, Kings and Chronicles
Painting on vellum
12¾"(32.5)×9⅛"(23)

This very handsome book, in excellent condition, was written at Cîteaux about 1200. It is open here at folios 143 verso and 144 recto, showing the elaborate initial at the beginning of Book IIII. The interlace pattern with the running dogs and the hunted rabbit in the centre was the kind of medieval conceit so much beloved of Burges himself. It is considerably earlier than any of his other manuscripts and of considerable importance, emanating as it does from the scriptorium of the mother house of the entire Cistercian Order. Its Transitional style is noticeably different from the more or less prettified Gothic of the rest of Burges's manuscript collection.
(BM Additional Manuscript 31831)   V.G.

Lent by The British Library

D.32

D.32 **Tennyson's Poems (5th ed., 1848)**

In the summer of 1854 Burges fell ill in Florence. While convalescing, he designed a book-binding studded with marble butterflies. When he returned home, this was the binding applied to one of his favourite books: Tennyson's *Poems*. Years later, in 1875, he employed one of his assistants Thomas Manly Deane (1851-1933), to illuminate its margins with watercoloured miniatures. These miniatures incorporated themes—and exactly posed figures—which appear again and again in Burges's designs: the mermaid, the sleeping beauty, the Lady of Shalott, St. Simeon Stylites etc.

For the Pre-Raphaelites, Tennyson's poems were sacred texts. And for Burges they supplied an endless source of inspirational detail. He used to tell young architectural students: 'paint the walls of your studios . . . illustrate your Tennyson'. The 'Day-Dream' illustration shown here reappears in the headboard painting of Burges's celebrated bed (B10).

Bookplate: 'Ex Libris Williemi Burges Anno Domini mdcccliii'.   J.M.C.

Lent by J. Mordaunt Crook

D.33 **St. Simeon Stylites**

1861
Pen and ink on Whatman paper.
15¼"(38.5)×11"(27.7)
Signed with the monogram WB.

This drawing illustrates Tennyson's poem of the same title. An entry in the artist's diary for 1861 reads, 'Finished S. Simeon Stylites'. R.P. Pullan describes the drawing as '. . . an excellent imitation of an old wood engraving. The saint seems to be at the point of death. A demon climbs up a rope to secure the parting soul, but he is frightened by the appearance of a galaxy of angels in the sky, bearing the saintly crown. The Gothic city in the background is designed in a masterly manner'. A sketch of the same subject exists in one of the artist's note books in the R.I.B.A.   M.A.

BN. xxvi (1874), 419
Pullan, *The Designs of William Burges* (1883), Pl.23

Victoria and Albert Museum

D.34 **Plaster Cast of a Mirror Case, Showing the Storming of the Castle of Love**
Diameter 4" (10)

Produced for the Arundel Society in the 1850's. The ivory original in the Museo Nationale (Bargello) in Florence. The scene of the storming of the Castle of Love is commonly found on gothic ivory mirror cases; there are, however, many variations of the basic theme, and the jousting knights in the foreground of this example are not often seen in the siege context.

The Arundel Society casts were a source of great interest and inspiration to Burges's circle, providing them with means for comparison, study and argument collected together in one place. On April 23rd 1856, such a discussion was reported at the Architectural Museum in Canon Row, Westminster, where a selection was on display, between Rev. W. Scott, G.E. Street and Burges (*The Ecclesiologist*, 1856). It was, however, a foreign example which Burges presented to the Archaeological Institute in 1857: '*Antiquities and Works of Art Exhibited.* . . . Mr. W. BURGES . . . a cast from a beautiful mirror-case of ivory, preserved in Italy, representing the Castle of Love.'   P.W., V.G.

Victoria and Albert Museum

D.33

D.34

D.36

D.35 **Ivory Leaf from a Polyptych**
Carved ivory
4⅝″(11.7)×2¾″(7)

One of a number of Gothic devotional ivories owned by Burges, this has for its subject the Crucifixion, with the sorrowing Virgin and St. John and Adam rising from the tomb below. A slightly crude specimen, it could be either French or German and dates from around the middle of the 14th century. V.G.
O.M. Dalton, *Catalogue of the Ivory Carvings of the Christian Era*, British Museum (1909) No. 274

Lent by the British Museum

D.36 **Ivory Panel**
Carved ivory
3¼″(8.3)×1⅝″(4.1)

A small tablet with a courtly scene of a lady and gentleman under a pair of gables with foliate crockets and trilobate arches below. Secular art of the Middle Ages was very greatly prized by Burges and his contemporaries, searching as they always were for sources for domestic decoration and non-religious designs for objects of art. This is a rather small and unspectacular example, but by Burges's day the really showy specimens like the Castle of Love ivories had mostly found their way into public collections. It is probably French and datable to the first half of the 14th century.

Dalton, *op. cit.*, No. 359. V.G.

Lent by the British Museum

D.37 **Casket Decorated with Bone Carvings**
Wood and bone
7½″(19.1)×8⅜″(21.3)×5¼″(13.3)

An early 15th century casket of the kind produced in Venice by the Embriaco family. This example appears in the R.I.B.A. album of photographs entitled 'Own furniture'. It appears on Plate 36, on the top left hand side of a set of openwork decorative shelves, surrounded by Islamic ivory boxes with pierced and carved decoration. The panels represent the story of Jason and the Golden Fleece.

Dalton, *op.cit.*, No. 401. V.G.

Lent by the British Museum

D.38 **Crystal Spoon**
Crystal, silver gilt and chalcedony.
l 4⅝″(11.7)

A fancy 14th or 15th century spoon with a silver gilt setting and a cupid's head carved from white chalcedony. There is a drawing of this spoon in the R.I.B.A. Album 'Metalwork' inscribed 'Crystal and silver gilt/From the debruges sale/C Baijly July 1865'. 'afterwards came into the possession/ of W. Burges/and at his decease was/selected by the British Museum'. Its origins are probably French or German. V.G.

Lent by the British Museum

D.39 **Sallett**
Iron
diameter 15¼″ (38.7)

A sallett probably of South German workmanship dating from the third quarter of the 15th century. This was perhaps the most significant item in Burges's own collection, and has featured in most scholarly publications on this type of helmet since his day. He himself published a similar 'salade' belonging to the Baron de Cosson in the *Archaeological Journal* in 1880 and had clearly studied the group with some care. The painted example in the Tower of London Armouries is described at length, another in the Ambras Collection is briefly mentioned, as is that in the Wallace Collection, but there is no reference to this sallett which may indicate that Burges acquired it very near the end of his life. Burges seems to have collected armour with the same romantic enthusiasm as everything else, using pieces of it to decorate Tower House along with the medieval bric-a-brac and the orientalia. However, the Baron de Cosson was probably one of the influences guiding him towards a genuinely scholarly approach to this particular field. Together they published a *Catalogue of the Exhibition of Ancient Helmets and Examples of Mail* in 1880, which defined certain types for the first time, and revealed certain others as fake. Along with the next twelve items this has been chosen from the Burges bequest, to show its range and quality.

Sir Guy Francis Laking, *A Record of European Armour and Arms through Seven Centuries* (1920), vol II, 26 fig 367

Lent by the Trustees of the British Museum

D.40 **Burgonet**
Iron; leather, linen
height: 11¼″ (28.6) width: 7½″ (19)

German, 16th century; of small size, the one-piece skull is remarkable for the height of its three combs, each crested by a row of embossed round-topped rectangular pyramids. The hinged cheekpieces are lined with linen. The plume-holder at the back of the skull is a restoration.
Marks: The peak is struck with a pine-cone (the Augsburg city mark), and an armourer's mark; a helm under a six-pointed star. The latter is the maker's mark of Desiderius Helmschmid.

W. Burges and Baron de Cosson, *Catalogue of the Exhibition of Ancient Helmets and Examples of Mail* (1880), item 88.

Ex collection Samuel Rush Meyrick
J. Skelton, *Engraved Illustrations of Ancient Armour from the Collection at Goodrich Court* (1830), vol 1, no. 25.

Lent by the Trustees of the British Museum (on deposit at the Tower of London Armouries)

D.39

D.41 **Close-Helmet**
Iron
height: 10¼″ (26) width: 9″ (22.9)

Of 'Maximilian' style, characterised by the shallow fluting of the skull, a manner of decoration popular in Germany in the late 16th and early 17th century. The visor is of so-called 'bellows' form. Two or possibly three plates to protect the nape of the wearer's neck are missing.
Marks: On the right side of the cheekpiece are three large letters; KXR, deeply struck.
Attributed to the Radziwill Collection; the letters KXR having been taken as the monogram of Krgystof Xiadz Radziwill.

Lent by the Trustees of the British Museum (on deposit at the Tower of London Armouries)

D.42 **Breastplate**
Iron
length: 15¼″ (35.6)

Of 'globose' form, this early 16th century Italian breastplate is etched with a Madonna and child, a military trophy, a motif of flames, and bands of strapwork.
Marks: Beneath the opening for the left arm is a cross and the letter G.

Lent by the Trustees of the British Museum (on deposit at the Tower of London Armouries)

D.43 **Piece of Mail**
Iron
length 8¼″ (21) width (at widest point) 5¼″ (13.3)

Each link is closed by a single rivet. This is an example of the type of mail in use in Europe in the 15th and 16th centuries.

Lent by the Trustees of the British Museum (on deposit at the Tower of London Armouries)

D.44 **Piece of Mail**
Iron
length 8¾″(22.2) width 8″(20.3)

Each individual link of this fine mail is closed by a small rivet. This mail is an example of the type in use in some applications in the later 16th and early 17th centuries.

Lent by the Trustees of the British Museum (on deposit at the Tower of London Armouries)

D.45 **Piece of Mail**
Iron
length: 6½″(16.5) width: 3¾″(9.5)

Possibly oriental; each of the large links being closed by a bifurcated rivet.

Lent by the Trustees of the British Museum (on deposit at the Tower of London Armouries)

D.46 **Sword Fragment**
Iron, gold
length overall 23¼″(59.1) width of quillons 7⅜″(18.6)

The excavated remains of a fine 'hand-and-a-half' sword of the 14th century, with a characteristic 'wheel' pommel and flaring straight quillons. The forte of the broad two-edged blade is inlaid in gold, on one side with a small heart, twice with a V, and with an animal, perhaps a unicorn. The other face has only the remains of another illegible animal mark.

Lent by the Trustees of the British Museum (on deposit at the Tower of London Armouries)

D.47 **Rondel Dagger**
Steel, iron, wood and velvet
length 21¾″(55.2)

An example of the classic 'knightly' dagger of the 15th century, and although found in the Thames, is probably German. Daggers of this type can be found on effigies and in manuscript illustrations, particularly those relating to the tournament.
The grip is of wood covered with brown (originally possibly red) velvet bound with iron wire, and is probably a restoration.

It was exhibited at the Archaeological Institute in 1862. 'By Mr. W. Burges—an ironspear-head found in the river Lea, at Bow Bridge, Essex, probably Saxon; also several mediaeval weapons, daggers knives, spurs, etc., found in the Thames, near Westminster Bridge, in forming the foundations of the Houses of Parliament.

Ex collection Samuel Rush Meyrick, presented by George Gwitt Esq.
J.Skelton, *Engraved Illustrations of Ancient Armour from the Collection at Goodrich Court* (1830), vol 2, Pl.cx, no.1

Lent by the Trustees of the British Museum (on deposit at the Tower of London Armouries)

D.48 **Sporting Crossbow**
Steel, wood, horn, bone and cord
length overall 25″(63.5) width of bow 23¼″(59)

A typical German sporting crossbow of the early 17th century.
A good example of this type of bow, in good condition, retaining most of its original fabric 'bobbles', some bone plaque inlays missing; the stock (or 'tiller') decorated on the sides with scenes and animals of the chase and on the underside at the butt with an engraved portrait of a crossbowman.
Marks: The steel bow is stamped with two marks; on the left limb with a bunch of grapes and on the right limb a large illegible mark, struck twice.

Lent by the Trustees of the British Museum (on deposit at the Tower of London Armouries)

D.48

D.49 **Cranequin (Crossbow Winding Mechanism)**
Iron, cord, and wood
length overall 13¾″ (34.9)

An example of the form of mechanism used to span sporting crossbows of the 16th and 17th centuries. It operates on the rack-and-pinion principle. The wheel is etched with hounds and a rabbit within floral scrollwork. The bar is stamped to the rear of the double hook with a shield-shaped mark: IK either side of three balls and above what may be a bird. A similar mark appears on a cranequin in the Berlin Zeughaus dated 1604. Either side of this mark is the possibly spurious date 1575. The bar is etched with a band of strapwork decoration, probably added at a later date.

Lent by the Trustees of the British Museum (on deposit at the Tower of London Armouries)

D.50 **Crossbow Bolt**
Iron and wood
length overall 15″ (38.1)

A typical crossbow bolt of a type used for war and for hunting during the 15th and 16th centuries. It is said to have been found complete in the tower of the Cathedral of Soest, Westphalia, in 1860, and to date from the 14th century, but the condition of the shaft and flights suggest that these must be a more recent restoration. It is one of a number brought back by Mr. A. Hartshorne and Mr. Petit in 1860.

Archaeological Journal, xxxv, 177

Lent by the Trustees of the British Museum (on deposit at the Tower of London Armouries)

D.51 **Crossbow Bolt**
Brass, wood
length overall 12¾″ (32.8)

A target bolt probably of 18th century date, with octagonal brass head equipped with a small iron sighting head. The original fletchings now broken off.

Lent by the Trustees of the British Museum (on deposit at the Tower of London Armouries)

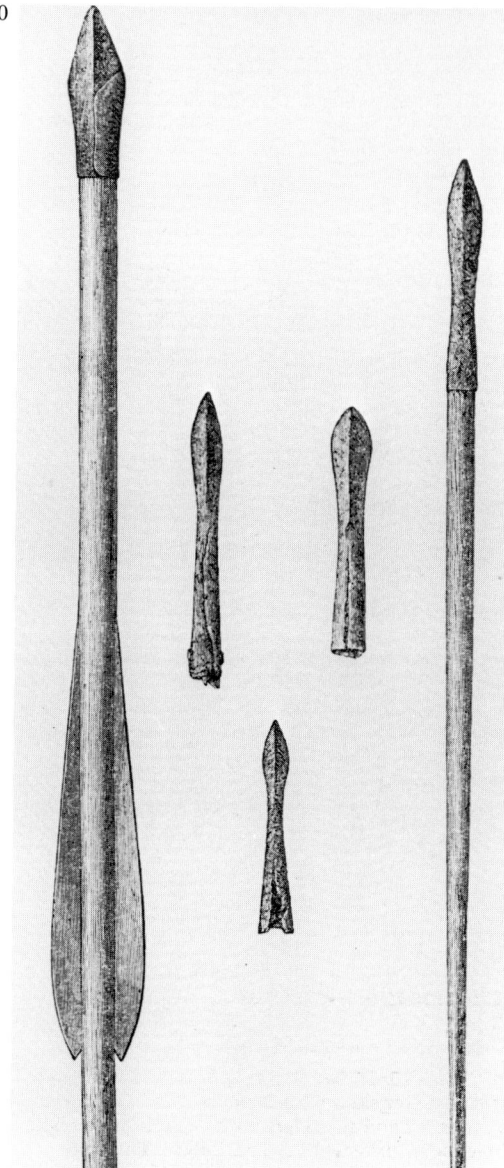

D.50 as illustrated in the Archaeolical Journal, *xxxv, 177*

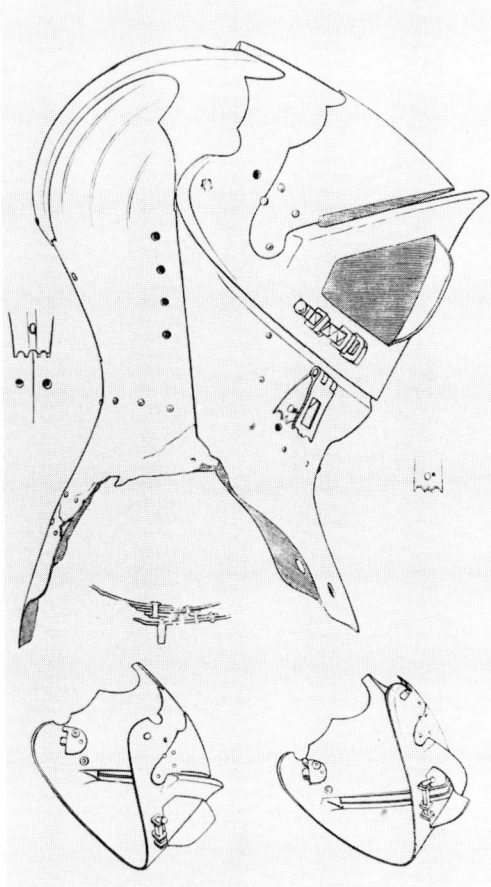

D.52 as illustrated in the Archaeological Journal, *xxxvi, 1879*

D.52 The Broadwater Helm
Iron
height 18″   width 15″

A Flemish or Italian jousting helm of about 1520, with shallow skull-piece covering the back of the head, neck and shoulders with a single centre bolt hole for securing it to the backplate. There are three ridges on either side of the skull piece and it is pierced with four holes at each side and with two more at the centre for laces from the quilted lining cap. Below the last is a single hole where the stem of a rondel was riveted. The front of the skull is formed by a large brow plate which is extended backwards to completely reinforce the comb and both this and the skull are pierced for a crest-stalk. The bevor, pivoted to the skull at the sides has a shallow cut-away at the centre in front of the wearer's mouth. The heavy visor with a long sight and strong medial lip has a rectangular opening for ventilation at the right side protected by a rightangle flange at its forward edge. The surface of the skull is deeply pitted by rust and the back of the collar is now much corroded. It has been broken across the centre and repaired with a patch. This splendid piece never, of course, belonged to Burges himself, but by his own account he was

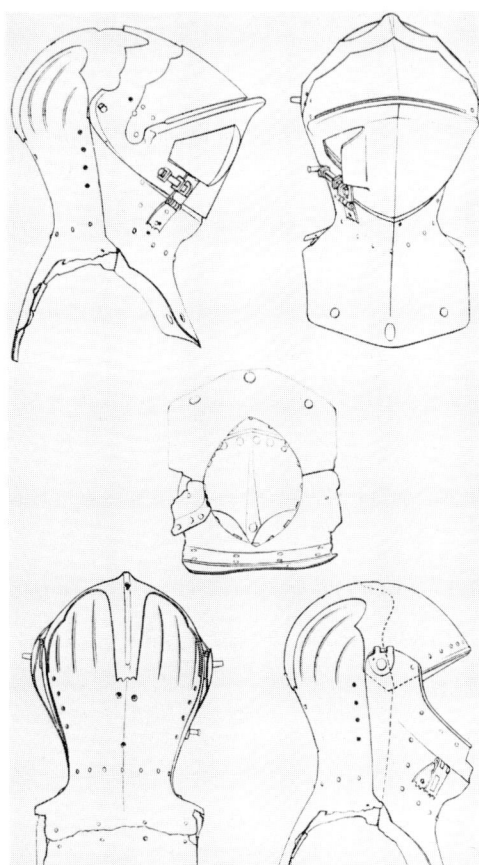

D.52 as illustrated in the Archaeological Journal, *xxxvi, 1879*

largely responsible for its survival. He wrote a lengthy article on it for the *Archaeological Journal* in 1879 in which he recounts that he found it 'lying on top of the altar tomb within everybody's reach, the visor loose and the lower part of the back piece broken off and detached'. He was allowed to bring it to London where he exhibited it at a meeting of the Archaeolgical Institute and had it carefully photographed. He then had it repaired, cleaned and repainted, before returning it to the church who owned it – Broadwater, Sussex. There it was placed 'at a sufficient height to be out of reach except by means of a ladder'. Burges tells us that it came from the tomb of Thomas West Lord La Warre whose family history he gives in some detail. He also carefully examined the tomb, subsequently going on to describe the helm minutely and compare it with related examples, finally making the extremely practical suggestion that a list should be published of all the helmets existing in churches so that 'a little might be done to prevent their removal, as no one would care to show an acquisition derived from a church'.

Sotheby's Sale Catalogue, 2 December 1974, lot 173

Lent by the Tower of London Armouries

Select Bibliography

J. Mordaunt Crook, *William Burges and the High Victorian Dream*, London: John Murray Ltd., 1981.

'Knightshayes, Devon: Burges versus Crace', *National Trust Year Book* i (1975-6), 44-45.

'Patron Extraordinary: John, 3rd Marquess of Bute' in *Victorian South Wales*, ed. P. Howell. London: Victorian Society, 1970.

'A Multi-Coloured Fantasy: Lost Treasures of William Burges', *Country Life* clxviii (1980), 1254-6.

'William Burges: The Dilemma of Style', *Arch. Rev.* clxx (1981).

P. Floud, *Castell Coch* (1974)

M. Girouard, 'Cardiff Castle', *Country Life* cxxix (1961), 760-63, 822-5, 886-9.

'Castell Coch', *Country Life* cxxxi (1962), 1092-5, 1174-7.

The Victorian Country House (1979), 273-290, 336-45.

C. Handley-Read, 'William Burges', in *Victorian Architecture*, ed. P. Ferriday, London, 1963.

'Notes on William Burges's Painted Furniture', *Burl. Mag.* cv (1963), 496-509.

'St Fin Barre's Cathedral, Cork', *Arch. Rev.*, cxli (1967), 422-30.

'Aladdin's Palace in Kensington', *Country Life* cxxxix (1966), 600-604.

'William Burges' in *Catalogue of the Drawings Collection of the R.I.B.A.* 1972, B, 117-8.

W.G. Howell, 'Castell Coch', *Arch. Rev.* cix (1951), 39-46.

T. Measham, *Castell Coch* (1974).

Victorian and Edwardian Decorative Arts (Victoria and Albert Museum, 1952).

Victorian Church Art (Victoria and Albert Museum, 1971).

Victorian and Edwardian Decorative Art (Royal Academy, 1972).

Marble Halls (Victoria and Albert Museum, 1973).

Morris and Company (Fine Art Society, 1979).

Acknowledgements

In compiling this catalogue we have relied so heavily throughout on one book — Dr. J. Mordaunt Crook's *William Burges and the High Victorian Dream* (John Murray, 1981) — that it has been impossible to acknowledge it as a source in every instance.

The following people have generously provided facilities for research, given up much of their time and, in some cases, made available the results of their own unpublished discoveries:—

At the Cecil Higgins Art Gallery, Bedford, Halina Grubert; James Berrow; for the Church of St. Michael and All Angels, Brighton, Rev Bernard Hopper, Prof. J.F.C. Harrison; Bord Fáilte Eirann; at the Fitzwilliam Museum, Cambridge, Prof. Michael Jaffé R.A. Crighton; The Very Rev. the Dean of Cork and Mrs. Hilary Carey; for Cardiff City Council, H.T. Crippin, Neil Jones, Geoffrey Parry, Pauline Sargent, Bruce Shard; for the Cork and Kerry Tourist Board, Richard Casey; The Very Rev. the Dean of Chichester; Mr. and Mrs. Trevor Ineson; at the British Architectural Library Drawings Collection, John Harris, Jane Preger, Nicholas Antrim; at the British Library, Daniel Waley, A. Payne, Shelley Jones; at the British Museum, Neil Stratford, John Cherry; for St. Paul's Cathedral, Commander Charles Shears; at the Society of Antiquaries, F.H. Thompson, J.H. Hopkins; at the Tower of London Armouries, A.V.B. Norman, Guy Wilson, Ian Eaves, Graeme Rimer; Eleanor Mallock; Rev. D.P. Mann; at Mountstuart, the Marquess and Marchioness of Bute, Catherine Armet; for the National Trust at Knightshayes, Hugh Meller, Mr. and Mrs. D. Crooks; at Newby Hall, Mr. and Mrs. Robin Compton, Rory Wardroper; at the Ashmolean Museum, Oxford, David Piper, Kenneth Garlick, Ian Lowe; The Provost and Fellows of Worcester College, Oxford, James Campbell, Lesley Montgomery; at the William Morris Gallery, Walthamstow, Norah Gillow, Jill Halliwell; Mr. and Mrs. Auberon Waugh; at the Welsh Office, Michael Thompson, Peter Humphries.

Help and support have been given by so many members of most departments of the National Museum of Wales and the Victoria and Albert Museum that it would be invidious to attempt to single out their individual contributions.